With very
+Love
S...

SPIRIT OF
BRITAIN
FIRST

'All my past life is mine no more,
the flying hours are gone,
like transitory dreams given o'er
– whose images are kept in store
by memory alone.'
John Wilmot, 1647-1680

As part of our ongoing market research, we are always pleased to receive
comments about our books, suggestions for new titles, or requests for catalogues.
Please write to: The Editorial Director, Patrick Stephens Limited, Sparkford, Nr Yeovil,
Somerset BA22 7JJ.

SPIRIT OF
BRITAIN
FIRST

The dramatic 20-year quest to return
a Bristol Blenheim to the skies

Graham Warner

Foreword by Lord Rothermere

PSL

Patrick Stephens Limited

First published in 1996

British Library Cataloguing in Publication Data:
A catalogue record for this book is available from the British Library

ISBN 1-85260-533-2

Library of Congress catalog card no. 96-075171

Patrick Stephens Limited is an imprint of Haynes Publishing, Sparkford, Nr Yeovil, Somerset, BA22 7JJ.

Designed & typeset by G&M, Raunds, Northamptonshire
Printed in Great Britain by Butler & Tanner Ltd, London and Frome

Contents

	Foreword by Lord Rothermere	7
	Introduction	8
	Prologue	9
Chapter One	Welcome to 'Blenheim Palace'	11
Chapter Two	'Someone really ought to do something about it'	19
Chapter Three	Scrap metal	25
Chapter Four	Wheels of fate	32
Chapter Five	The Team	39
Chapter Six	Evolution of 'Britain First'	46
Chapter Seven	The airframe takes shape	58
Colour Section	*The first restoration*	65
Chapter Eight	Restoration dramas	77
Chapter Nine	Vital systems	85
Chapter Ten	The beating hearts	94
Chapter Eleven	Towards roll-out	105
Chapter Twelve	The forgotten bomber	114
Chapter Thirteen	Take-off!	124
Chapter Fourteen	Disaster at Denham	131
Colour Section	*The second restoration*	137
Chapter Fifteen	Aftermath	148
Chapter Sixteen	Starting from scratch	157
Chapter Seventeen	Our finest hour	172
Appendix 1	Obituary of Ormond Haydon-Baillie	183
Appendix 2	Bristol Aeroplane Company Type Numbers (multi-engined aircraft)	184
Appendix 3	Some Blenheim 'firsts'	185
Appendix 4	Principal Bristol piston aircraft engines	186
Appendix 5	Citations for Victoria Crosses	188
Appendix 6	The Blenheim Appeal announcement	191
Appendix 7	Accident Investigation Board Report No 11/87	193
Appendix 8	Flight Test Notes G-BPIV	195
Appendix 9	Obituary of John Larcombe	198
Appendix 10	Letter from AOC 11 Group, Royal Air Force	200
Appendix 11	'Blenheim': a poem by Richard Passmore, 1987	202
	Acknowledgements	204

Lord Rothermere naming the Spirit of Britain First, and (below) with John Romain.

Foreword

by The Rt. Hon. The Viscount Rothermere

I was delighted to name the second restored Blenheim *The Spirit of Britain First* in honour of my Grandfather who, back in 1934, commissioned an aircraft from the Bristol Aeroplane Company in order to demonstrate that the British aircraft industry could produce a machine ahead of any other in the world at that time. As the first Secretary of State for Air he was filled with foreboding at the advanced machines being developed for the Luftwaffe, and concerned at the shortcomings of contemporary and proposed Royal Air Force equipment.

He named his aeroplane *Britain First* and presented it to the Air Ministry – it became the prototype for the Bristol Blenheim. Blenheims were a vital and widely-used weapon in the hands of the RAF on all fronts during the first few desperate years of the war, frequently pressed into action against overwhelming odds. Their exceptionally brave crews earned the respect of their wartime peers, but the considerable contribution made by Blenheims to the war effort is only now becoming appreciated.

This belated recognition of the historic importance of the Blenheim is due in large part to the efforts of Graham Warner and his Team in putting a Blenheim back into the skies – not once but twice. Fortunately I was able to witness their first Blenheim performing, and was disturbed by its loss so soon afterwards. I had admired the beautifully-restored craft, and it saddened me that all the hard work and effort put into it by the small Team over some 12 years had been destroyed in a few seconds.

That the Team accepted so readily the daunting challenge of starting all over again to recreate another flying Blenheim shows that the Spirit is still alive. We are indebted to John Romain and all who worked on both restorations for overcoming numerous intractable engineering problems so successfully. We are indebted especially to Graham Warner, not only for his tremendous efforts in inspiring and leading his Team for so many years through all the difficulties, but also for depicting the saga so well within these pages.

Introduction

I have tried to set out this story in a succinct but straightforward way: describing the efforts of a small team at Duxford to put the derelict shell of a wartime Blenheim back into the air, and how they had to do this not once but twice. I will tell you who did it and why they did it, not just how they did it. For this is essentially a human story about the personalities of those involved, and covers a wide range of human emotions.

The 20-year saga has been considerably condensed and simplified; this results from my desire to reach and retain the interest of a readership well beyond that of aviation experts and enthusiasts alone. Thus technicalities have been avoided, facts and figures kept to the minimum, statistics and items that would restrict the flow of the narrative moved to the Appendices, and engineering and aeronautical terms explained in layman's language. Although I have tried to find the happy medium, I hope that aviation engineers and experts will forgive me for not being sufficiently technical, and that the ordinary reader will pardon me if I have sometimes become too technical!

I am concerned that my attempts to shorten and simplify the story will result in a failure to convey adequately the sheer volume of demanding, often repetitive, but always grindingly hard work that was put in by the team over so many years. They are mainly volunteers, working in their spare time; their dedication is unmatched, and the excellence of their skills is amply demonstrated by their success in restoring two Blenheim hulks to airworthy status. Their constant effort throughout such a lengthy period is unsurpassed.

As you watch the one and only Bristol Blenheim flash by and curve up into a graceful wing-over at an air display, reflect on the two main themes of the story unfolded by this book. Remember the courageous Blenheim crews who faced without flinching such daunting odds over 50 years ago when Britain fought alone. Recall the brave 'Blenheim Boys' – those unsung heroes whom we salute with our flying Blenheim – and join with us in paying them overdue tribute. Muse on the very many Blenheim crews who sacrificed their lives for their Country.

Think too of the triumphs and tragedies experienced by the Blenheim restoration team, dwell upon their delights and disappointments, ponder the problems they over-came and the difficulties they defeated. Pause to consider the years of unremitting hard work that went into returning a Blenheim to the skies. Then give thanks for the achievements of the Blenheim Team, for these young men are the present-day heroes of this modern Blenheim saga – just as the original RAF crews were the youthful heroes of those desperate wartime years. Both have shown the same selfless 'Spirit of Britain First': this book is dedicated to them.

Prologue

On a raw Sunday evening in January 1987 I was with the Blenheim Team in the hangar at Duxford; a rain-coated and becapped visitor to the Museum stood at the partly open hangar doors with his head inclined to one side. He was studying our Bristol Blenheim, by then almost completely rebuilt, and watched for a while as the Team worked away.

'How long have you lot been doing that Blenheim now?' he enquired.

At least he knew what it was.

'Over 12 years,' I replied, 'but we're nearly there now, thank goodness', adding, 'It seems an age since we started.'

'How do you manage for spare parts then?' was his next query.

'There just aren't any!' was my response. 'When we find any component that we can't repair, we have to make a new one – using the old part as a pattern.'

'What did you do about the engines? They look like new to me' was his following question and complimentary comment.

'We had a couple of dozen 50-year-old engines, left out in all weathers, seized and virtually scrap, and had to strip all of them right down to get enough parts to rebuild two good ones.'

I liked to enlighten those visitors who showed more than just a casual curiosity just how comprehensive, lengthy and painstaking the rebuild had been, so I added:

'In fact, the entire airframe, engines, propellers and aircraft systems – all derelict – had to be completely stripped and fully restored to put her back into airworthy condition.'

'There's not another Blenheim still flying anywhere, is there?' he then asked.

'No, this will be the only one in the world,' I replied proudly.

He took off his cap and scratched behind a very wet ear.

'How much has it all cost then?' was his final question.

'A hell of a lot of hard work and well over £300,000,' I answered.

He sucked his teeth and replaced his cap.

'Well, I think it just wasn't worth all that effort and money.

'For, after all, Blenheims didn't do very much in the war, did they?' he opined, and wandered off into the drizzle.

That remark, whether his carefully considered opinion or merely thoughtless, brought home to me just how the Blenheim had become largely forgotten, and made me determined that we would restore not just the aircraft itself but also its reputation. My personal campaign to put the poor old Blenheim right 'back on the map' – where I thought it deserved to be – commenced at that moment.

I did not know then that the Blenheim we were looking at would indeed, to our great delight, fly successfully within a few months, only to be destroyed, to our deep dismay, in a needless crash less than one month later. Certainly, on that damp day, I could not even begin to imagine that we would be forced to start the whole lengthy restoration process all over again.

Let me take you back to the beginning of our 20-year saga to put a Blenheim back into the air, and back on the map, again.

Chapter One

Welcome to 'Blenheim Palace'

During the early 1970s Ormond Haydon-Baillie, a young Royal Air Force Flight-Lieutenant pilot, was seconded to the Royal Canadian Air Force to fly North American Sabre jet fighters at Cold Lake, Manitoba; he came from a good family and was a very skilful and enthusiastic pilot. Ormond fell in love with, and purchased from Bankstown, Australia, a surplus but airworthy Hawker Sea Fury piston-engined single-seat fighter that had seen active service during the Korean War with the Royal Australian Air Force (still under its RAF serial number WH589). He had this crated and sent to Canada where it was registered CF-CHB, re-assembled, and put back into Second World War RAF Fighter Command camouflage. With a typical flamboyant touch he had his initials OH-B applied as the spurious squadron codes.

Ormond revelled in flying this personal classic 'warbird'. He flew it to the 'States and competed in the Air Races at Reno, showing obvious enjoyment and enthusiasm. In November 1973 he ferried it via Iceland to Southend Airport in England, where it was registered as G-AGHB. He also bought a couple of Lockheed T33s – the two-seat advanced jet trainer version of the famous P80 Shooting Star fighter – had them

Ormond Haydon-Baillie enjoying his Hawker Sea Fury WH589.

'civilianised' (as CF-IHB and CF-EHB) and ferried them also to Southend (where they became G-OAHB and G-WGHB respectively – the WG to recognise the initials of Ormond's brother Wensley). These three airworthy aircraft formed the nucleus of what was to become virtually his own private air force.

But he also had some other very exciting discoveries on their way by sea to the UK. These became the quintessential elements of the saga I now relate.

For Ormond had discovered the airfames of several completely derelict 'Bolingbrokes' laying abandoned on various inaccessible farms and similar locations deep within the vastness of Canada. He was aware that they were in fact Bristol Blenheims built under licence in Canada during the war, and that there was not a single Blenheim flying anywhere in the world. So in 1973 he purchased from Wes Agnew, a renowned Canadian collector, two of the most complete airframes that he could find – Royal Canadian Air Force serial numbers 9896 and 10038; they had both been manufactured in 1942 and seen wartime RCAF service. Wes had bought several as war surplus in 1946 (reputedly at $50 each!) and they had been stored – or should I say left out? – in the open ever since.

Ormond also gathered together as many engines as he could track down, plus various useful spares such as control-surfaces, wheels, undercarriage units, propeller blades, a gun turret, etc, – mostly badly damaged. He had the whole lot dismantled into major components during 1973, and shipped them over to England in 1974.

When I say 'the most complete airframes', they were of course very far from complete, having stood out in all weathers for over 40 years; Canadian winters are particularly cold and harsh, although the climate is generally quite dry compared with that in Europe. Apart from being continuously exposed to the destructive forces of the elements, the airframes had been vandalised, robbed of any parts the farmers found useful, used as playthings by two generations of children, and invaded by all sorts of plant,

Where both our restored Blenheims started their lives – a 1942 photograph of licence-built RCAF Bolingbrokes on the Fairchild production lines.

One of the derelict airframes as discovered in Canada in 1973.

insect and animal life. Their cockpits had been completely gutted, they had been used for target practice, and had of course generally suffered very severely from the ravages of time.

Thus the shipping of these decrepit Blenheim components to England marked the

Leaning against the wall in the corner of a hangar was a centre-section with the wheels folded into the rusty frames.

The components of RCAF 10038 start their long journey from the Canadian Prairies to the UK.

beginning of the long, long journey that would see one of these derelict wrecks finally resurrected to take to the skies once more as an airworthy Blenheim – indeed, the only airworthy Blenheim in the world. This extended journey would involve both triumph and tragedy, an enormous amount of hard work, many unexpected problems and difficulties, moments that were heart-warming and others that were heart-breaking, much fun and laughter plus quite a few tears.

Ormond's aircraft collection grew rapidly over the next couple of years, for he purchased a batch of ex-Luftwaffe North American Sabres in West Germany, a Gloster Meteor Mk 8 and a Canadair CF100 all-weather fighter in the UK, some derelict Spitfire wrecks used as decoys in India, plus two de Havilland Chipmunks and another T33 'T Bird' (N12420) for use as a 'spares ship' for his flying examples. His intention was to attempt to make airworthy once again at least one example of each type of these ex-military aircraft, if and when this was possible, so that they could eventually join his Sea Fury and T33 back in the skies. Then they could take part in air displays, as well as photography and film work, or be traded for other exciting 'warbirds'. He was conscious too of the personal satisfaction, great enjoyment and excitement he found in flying them. However, he found that accommodation, workshops and hangarage for his expanding collection was becoming a problem, as storage charges and landing fees at Southend and elsewhere were mounting.

Fortunately, Ormond had found that the famous former Royal Air Force Station at Duxford near Cambridge, which although built during the First World War and kept in constant use by the RAF (or the USAF during the latter part of the Second World War) right until 1961, was at that time laying empty and unused. This was while the various authorities concerned – the Ministry of Defence, Department of the Environment, Cambridgeshire County Council, the Home Office, and the influential University that owned much of the land – were trying to decide whether it was to become a prison, a sports centre or even a housing or industrial estate, with the airfield itself reverting to agricultural use as farmland.

He heard that the Imperial War Museum at Lambeth was using parts of the Duxford site for storage purposes, so he investigated further and in 1974 was able to wangle accommodation there for his embryonic collection. He moved the Sea Fury and T33s from Southend into a hangar at Duxford and the great pile of Blenheim/Bolingbroke airframe parts with all the engines, which had arrived at Harwich in the meantime, into two adjacent and very dilapidated buildings. One of these was the former Station Armoury; with its barred windows this was the most secure building on a site, which suffered from widespread vandalism. This building – Numbered 66 – was immediately christened 'Blenheim Palace', and is still known as that today!

Ormond's Sea Fury thus became the first aircraft to fly from Duxford regularly since the last Royal Air Force aircraft – a Meteor NF14 flown by Air Vice Marshal Bateson, an ex-Blenheim and Mosquito pilot – had left the airfield some 16 years earlier in July 1961. Now there are over 50 active ex-military aircraft based there!

One other burst of nostalgic flying activity had taken place prior to the general revival initiated by Ormond in the 1970s, for the empty site and airfield at Duxford had been used extensively during 1968 for making the epic feature film *The Battle of Britain*. Spanish-built Heinkel He 111s, Junkers Ju 52s, and Messerschmitt Me 109s shared the hallowed turf – base of Douglas Bader's controversial 'Big Wing' fighter operations during the real battle in 1940 – with various ex-RAF Spitfires and Hurricanes gathered together by Hamish McHaddie for the film. These aircraft, sold off afterwards by the film company, formed the foundation of the worldwide move-ment to collect former 'warbirds' and preserve them in flying condition, for example by the 'Confederated Air Force' at Harlingen in Texas.

During the filmed re-creation of a German air raid on an RAF airfield one of the large hangars had been blown up very spectacularly. In fact, so well-built were these First World War 'Belfast'-type hangars, with their huge wooden trusses supported by

The components installed in 'Blenheim Palace' at Duxford; the stripping down of interior fittings has commenced.

massive brick piers, that it took the film company two attempts, the first explosion only blowing off one of the doors. The publicity that the film company obtained for this 'realism' backfired, for it caused quite a fuss amongst traditionalists upset at what they saw as part of their heritage being destroyed 'just to make a film'. This led to a move to get these early hangars 'listed' to prevent any further such destruction, and the Imperial War Museum at Lambeth was called in as an appropriate authority to confirm their historic importance. After doing so, the IWM arranged with the MoD to store some of its vast collection of military artifacts there, using Duxford merely as an out-station of Lambeth for storage purposes, and at that stage with no intention of opening the site to the public.

The East Anglia Aviation Society also gathered together at Duxford some aircraft artifacts that they had recovered from various East Anglian crash sites, and provided volunteers to work on the IWM aircraft in one of the hangars. Ormond too soon gathered around him a small team of volunteer enthusiasts to help him maintain his aircraft and keep them clean. Two of the keenest members of this ad-hoc team were John Romain, a 15-year-old aircraft engineering apprentice at British Aerospace at Hatfield, and William Kelly, a 13-year-old local schoolboy. Both of these young enthusiasts, but particularly and vitally John, became inextricably entwined with the Blenheim, and are still heavily involved with it to this day!

David Tallichet's Consolidated B24 Liberator 'Delectable Doris' was based for maintenance at Duxford for a couple of years while on its way from India to Chino in the States. The Shuttleworth Trust and one or two other enterprising private owners, quick to take advantage of such a 'free' and unrestricted airfield with extensive storage facilities, also based their active vintage aircraft or restoration projects there – the major overhaul of the Shuttleworth Spitfire Vc was the first example of such work carried out on an airworthy aircraft at Duxford.

The IWM arranged an Open Day in 1973 and was surprised by the large number of visitors who turned up despite inclement weather. News of this activity soon spread among aviation enthusiasts, and in April 1975 the Duxford Aviation Society was formed by the part-time volunteers to assist the IWM in various conservation and restoration projects.

After an inconclusive Public Enquiry, which reported in 1975, the IWM completed negotiations in February 1976 to take over all the buildings on the site, plus the apron and control tower, and (apart from the Open Days) the site was first opened to the public for a couple of months from June 1976. A 'Department of Exhibits (Duxford)' was set up at the IWM head office, with Ted Inman and Martin Garnet in Lambeth and Dr Charles Rhodes and Peter Loveday at Duxford. This set the site and airfield firmly upon the path that was to lead to Duxford becoming the pre-eminent European aviation museum and the most important centre worldwide for airworthy ex-military aircraft and major restoration projects that it has become today.

The flying at Duxford was very uninhibited in those early and carefree days, with Cambridge University Gliding Club members sometimes being scared out of their wits by a 'warbird' blasting past; very low flying and spectacular 'beat-ups' were not unknown. Ormond was the leading light in this thrilling aerial activity, and Neil Williams too gave several impromptu aerobatic displays. But it all became far more controlled when, early in 1977, Cambridgeshire County Council purchased all of the airfield south of the apron, including the runway, and agreed to operate it jointly with the IWM as a properly licensed and regulated airfield.

The growing amount of activity and rapid rate of expansion of the entire Duxford facility throughout the 1970s was exciting the keen interest of aviation enthusiasts. The

'The flying at Duxford was very uninhibited in those early and carefree days . . .' – Ormond in his T33 'Black Knight' just a few feet above a cornfield adjoining Duxford Airfield, causing photographer John Rigby to duck!

media coverage of the Concorde flying in to land for its last time at Duxford on 20 August 1977, just before commencement of the building of the new M11 motorway, aroused great interest among the general public too, especially as the eastern third of the main runway was lost to the roadworks immediately afterwards.

This decade of energetic expansion was fuelled by the Imperial War Museum, which at last had the space to enable it not only to display items previously kept in storage, but also to acquire many more major exhibits; the Duxford Aviation Society, which solicited civil airliners for preservation as soon as they were withdrawn from service; and various private owners and collectors. Apart from Ormond and the Shuttleworth Trust, these now included Mike Russell, with his 'Russavia' collection of Miles Gemini, BAC Drone and DH Tiger Moth restoration projects, plus half a dozen vintage gliders; Sandy Topen, with his Vampires V and T11, Meteor NF14, plus Piston- and Jet-Provosts; Jeff Hawke, with Meteor IV, Javelin, B25 Mitchell, DC3 and Beech 18; and Robs Lamplough, a well-known collector (about whom much more will be heard later!) who moved in his ex-Israeli Mustang and Spitfire restoration projects in 1976, and flew in with his Harvard and Beech 17 'Staggerwing'.

This was an extraordinary period of expansion at Duxford and many important aircraft, including the TSR-2, which led the world in advanced aviation technology, and those from the pioneering Skyfame Museum at Staverton near Gloucester, were saved from the scrapman's axe. Great credit is due to the IWM, the DAS, and the private owners and collections, for the consequences of their foresight, shown throughout the 1970s, are exhibited in the 1990s – and will be in the next century – to interest and inform present and future generations.

Meanwhile, in 'Blenheim Palace' the long-term Blenheim restoration process had commenced, albeit in a fairly leisurely way. The fuselage of 10038 had been stripped of all internal fittings, placed on trestles, partially paint-stripped, and a couple of damaged skin panels had been removed. But work on it was very low-key; the maintenance of Ormond's flying aircraft naturally took priority and members of the team often had to rush off to places like India or Germany to rescue other aircraft or components that he had acquired. Both Blenheim centre-sections and wings, together with the fuselage of 9896, were stored untouched at the back of a hangar, while the entire building next door to 66 was piled high with engines and all the other airframe components and various bits and pieces.

Ormond was a dynamic and charismatic leader, always at the hub of the activity at Duxford. His infectious enthusiasm and single-minded determination inspired his helpers; he cut through red tape incisively and delighted in brow-beating bureaucrats. His obvious love of flying was soon shared by his Team, and the great interest it aroused was noted by others at Duxford, in particular and most perspicaciously by Ted Inman, newly appointed Keeper by the IWM. Together they did much to establish the basis of the unique and highly successful combination of a major national museum (comprising only static exhibits) working closely with privately-owned, live, exciting flying aircraft that has made Duxford the internationally acclaimed major public attraction it is today.

However, fate dealt a terrible and tragic blow, for in July 1977 Ormond Haydon-Baillie was killed in a flying accident at an air display in Germany. How deeply his loss was felt by all at Duxford is shown in the obituary notice in the Duxford Society Newsletter of December 1977, reproduced as Appendix 1.

The sudden loss of his enormous energy, enterprise and enthusiasm seemed, in the words of one of his Team, 'just as if someone put the light out'. Ormond had been carrying out a photo-sortie in an Italian P51-D Mustang, formating on a much slower camera aircraft, when it appears that he made the one fatal error that cut down such a brilliant leader and pilot. Most sadly, a hero-worshipping German teenaged lad, so thrilled at the chance to go up in the Mustang, was killed too – fate can be very cruel.

The driving force had gone. The Team were left leaderless and became uncertain as to the future of the collection, so they soon dispersed; some joined other projects at Duxford, others drifted away completely. Meanwhile the Haydon-Baillie family decided that Ormond's entire collection was to be broken up, and it fell to his brother Wensley to make the arrangements for disposal. Apart from the personal tragedy, his loss was most unfortunate, for after decades of neglect the work on the Blenheim restoration project had at long last actually been put in hand, but now it had to be abandoned.

Thus the infant Blenheim restoration project ground to a complete halt. 'Blenheim Palace' became disconsolate, darkened and deserted once more. The Blenheim components were forsaken and rested in silence again, gathering the dust; soon the IWM wanted them removed as it needed the space. It seemed as if the poor Blenheim, abandoned and neglected for so many years, was destined – even as its lengthy restoration to airworthy status had finally just commenced – to remain earthbound, and that it would never be able to take to the skies again.

For myself, I had not yet set foot in Duxford so was completely unaware of any of these sad events, only learning about them later. So how did it come about that my footsteps were pointed in the direction of Duxford – and towards the Blenheim?

Chapter Two

'Someone really ought to do something about it'

During this period – the late 1970s – 'The Chequered Flag', a well-known sports-car garage in West London that I had founded some 20 years earlier and still ran on a day-to-day basis, had sponsored Robs Lamplough for a modest amount in a few Historic Car Races with his front-engined P25 BRM. I had met him some ten years earlier when the 'Flag and he were both involved in Formula Three racing; he was then an enthusiastic amateur owner/driver and we were running the F3 Brabham Team for the works with a good measure of success. When, one day in 1978, Robs mentioned quite casually that he 'had some Spitfires and Mustangs up at Duxford', I will admit that I was fairly sceptical and took this news with the proverbial pinch of salt. So, shortly afterwards, I tracked down a telephone number for the Imperial War Museum at Duxford and contacted them. Yes, they did know a Mr Lamplough, and yes, he did have some Mustang and Spitfire projects there.

That July I had flown with him in his Harvard to Silverstone to see the British Grand Prix, as the BRM was entered in the Supporting Historic Car Race. We had an enjoyable day, Robs leading his race for a few laps before fading away to finish third, and I met and chatted with several old friends from the 'Flag's racing days such as Frank Williams, Innes Ireland and Keith Duckworth. So when Robs invited me to visit Duxford, and offered to show me round his projects, I accepted with considerable curiosity as to what I would be able to see there.

What I did see there was quite an eye-opener, as it appeared to my uninitiated eye to be just a load of bent and battered metal that seemed fit only for the scrap-yard! In an old hut we climbed over great piles of damaged and corroded alloy, with odd bits of broken and rusty metal here and there, some parts of which were, to me at least, only barely discernible as belonging to Spitfire airframes. They were the remains of at least three Israeli Spitfires that had crash-landed on the Golan heights during the first Arab/Israel war, had been stripped of useful parts and abandoned. Robs found the remains still laying there many years later, and the Israelis said, 'If you want to go to the trouble and expense of taking them away, then you are welcome to do so.'

So he did! He also found a Russian T33 tank that had been supplied to the Syrians, and presented it to the IWM if they would cover the costs of shipping the entire consignment back to Duxford. In fact, however badly damaged the exterior alloy panels of the Spitfires were, the hot and dry climate had preserved the interior frames and stringers of the fuselages, as well as the spars and ribs of the wing and tail sections, remarkably well. As an experienced collector and restorer, Robs knew that these decrepit components were sufficient to form the basis of one or more aircraft rebuilds.

In another hut were three P51 Mustang fuselages – still with the faded Israeli markings visible – plus a few battered wings and tails, and a huge pile of other bits and pieces. They were in marginally better condition than the Spitfire components, but any rebuild was clearly a most formidable undertaking. Even many years later, having gained a far greater insight into the difficulties of such major rebuilds, it still seems to me quite remarkable that at least one of these Spitfire wrecks, as well as a single Mustang re-created from all those damaged P51 components, are now actually flying!

In a hangar Robs showed me his YAK 11, the Russian equivalent of the American T6 (Harvard) advanced fighter-trainer, undergoing a complete rebuild – unlike the others this was at least a complete and recognisable aircraft. Supplied by the Russians to the Egyptians, it had force-landed in Cyprus during its ferry flight in the 1960s. Also in the hangar, and being worked on, was a Boeing B17 Fortress and a North American B25 Mitchell that had obviously been standing out in all weathers for a long time.

Lurking in a back corner of this hangar were some more derelict aircraft components, soon to assume a far greater importance and significance to me – though I was entirely and blissfully unaware of this at the time – for laying on some old tyres was the dusty main fuselage shell and gutted nose portion of a Bristol Blenheim, with some faded yellow paint and the remains of an RAF roundel still visible. Stacked against the wall in the corner on some more old tyres were two decrepit centre-sections, complete with rusty engine mountings and undercarriage frames. Some dim memory from my days as an ATC cadet at school allowed me to recognise the fuselage as belonging to a Blenheim, due to the odd shape and asymmetric framing of the 'scalloped' nose where the glazing had once been. I mentioned this to Robs, but made no other comment.

At that stage the Blenheim as an aircraft meant nothing to me at all. I could only remember, albeit vaguely, reading that the RAF had used them as a 'stop-gap' bomber at the beginning of the war, but I had never actually set eyes on one before. Completely unbeknown to me at the time was that over the next 17 years the Blenheim would come to mean more and more to me – indeed, to dominate my life! I would learn that it was far, far more important to the RAF than just the 'stop-gap' bomber I had recalled. I could not foresee or even imagine that my eyes would witness that forlorn mound of wreckage growing gradually to become once more a beautiful, living, flying aircraft.

Looking through the windows I saw the bare fuselage and nose of a Blenheim.

This nose section had been partly stripped out; note the tattered remains of the seat harness under the pulley on the back of the pilot's seat chassis.

Later that morning, through the window of the workshop diagonally opposite the hut where Robs' Spitfire components were stored, I saw the main fuselage and nose section of another Blenheim. It was clearly a sister to the one in the hangar, as some

The rear fuselage mounted on trestles and partly paint-stripped. An outer wing is laying on trestles beside it.

similar faded yellow paint was visible, although this fuselage was mounted on trestles and had been partly paint stripped. The empty shell of the nose stood alongside; both were dusty and seemed strangely uncared for. I could see a pilot's seat on a tubular frame and several other components laying around.

Peering through the murky windows of the next door building we could see many rusty and filthy dirty engines, some mounted on engine frames, all in various states of dilapidation and with many parts missing, plus a huge mound of other damaged air-frame components such as a couple of rough-looking tailplanes, two dented fins with the vestigial remains of rudders hanging on the back, a very battered gun turret, some old wheels and brake-drums, plus many other bits and pieces. They looked similar to the pile of derelict Spitfire components in Robs' hut. But no one was working in either of the darkened buildings, and it all appeared neglected and somewhat forlorn, so I asked Robs to tell me about it.

He confirmed that what we had seen formed the basis of two long-term Blenheim projects – one a hoped-for restoration to possible flying condition, with the other to be restored eventually as a static exhibit – and that they both had indeed been abandoned, for their owner, Ormond Haydon-Baillie, had been killed in a tragic aircraft accident just over a year earlier. I said that this was a great pity, particularly as the long-overdue restoration had apparently only just commenced, and as I knew that there was not an airworthy example of the Blenheim anywhere. To me it was sad to see such an eminently worthwhile project cut off just when, after a delay of many years, it had been started. The seed had been sown in my mind.

We repaired to an excellent lunch at the Chequers Inn at Fowlmere; from the photographs of P47 Thunderbolts and P51 Mustangs on the walls, this had clearly been a favourite wartime watering-hole for the USAF personnel based at nearby Duxford and Fowlmere airfields.

The four best engines in 'Blenheim Palace' prior to stripping down, laid out for the first Duxford Open Day in 1975. On the bench are a stern section, a partly dismantled fin, undercarriage components, and a pilot's seat.

But I couldn't get those abandoned Blenheim remains out of my mind. The seed had found fertile soil and was starting to sprout. So I quizzed Robs about what was likely to happen to them, and about the set-up at Duxford generally. It seemed to me most regrettable that the proposed Blenheim restoration would not now be carried out, for I felt strongly that it really should. I hadn't at that stage begun to consider consciously that I might become involved personally. I regarded it as 'one of those things that someone ought to do something about'.

Robs had known Ormond well, and told me that he had been a great driving force behind several of the main restoration projects at Duxford, and that he was at the centre of the flying activity there, so was sorely missed. He explained that Ormond, like himself, had gathered a crew of keen volunteers to help him with much of the maintenance work on the flying aircraft, and more especially on the major restoration work, as it was simply not viable to have such work carried out at commercial rates. He went on to inform me that Ormond's family had decided reluctantly to break up his collection of aircraft and aviation projects as they were not able to continue with them, and that his brother Wensley was acting for the estate in their dispersal and disposal.

Robs explained that the situation was becoming complicated, as now that Ormond's three T33s, his Sea Fury and his Chipmunks could no longer be flown, and work on the Blenheims and all his other restoration projects had come to a halt, the IWM was pressing ever harder for the removal of all of these aircraft and projects from Duxford as it needed the space itself. This was proving difficult, as such exotic ex-military aircraft, even if fully airworthy, are by no means easy to sell, especially within a given time limit; and to find a purchaser for such a large collection of derelict aircraft components, even when they are portentously termed 'important restoration projects', was very much more difficult. Further, no formal tenancy agreement had been drawn up for the considerable amount of space occupied by Ormond's aircraft and projects at Duxford, the family had begun talking of 'their occupancy rights as tenants', and the whole situation was getting very tricky.

If Ormond's restoration projects, especially the Blenheims, were to be dispersed away from Duxford – a dispersal that appeared to be approaching rapidly – it was clear that the likelihood of the undertaking of a comprehensive rebuild of one of them back to full flying status would become so remote as to be almost inconceivable. And even if the unrestored airframes and components were allowed to remain at Duxford, the prospects for the continuation – yet alone completion – of the Blenheim rebuilding project, as things stood with the Haydon-Baillie family, remained non-existent.

The seed had now taken firm root. It now seemed to me a grievous shame that the intended Blenheim restoration had foundered, and I felt that these once famous warplanes deserved a far better fate than being allowed to simply fade away. I would have much preferred to have been told that the prospective rebuild was going to be persevered with by the family through to completion in flying condition, but alas this clearly was not to be. Therefore the very availability of the forsaken Blenheim project at the time of my arrival on the scene at Duxford appeared particularly fortuitous.

The seed was now a little plant growing in my mind, and had formed itself into the notion that I should at least look into the possibility of taking over the Blenheim restoration, and investigate if this was feasible, or even possible.

Robs agreed with me that it was a pity that the restoration had foundered, and said that it would soon be dispersed, and probably lost forever, unless someone could be found soon with sufficient time, money and dedication to take over the undertaking. We speculated about who would be likely to assume the responsibility for such a supremely difficult project, and be able to see it through to completion – clearly he did not want to do so himself. It was all very well us both saying 'Someone really ought to do something about it' when each of us actually meant 'someone else, but not me!'.

But he did not know that even then the seedling was seeking the light, and I was wondering if that 'someone' could possibly be me. When I hinted at this tentative interest, he became most enthusiastic and said that 'the restoration of old warbirds to flying condition is absolutely fascinating', adding that it was 'far more challenging and satisfying than rebuilding old racing cars'. He assured me that I would love 'the aircraft restoration scene', and said that he believed that I possessed the temperament and ability – plus of course the money – to 'make a real go of it'. When Robs is 'all fired up', as he was then, his great enthusiasm is highly contagious, and it applied a dose of fertiliser to the tender plant so that it grew rapidly into a firm intention!

While driving back to London I turned over the known facts and options in my mind, for I was beginning to explore and develop the idea that, through my garage company, I might be in the position to 'do something about it' and take over the Blenheim project. I already viewed it as a clearly desirable and worthwhile objective; it might even make sense as a very long-term investment, and our Company Articles allowed it. So it did appear to be feasible as long as we could control the rate of expenditure on materials, labour and general overheads and not let them run away.

It seemed to me that I could keep this expense under control by three main methods: first by simply taking our time on the project – spreading the expenditure over many years if necessary – as we were not bound by any rigid time-scale. Second, by the continued use of mainly volunteer labour as pioneered by Ormond and Robs. And third, by agreeing suitable arrangements with the IWM for the continued use of facilities at Duxford, which obviated the need to pay rent and rates. These appeared to me to be the three key elements in maintaining this essential control of costs.

But when trying to review as dispassionately as possible the overall prospects of this daunting restoration project, and the intended commitment of my company and myself to it, certain fundamental questions needed to be asked – and satisfactory answers obtained if possible – before, and not after, we became committed.

Primarily, did I really want to become so involved personally when I had more than enough to do as it was? Could my Company afford to take on such an obviously costly undertaking? Was it not most likely that it would turn out to be a 'pig in a poke' anyway? Was the proposed restoration to flying condition, however desirable and laudable an objective, even possible, let alone viable? For I knew that I could not get very excited about rebuilding a static aircraft. Could the IWM be persuaded to allow it to remain at Duxford? Would the volunteer team Ormond had gathered together wish to become involved in the project again? Could the Civil Aviation Authority be satisfied that the rebuild would be carried out to full airworthiness standards in order to issue the necessary Permit to Fly upon completion?

Or was it all just a pipe-dream anyway?

Had I realised at this early stage that Fate would decree, some nine years later and at a particularly traumatic and fraught time in my life, that once more it would be necessary to ask myself most of the self-same questions, and this time be faced with finding the answers without the resources of my garage company behind me, it is almost certain that I would have balked at taking it on in the first place.

I remembered reading once 'There is more pleasure in building castles in the air than on the ground', which seemed very apt in the circumstances. Incidentally, I looked up the source of this adage recently, as I thought it might make an appropriate inscription to place at the beginning of this tome; it was quoted as being by Edward Gibbon from his 'Miscellaneous Works' of 1796!

Chapter Three

Scrap metal

The time had now arrived to address these questions as realistically as possible, and attempt to find some answers to them.

Robs put me in touch with Wensley Haydon-Baillie who was handling the dispersal of his late brother's estate; I telephoned to express my interest in the Blenheim components and to make a few general enquiries. I then went to see him to try and establish exactly what was available and at what price. This was not easy as no inventory existed and he was reluctant to indicate the price range he had in mind, although hinting that it was a substantial sum – being an astute businessman he was attempting to persuade me to make an initial offer. But I felt that if I 'went in' at too high a figure he would shake my hand instantly to confirm acceptance!

Although I could look around the components stored in the corner of the hangar at Duxford again, and did so, it proved difficult to gain access to the workshops. The IWM was being very cagy, but after I wrote to explain the position, they agreed to allow me 'limited access for inspection purposes only'. So I duly signed a chit to this effect at the Guardroom and, accompanied by a Warder who clearly thought I was certifiable, was permitted to make a brief inspection of the components stored in 'Blenheim Palace' and the adjoining building. The small storeroom remained locked throughout this visit.

It was all rather depressing. The main fuselage that I had seen through the windows sitting on trestles was just a bare shell; it had been partly paint-stripped and two skin panels had been removed, and the interior was bare of all fittings, though retaining the original paint, flaking off in many places. Generally, it appeared to be structurally quite sound. The nose section was in a similar condition – the cockpit had completely vanished, having been gutted of all internal fittings – but was also not paint-stripped internally, and it was only partly so externally. Various components lay around: the tubular chassis for the pilot's seat and controls, with the seat itself, the control column and rudder pedals, was on a bench; the rear fuselage section, with bent tailwheel fork below and battered fin above, stood on the floor separated from the main fuselage; and a badly damaged outer wing, with most of the trailing-edge sections behind the rear spar missing altogether, lay on two trestles, but no work appeared to have been done on it. Several piles of muddled cables, scrap wires and twisted piping, as stripped out from the interior, lay around. It was clear that the amount of restoration work carried out up to that stage on the basic airframe had, almost literally, barely even scratched the surface, for an immense amount of crucial, costly and complicated reconstruction work still remained to be done.

We went through the connecting passageway to view the mass of engines and other

Above left *'It was all rather depressing'* – *a wing, showing the damaged and corroded skin panels, each numbered prior to removal.*

Above right *The same wing showing the skeletal remains of the aileron.*

components stored next door, and their condition was even more discouraging. The 20-odd engines were all as recovered and remained untouched; those areas not covered by the black, caked residue of oil, grease and dirt showed considerable surface corrosion – rust on the steel components and white on the alloy ones. Some engines were still in

The interior retains the original paint, flaking off in many places. The turret seat can be seen, with the lap-harness hanging below and part of the hand controls above.

The nose section was in similar condition, 'gutted' of all internal fittings but not paint-stripped.

their mounting frames, many were not; several still had their stainless-steel exhaust-collector rings attached, although very few of these appeared serviceable. Not one of the engines appeared to be complete; nearly all were missing major and vital parts altogether, such as complete cylinder barrels, carburettors, manifolds, ignition harnesses, valve-gear, magnetos, etc. Most had lost the all-important engine-driven ancillary pumps for the oil, fuel, hydraulic, vacuum and pneumatic systems, as many alternative uses for these expensive items had been found by the Canadian farmers. Being a very self-sufficient breed they are adept at this – they rarely throw anything away!

Inspecting the interiors of the crankcases of several of the engines, possible where one or more cylinder barrels were missing, and with the aid of a torch, showed that the connecting-rods, pistons and interior surfaces appeared to be in a remarkably well-preserved condition. They were all covered with a light film of oil, which had certainly helped over the years to protect them from the elements.

It seemed therefore that it might be possible that sufficient material could be extracted from this great hoard of 45-year-old and incomplete engines to provide the necessary components to be overhauled and made fully serviceable to provide the two good engines that we would need. It was still an unknown factor whether or not it was possible, on such old and derelict engines, for this major reclamation work to be carried out to the very exacting standards and tolerances so rightly required for aircraft engines.

The great piles of miscellaneous parts and bits and pieces from the airframes, engines and aircraft systems laying at the far end of the building were in very poor condition, and provided an even more sobering sight. These piles contained most of the collected items: control rods and levers, yards of cables, pulleys, chains and sprockets; reams of electric wiring, switches and components; some broken instruments; numerous brackets and fittings; and very many lengths of pipework, hoses, oil- and fuel-lines, etc. These were all as stripped out from the nose and main fuselage sections, the engine and undercarriage bays, etc, and had apparently been discarded as being incapable of further use.

Some of the other major airframe components laying around these piles were more easily identifiable, but in an equally distressed and dilapidated condition: main wheels and tyres with rusty brake-drums, axles and brake shoes; two battered tailplanes with the skeletal remains of the elevator frames, plus two fins with the parts of the rudder frames still attached (being fabric-covered, the elevators and rudders had apparently been nibbled away by hungry cows and other animals!); a section cut like a huge slice from a rear fuselage but including most of a turret (used for years as a plaything by generations of children); and some dented fuel and oil tanks.

Equally bent and battered, and (to me at least) practically unidentifiable, were hundreds of pieces both large and small of scraps of alloy in a great variety of weird shapes and sizes: fragments of fairings, partial remains of cowlings, remnants of various skin panels, pieces from inspection covers, parts of flaps, hatches, etc.

All in all it looked to me like a huge and virtually impossible metallic jigsaw, with far too many damaged and missing pieces – and no picture to guide assembly!

I looked up what I could about Blenheims in the few aviation books that remained from my earlier days, and visited Chiswick Reference Library to see what more I could find out. I discovered that they had been a very important aircraft to the RAF, and was surprised that they had faded away as far as they had in the public memory.

The next step I took was to seek the advice of someone far better qualified than I was to assess the practicability, or even the possibility, of the proposed restoration to flying

Piles of battered alloy panels, two fins and the skeletons of rudders and elevators – being fabric-covered, these had been nibbled away by hungry cows and other animals!

condition of this mountain of what was, in effect, little better than scrap metal.

I had spoken with Norman Chapman, an ex-RAF fitter who, it turned out, had worked on many Blenheims during the war and was then Robs's aircraft engineer working on the YAK 11 rebuild. He was very keen to see the Blenheim project rescued and pointed me towards his friend Fred Hanson, another ex-RAF fitter and by then a vastly experienced and fully-licensed aircraft engineer, who was responsible for 'signing off' the Duxford-based B17 Flying Fortress 'Sally B' amongst others, and was nominally the engineer supervising the work on the Blenheim. He should be able to give the definitive answer to the most important question of all – was the proposed restoration to airworthy status possible or not?

A meeting with Fred Hanson at Duxford was arranged. We poked and prodded at the Blenheim remains in the hangar and workshops once more and made some notes as we went along. These became ever more depressing, with a growing list of very serious difficulties, such as the mainwheel tyres being unserviceable and no longer made, the propellers being beyond repair and likewise unobtainable, with many more major items found to be missing or too damaged to be used. Plus the fact that no manufacturer's drawings, or any new replacement parts for either engines or airframes, were available at all. This much we had established during a brief preliminary survey – and no doubt many more problems would be discovered as restoration work progressed.

At the end of the day we sat on a bench overlooking the peaceful, deserted airfield, a scene unchanged from Duxford's earlier days, and fortunately remaining unspoilt by electricity pylons or housing or industrial estates. The trees, hedges and fields leading over the brow to the south of the airfield were still as they had been when seen by wartime crews wondering what tomorrow would bring. Fred and I held a serious discussion about the feasibility of the proposed restoration. He explained that the aircraft would have to be put on the United Kingdom Civil Register so that the Civil Aviation Authority Surveyors could monitor and approve the work as it progressed, and that we would have to keep detailed records so that they would be able – if entirely satisfied – to issue the Permit to Fly upon completion of the rebuild to flying status. Even as we spoke I could imagine the rebuilt Blenheim taking off against that timeless backdrop – I always did have a vivid imagination!

However, Fred was extremely dubious as to whether this rebuild would be possible, and clearly had grave reservations. I tried to press him to give his firm opinion as to whether any of these known difficulties would prove to be insurmountable or not. He was, naturally, reluctant to commit himself to any such opinion, as there were far too many unquantifiable factors. He thought that, if some such factor – known or unknown – did make it impossible to restore the Blenheim to full airworthy condition, then 'we would end up with an excellent static exhibit'.

This was not what I wanted to hear. Although I had to respect his opinions, as he – not I – was the highly skilled professional aircraft engineer, I tried to prevail over his perfectly valid misgivings by saying, 'If man made it once, man can make it again', 'Where there's a will there's a way', and other such fatuous remarks, trying to overcome his objections one by one. Upon reflection, I feel now – many years later – that I was being both unreasonable and naively over-optimistic in attempting in this somewhat facetious way to talk him out of his doubts and justifiable reservations.

However, he agreed that it *should* be done, and I continued to persuade him to agree that it *could* be done – even if it took several years and cost a substantial sum – assuring him that I was prepared to expend considerable amounts of both time and money. He did finally, and somewhat reluctantly, agree, 'providing I had a bottomless pocket'. Little did I know what I was really letting myself in for!

The next step was to meet the former members of Ormond's 'Black Knight' Team and see if they were willing to rejoin the project and get it moving forward once more. Obtaining a couple of their names and telephone numbers from Wensley, and through those two contacting the rest, we arranged a meeting one evening at the Chequers in Fowlmere.

They were a youthful and cheerful group. One who stood out by his keenness and the astute accuracy of his questions was young John Romain. They were encouraged when I related Fred Hanson's opinion that it could be done, but anxious to learn that I was aware of the great amount of work needed, and seeking assurance that I was willing to see the project right through to the end. I think that they were worried that I might lose interest and give up in the face of the great difficulties that they realised were bound to occur in such a mammoth task.

I told them that I did appreciate fully the immense scale of the work involved, and was able to reassure them of my utter determination to complete the restoration. I said that I was sure that we would be able, between us all, to find ways to overcome or 'get around' the many problems that would doubtless arise.

They were most enthusiastic and delighted that the abandoned Blenheim projects would be retained and not dispersed, readily agreeing to return to restart the restoration work as soon as the necessary arrangements had been concluded. I thought, somewhat fancifully, that far from being a 'Black Knight', I must have appeared like the proverbial 'White Knight' riding to rescue the Blenheim when all seemed lost! However, the most significant thing to come out of that evening was that the Team had answered another of the important questions in the affirmative.

The next question requiring urgent resolution was whether or not suitable arrangements could be made with the IWM for the airframes and engines to remain at Duxford and for facilities to be made available for the restoration work to be carried out there on a long-term basis. This was far from easy. For, following the difficulties it was experiencing in attempting to regain use of its own premises when it had repeatedly requested Wensley to remove the aircraft and restoration projects from Duxford, the Museum was determined not to allow the establishment of any sort of tenant/landlord relationship. I asked them to grant a lease on the workshops and to enter into a rental agreement for the part of the hangar space that we would need to carry out the final assembly work, but the IWM was unwilling to do either. To me, security of tenure was important so that we could plan forward and be able to carry out the rebuild on a sound and business-like basis. Also, it was clear that we needed to spend money on improving and equipping the workshops, office and stores, and did not want to be asked to leave as soon as we had done so!

Protracted negotiations followed. I could not obtain any form of lease or rental agreement from the Board of Trustees and thus had no security of tenure at all, which was worrying. I had to be content with an agreement, renewable on a three-year rolling basis, that they would make sufficient space available in return for our providing suitable aircraft – including the Blenheim in the course of the rebuild – on long-term loan to the IWM as public exhibits. That basic agreement, in slightly modified form, continues to this day. I also negotiated further with Wensley and reached agreement on a mutually acceptable purchase price for the project, and he subsequently sent me a sales contract for signature.

Thus most of the major questions had been answered affirmatively: the rebuild to flying condition not only *should* be done, but *could* be done; if all the work (and the paperwork!) involved was done properly, the CAA would be able to issue a Permit to Fly upon completion; the Team was ready and willing to restart the restoration;

'Surrounding heaps of virtual scrap' pair of skeletal rudders in front of two tailplanes; axles and brake-shoes to fore of pile on left; a turret section on the right 'cut like a huge slice from a rear fuselage'.

arrangements could be made for it to stay on at Duxford; the project was available for purchase; and my company was in a position not only to take it over but also to be able to control the costs.

But other vital questions still required answering, and I alone could provide the answers. Did I really want to take on such an onerous task, and was I right to commit my company and myself to such a burdensome long-term financial liability? The answers were difficult to find. I realised that this commitment was far from prudent from the business point of view, especially in light of the number of known difficulties, and the advice that other major problems, at that stage unknown, were bound to arise in the course of the work. I wondered if I did have enough perseverance, application and determination to see this daunting task through to the end – only time could answer that one. My heart was strongly tempted to go ahead, but my head knew it would be unwise to merely 'turn a blind eye' to the obvious cost and the great risks and difficulties involved. Few can disagree with the conclusion that it would have been far more sensible for me to simply 'walk away' and leave it alone. Clearly I was standing at a major fork in life's road and the signposts were contradictory.

For even I, the eternal optimist, understood fully that it would be very much an uphill struggle to complete the restoration of this derelict old hulk and the surrounding heaps of virtual scrap and turn it all back into a Blenheim in full flying condition once again. Many people said that it couldn't be done. Certainly it was an undertaking not to be taken on lightly and I had been warned very clearly that the prognosis was not at all good. Indeed, the situation reminded me – from my days as a choir-boy many years before – of the quaint phrase in the preamble to the Marriage Service admonishing participants that the estate of Holy Matrimony was 'not by any to be enterprised, nor taken in hand, unadvisedly, lightly or wantonly'.

Chapter Four

Wheels of fate

It may help you to understand how I attempted to arrive at the answers to these remaining but vital personal questions, if I provide a brief summary of my own background and the factors that influenced the development of my interests and personality.

I was the youngest of three sons and was brought up as a baby in London, then as a child in Twickenham during the war. Our father had a couple of drapery shops, and we, as a family, had no aviation connections or ambitions whatsoever, so it was quite impossible to foretell that all three boys would eventually become pilots. My father served in the Army throughout the Second World War; being just too old for front-line service, he drove a desk not a tank.

I followed my two elder brothers into the Scouts, which seemed a great adventure to me. Alex, the eldest, was Troop Leader; he volunteered for pilot training in the RAF in 1941 immediately he was old enough to do so. The middle brother, Kennett, became Troop Leader too, and when he left school later in the war he trained as a design draughtsman, so did not join the Forces. They both attempted to satisfy the voracious curiosity of their younger sibling. For my part, I tried to follow the good examples of leadership they had set me, as I looked up to them both, and a few years later I in turn became Troop Leader. As Alex had joined the Royal Air Force it seemed natural for me, when I was old enough, to join the Air Training Corps as a Cadet – later I rose to Flight Sergeant, although the war was over by then.

Thus it was entirely due to the example and influence of my eldest brother, during those formative boyhood years, that I acquired and later developed my own strong interest in aviation, which, resurrected many years later, led to my direct and deep involvement in the Blenheim restoration. If Alex had decided to join the Navy or the Army instead, I might one day have become involved in restoring a boat or a military vehicle, but certainly not a Blenheim! More likely it would have been a sports-racing car, resulting from my later strong interest in cars, mainly due to the influence of Kennett.

Alex noted the early part of his RAF career in the front of his copy of *Aircraft of the Fighting Powers*. Thus I know that in September 1941 he, like many tens of thousands of other hopeful young men both before and after, joined the RAF at Lord's Cricket Ground passing through the Air Crew Reception Centre at Regents Park. Alex went to No 8 Initial Training Wing at Newquay, and (via Posting Wings at West Kirby and Heaton Park and the ACDW at the Grand Hotel Brighton) to No 9 ITW at the Shakespeare at Stratford-upon-Avon. Then he went on to Tiger Moths at 22 EFTS at Cambridge, the course moving a week later to 29 EFTS at Clyffe Pypard near Swindon. Later he was on Ansons at Penrhos and, I believe, Whitleys at 24 OTU Honeybourne. Didn't some of these RAF Stations have lovely names!

Alex, my eldest brother, who sparked my boyhood interest in aircraft. Soon after his 20th birthday he was killed in action to join the 55,573 men of Bomber Command who lost their lives during the war.

His notes stop at this point, but I know the OTU was equipped with Whitley Vs, and he had half completed a scale model of a Whitley complete with all the crew positions. Here he would have 'crewed up' with the other young men who were to share his fate, going on to a 4 Group Heavy Conversion Unit (1652 or 1658) in Yorkshire. Finally, at the end of 1942, he was posted on to Halifax Mk IIs with his operational unit, No 102 'Ceylon' Squadron, based at Pocklington.

His RAF nickname was 'Plum', after the famous cricketer Sir Pelham Warner, and he celebrated his 20th birthday with the Squadron early in 1943. A few weeks later his Halifax was shot down by flak when crossing the Danish coast at low level on the way back from bombing Stettin on the moonlit night of 21 April 1943. The dreaded telegram arrived at our home: '. . . regret to inform you that 1318828 Sgt A. F. Warner is reported missing in action'. We hoped that he had baled out, or 'ditched' in the sea, had been taken prisoner, or evaded capture as many aircrew did, but we just did not know, and had no means of discovering, what fate had befallen him and his fellow crew members.

Even a letter some months later stating that he 'must now be presumed killed' did not ameliorate the desperate uncertainty as to his fate, which was most distressing to our family, mother especially, as it must have been to the thousands of other anxious families in similar circumstances. Two of the crew did survive to become POWs and confirmed some months later through the Red Cross that the other five crew members, including Alex, had indeed been killed and given a military funeral in Denmark. This news removed the dreadful uncertainty, but could not alleviate the grief and sorrow we all felt.

Although I was only a small boy at the time his loss affected me greatly and certainly altered my outlook on life. He left me his collection of aeroplane models and books, including the first two volumes of *Aircraft of the Fighting Powers*. I added the other five volumes as they were published, and many other books and magazines about aviation and the RAF, reading them all avidly. As mentioned, I was in the ATC and the Scouts, forming an Air Scout section, and became so interested in flying that in 1951 I too joined the RAF when old enough.

My knowledge of the significant contribution made by Bomber Command to the war effort grew steadily. I had read that Bombers were the only major offensive weapon available to this country for several years, and I learned too something of the enormous cost both in industrial and human terms of this tremendous and unremitting effort.

Looking back now, I can see that Blenheims were scarcely mentioned, which explains why, when I first saw the Blenheim remains at Duxford some 30 years later, I had merely the vaguest recollection of the type and thought that they were merely a 'stop-gap' bomber used for a short period at the beginning of the war. As far as I knew, my brother had not flown in Blenheims, though he certainly would have seen plenty of them during his training through 1942, thus they had no direct link to him or consequent appeal to me.

After surviving the usual Selection Boards, thorough medical examinations and Aircrew Aptitude Tests at North Weald, I did some 'square bashing' at No 3 Recruit Training Wing at Bridgnorth – where the few of us who wore the white aircrew flashes in our forage caps soon learned to leave them off to avoid the special attentions of the more sadistic NCOs! Soon after passing the Pilot's Grading School on Tiger Moths at Shellingford I persuaded the Aircrew Transit Centre at South Cerney to post me to 4 FTS at Heany in sunny Southern Rhodesia (as it then was) rather than 2 FTS at chilly Spittlegate, by claiming (quite incorrectly) that the family had friends in Bulawayo. Following the usual 18-month RAF pilot's training course – six months ground training, six basic flying and six advanced flying training on Harvards – I gained my 'wings' as a 19-year-old, and thought I was the 'bee's knees'.

That I wasn't nearly as good as I thought I was is demonstrated by the very lucky escape I had, both from what could so easily have been a fatal accident, and from being court-martialled or at least suspended from the course in disgrace. A few days before the 'wings parade' I was sent up to fill in a few more solo flying hours and indulged in the fascinating but strictly forbidden practice of low flying – and I mean grass-cuttingly low, for the greater the risk the greater the thrilling sensations of speed. With the adrenalin flowing freely, I saw two trees on the crest of a slight brow; the gap in the middle appeared wide enough for a very steep turn between them, and this I attempted. However, I didn't get the aircraft quite vertically banked for – while glancing at the lower wingtip which was a couple of feet from the ground – the upper wingtip struck the other tree, wrenching the Harvard violently over into the start of a cartwheel in that direction.

How I missed the ground I don't know – the heave on the stick and rudder was instinctive. The poor aircraft was vibrating and shuddering so severely that I could only just keep it in the air. I could see that the wing was badly damaged – the leading edge was stove in with bits of branch jammed in it, the pitot tube had gone (and with it any indication of airspeed), and fabric was flapping from the aileron. It required lots of rudder to keep it straight, and maximum power to keep it flying at all; if I reduced power even slightly the damaged wing buffeted so badly that it was clearly on the point of stalling, which would have flipped the aircraft on to its back.

I was badly shaken, but somehow managed to struggle up to about 800 feet and stagger back to Heany, with the engine cylinder-head and oil temperatures rising alarmingly. I called an emergency on the RT and flew it straight in, even pulling off quite a good landing.

The Flight Commander was rightly furious and made it clear that I was for the 'high jump', but later he cooled down and helped me to concoct an Accident Report blam-

'I gained my "wings" as a 19-year-old, and thought I was the "bee's knees".'

ing 'loss of height following an engine misfire due to mishandling the mixture control when overshooting from a practice forced-landing'. This didn't wash with the Wing Commander Flying, who made me fly to the practice forced-landing area, which had very few trees indeed, and show him which one I had hit, as the evidence made it abundantly clear that I had struck a tree. Of course I was unable to do so, so he told me to take him to the right one, which I did. On seeing it he said, 'You must be off your bloody rocker.'

When we got back we had a long talk in his office, and I was aware that my entire future depended on the outcome. He had inspected the damage and said that it was amazing that I was able to fly it back, although he could not forgive the foolhardy low flying. He added that the country had invested heavily in my training, and although I had shown that I did not deserve this investment, the course had just been completed satisfactorily, so it seemed wrong to allow one stupid lapse to deny the taxpayer the benefit of all my training. I could see that a life-line was being extended. He instructed me to withdraw the original Accident Report and submit a more truthful one, adding, 'This is definitely your last chance. You seem quite good at stringing words together, so have it on my desk in the morning. Dismiss.'

I saluted and left, to toil through the night on the fateful report. It worked, because although reprimanded, I was not suspended and was relieved to be awarded my wings a few days later.

I relate this salutary tale, not only because it describes a major crossroads in my life caused by the foolish over-confidence of youth, but also because it helps me to convey a little of the sheer exhilaration that several Blenheim pilots have told me they experienced when engaged in low-level attacks – an exhilaration that even overcame their fear of the great dangers they knew they were being exposed to. Often they were hedge-hopping to death or serious injury, but they still – some $5^{1}/_{2}$ decades later – recall the thrill and excitement rather than the danger.

Back in the UK, we Rhodesian-trained pilots found the weather to be a rude shock after becoming used to constant sunny skies; and pilot navigation was far more difficult over England's crowded terrain compared with our easy task out there with so few major features. We all had to complete bad-weather flying courses at South Cerney. I applied to go on to Canberras and, after months of leave and a spell as second-pilot on a Lincoln Squadron, I finally got on to Meteors and Vampires. Nowadays I have seen these flying at air displays as 'The Vintage Pair', and, after a long career, the Canberra has also become an out-of-service classic!

I loved the actual flying, but whole-heartedly disliked the 'red tape' and petty bureaucracy endemic to the Forces, so when 'my time was up', and without getting as far as a Canberra cockpit, I returned to Civvy Street. Aircraft were no longer part of my life.

At that time I liked to run about in little open cars; some even had sporting aspirations, but in reality they were 'old bangers' worth only a few pounds. So when pals still in the RAF asked me to 'find them one like that', I did, and sold several MGs and the like at a small profit. This small one-man business soon developed through personal contacts, local advertisements and purchasers 'coming back for more', and it seemed a pleasant enough way to earn a living. Besides, having found that I liked speed, I really wanted to become a racing driver and had observed that most of the then leading drivers owned garage businesses, so thought that I would follow that road.

My surviving brother Kennett and I followed motor racing closely; he did a few sprints and hill-climbs and I raced a Kieft at Castle Combe, but a wheel came off – the shoestring we ran it on wasn't long enough! Kennett was then a design draughtsman with Connaught Engineering in Send, and helped to develop their L3 Sportscars, and type A Formula 2 and type B Formula 1 racing cars. The latter, in the hands of Tony Brooks at Syracuse in 1955, was the first British car to win a Grand Prix for 31 years.

When Connaught ran out of funding in the late 1950s, Kennett went into the electronics industry, helping to design the radar for the ill-fated TSR-2. The local Council objected to a car business being run from the garage at our home, so I drifted into another sportscar garage. I had met (through often finding ourselves as rival bidders on the same sportscars at car auctions) the proprietor of 'Performance Cars' on the Great West Road, and he – also an ex-RAF pilot – offered me a job on the sales staff. They then dealt in sportscars on a large scale, and I soon learned what to do and – more importantly – what not to do in such a business.

I then ran the sportscar department for a garage in Purley for a year to see if I could manage such an enterprise on my own. Thus I felt equipped to run my own business specialising in sports and Gran Turismo cars – now termed 'classic cars' but in those days just our normal stock in trade. So I started 'The Chequered Flag' in a small showroom in the Fulham Road, soon moving to far larger premises in Chiswick further to the west of London. I didn't wish to call it 'Graham Warner Motors' or anything similar, as I've never pushed my own name forward, but wanted a distinctive yet easily remembered name. I toyed with naming it 'Pits and Paddock', but am glad that I didn't! The business was successful and enabled me to indulge my passion and go motor racing properly at last.

The 'Flag prepared and entered cars, always well presented in a striking black-and-white colour scheme, initially in the International Sports and GT categories, then in the main single-seat formulae, for some 15 years, with varying degrees of success. In the early days I was lucky enough to win quite a few races both at home and on the continent, mainly in Lotus Elite-Climax and Elan-Cosworth GT cars with the registration LOV 1. The crowds loved to see such small cars dicing with much larger ones; at one stage I held the outright or class GT lap records at all the English circuits, and some of the continental ones. This led to the offer of a 'works' drive for Aston Martin, and I drove the Zagato Astons 1 VEV and 2 VEV, being Jim Clark's team-mate in the TT at Goodwood. I also tested the powerful DBR1 3-litre sportscar there, and was asked to drive it in the 1000Ks at the Nurburgring, but declined as I felt that I could not produce competitive lap times in an unfamiliar car on the unknown and notoriously tricky 14-mile circuit – and I didn't want to drop it in the ditch at a major World Championship event! I wasn't asked again!

Motor racing was great fun in those days and there were many larger-than-life characters who enlivened proceedings; I know that it has grown far more sophisticated and computer-dominated nowadays, and that the commercial and financial pressures are now colossal, but many drivers seem to take themselves rather too seriously and do not appear to enjoy it all as much as we did.

The GT class in racing was the closest to the types of car we sold, and we hoped, probably wishfully, that our participation promoted the business. Apart from Lotuses, we ran a couple of Shelby Cobras, a 4.7- and a 7-litre, and won the first 1,000 km race at Brands Hatch with the latter, the only FIA International Race ever won by a Cobra. As far as single-seater racing was concerned, the 'Flag designed and built about 100 Gemini FJ cars – the first car ever to use a Cosworth-Ford engine, and the car in which Jim Clark made his debut single-seat drive – and ran 'works' F3 cars for Brabham, McLaren and DAF (to demonstrate their 'Variomatic' band-driven transmission). We won quite a few races with the former marque, but very few with the latter two.

Apart from Jim Clark, Graham Hill and Jackie Stewart, also future World

My Chipmunk and Elite were both finished in the white-and-black Chequered Flag 'house' scheme.

Champions, drove for the 'Flag, as did many other famous drivers, who were helped on their way in the early stages of their careers. By the late 1960s I had hung up my own crash helmet to concentrate on running these various teams, for we also ran the odd F2 car and rescued the struggling Token F1 Team before moving on to a Formula 1 Brabham, which proved a very expensive mistake! This almost ruined the firm and we withdrew from racing.

In the mid-1970s we were tempted into international rallies with a Lancia Stratos. This was quick but fragile – we led many events, but it lasted long enough to win only a handful. We tried with factory-backed TR7-V8s and a Porsche 3-litre RS Carrera, but to no avail. This marked the end of the road as far as serious participation by The Chequered Flag in motor sport was concerned. I have outlined this long and close commitment to racing and rallying to show that, as well as running the garage business itself – though the day-to-day management was in the hands of the various departmental heads – I was so heavily involved in cars that they were virtually the 'be all and end all' of my life. Aircraft played but a marginal part in it at that time; although I had bought a Chipmunk for a plaything a few years earlier – it too was painted black and white! – I didn't have time to fly it more than occasionally, and soon sold it. Also, Kennett surprised me by announcing that he had gained his Private Pilot's Licence and persuaded me to share a Cessna with him, but I was too busy to take more than the odd trip in it. For many years my entire life revolved about The Chequered Flag and motor cars.

However, although the 'Flag had withdrawn completely from motor sport, in the late 1970s we did have one final and fateful fling with it. This was the link through historic car racing with Robs Lamplough and his BRM, which, as related earlier, led directly to my own involvement with the Blenheim.

For, by accepting the mainly positive answers to my queries and discounting the more negative ones, I had convinced myself that it would be fitting and entirely appropriate for the 'Flag to take over the Blenheim restoration. Therefore, for better or worse (also a phrase from the Marriage Service – it did seem rather like getting married!) I decided to go ahead, and commenced to finalise the necessary arrangements straight away. Thus motor racing was not only instrumental in causing aircraft in general to re-enter my life, but also, within just a few years, for one aircraft in particular to occupy the very centre of it. The wheel of fate had turned full circle.

Chapter Five

The Team

The Wedding Vows were made, the Agreements and Contracts soon signed, sealed and settled: now the Team could get weaving on the restoration work again. We surveyed the airframe and other components as thoroughly as possible and planned a sequence for the rebuild of the major airframe sections; it was decided that the engines would have to be dealt with separately. The Blenheim restoration project was retrieved from its state of desuetude and put back on the road.

We equipped the workshops with a range of tools and equipment such as a compressed-air system with coiled overhead leads for the air-driven drills and riveting guns – the high-pitched 'bzzzz' of the 'windy' drills and the loud 'brrp-brrp' of riveting were sounds to be heard constantly in 'Blenheim Palace' over the next few years! We erected workbenches and racks of shelving in both sections of the workshops, added proper strip-lighting, and redecorated right through. Over the months we fitted the workshops out with pillar-drills, bench and mobile grinders; gas, electric, and arc welding equipment; a small lathe, vices, surface plates, clamps, measuring devices and gauges; and so on. We also decorated the office, and installed telephones, office furniture and equipment, so that the paperwork could be looked after better. The 'crew room' section had an old electric kettle, but we added a refrigerator, microwave oven and coffee-machine so that the Team could be looked after better too!

They certainly needed frequent mugs of hot beverages in the cold weather as a heating system was not installed in the workshops until several years later. The fact that the Team were willing to leave the warmth and comfort of their homes right through the winter months to continue working in unheated workshops or hangars at Duxford demonstrates their dedication to the restoration.

We gathered together copies of all the repair and maintenance manuals that we could trace from both the Filton and Fairchild companies, as the original and licensee manufacturers, together with all the RAF and RCAF manuals, notes and diagrams on the airframes, engines, systems, carbs, props, turrets, controls, etc, that we could find, or were donated to us, and studied them carefully.

It was decided to give the ex-'Black Knight' team a fresh identity, so we adopted the name 'The British Aerial Museum' – with the sub-title 'of Flying Military Aircraft' – to describe our main activity, which, starting with the Blenheim, would be restoring then operating airworthy (as opposed to merely static) ex-military aircraft. Incidentally, this latter phrase has been replaced colloquially by the apt term 'warbirds', which originated in the United States.

The new Museum title, soon shortened to 'BAM', was on our blue letterhead, with a circular logo of the name around a three-bladed propeller. It was designed to carry more weight in our correspondence with the aviation industry, various authorities such as the CAA, overseas museums and so on, that we needed to contact. This attractive logo also appeared on the Team's new blue overalls. The fresh identity, the re-equipping of the workshops, but above all the resumption of active work on the Blenheim restoration itself, revitalised the Team and gave them a new sense of purpose.

Talking of 'the Team', this is a suitable point to describe and attempt to flesh out for you some of the characteristics of the individual members. They built the aircraft, not me. It was their dedication, their sheer hard work put in over many years, and their collective ability to overcome numerous seemingly insoluble problems, that put the Blenheim back into the air. The credit is due to them, not me.

First and foremost is John Romain. Quite simply, without him the world would not be able to see a Blenheim back in the skies again. The road has been a very long, eventful and arduous one for him too, for he has been deeply involved with Blenheims for more than half his life! No one else has worked harder, or for longer, on the Blenheim restorations; no one else has overcome so many of the problems and difficulties encountered along this lengthy, obstacle-strewn road with such ingenuity and perseverance.

Today John is deservedly famous for his spirited but sensitive demonstrations at the controls of the Blenheim and other 'warbirds' as our Chief Pilot; then he was a lowly apprentice with British Aerospace at Hatfield. Entirely through his own efforts he has progressed all the way from being a fresh-faced, long-haired teenager, one of Ormond's unknown part-time volunteer helpers, to his present positions as Managing Director of our associated Aircraft Restoration Company, and Chief Pilot and Head of Engineering

John Romain climbing from the cockpit after giving one of his spirited but sensitive displays in the Blenheim.

at BAM – still fresh-faced, but now with short hair! He is widely respected for his depth of aviation engineering knowledge – especially concerning rebuilding and operating the types of ex-military aircraft that we handle – and is rightly renowned among his peers as an excellent Test and Display Pilot.

Following several years as a volunteer working on the Blenheim in his own time while still an aeronautical engineering apprentice, on completion of his training with BAe John joined BAM full-time in July 1980 as a qualified aircraft engineer. Over the next few years, all the time gaining valuable practical experience, he studied for and passed many examinations and tests to obtain his full CAA licences on the airframes, piston engines and propellers of all the different aircraft that we work on. Thus he was authorised to assume full engineering responsibility for all the restoration work, and 'sign off' the work-sheets. In addition, he also obtained his Private Pilot's Licence, and in due course his Instrument and Night Ratings, then his Commercial Pilot's Licence. He now has CAA Display Authorisations for Chipmunk, Auster AOP9, Storch, Jungmeister, Flycatcher, Harvard, Beech 18, B25 Mitchell, Catalina, Corsair, Spitfire and Mustang – not forgetting the Blenheim, of course! All in all, it is a remarkable record of self-improvement that shows what can be achieved by an intelligent young person endowed with strong ambition, perseverance and self-discipline.

As you can see, John has worked hard and made impressive progress, but his success has not changed his cheerful, outgoing, ingenuous and amiable nature. No one else at Duxford is as universally popular or as well thought of for being unfailingly helpful. Always ready with a friendly grin, his pleasant, open and straightforward manner conceals his incisive intelligence and a single-minded determination to get what he wants.

Incidentally, I have noticed this tenacious, somewhat combative edge in others who are also fairly short in stature, such as Jim Clark and Jackie Stewart. John is fortunate indeed to look about ten years younger than his age, but did not appreciate this attribute when, well into his 20s, he sometimes experienced difficulty in getting served in pubs!

I am convinced that no one else in the world today has a better or more intimate knowledge and understanding of the entire detailed construction and operation of Blenheim airframes, engines, propellers and systems than John Romain, for he has been working closely and constantly on them for almost 20 years now, and literally knows every single nut and bolt. The Team is most fortunate to be headed by such an exemplary engineer, who is also a sound, skilled and sympathetic pilot, for this combination of abilities is rare.

Some of you may have read my earlier book, *The Forgotten Bomber*, in which I paid this tribute to John: 'If a Distinguished Service Order could be awarded in the aircraft restoration movement, he certainly deserves one!' This sincere compliment still reflects the high regard in which I hold him, and I know that many ex-Blenheim crews agree with me.

John's wife, and mother of his two little boys, is Amanda, the engaging younger sister of Robert Jackson, who was one of Ormond's original band of volunteers and put in a lot of work on the first Blenheim. He is now a family man too, but had to give up working at Duxford as he had to run the family building business when his father retired, but we still see him from time to time.

As John and Amanda left the beautiful Whittlesford village church on their wedding day, a Spitfire from Duxford, flown with his usual elan and impeccable timing by 'Hoof' Proudfoot, an ex-RAF Harrier pilot, did a slow roll overhead, which was a nice touch. During the marriage service the vicar reminded the congregation that John was already married to a Bristol Blenheim, so much tolerance and understanding would be needed! It appears that I am not the only one to regard deep involvement with the Blenheim project as akin to being married to it.

Another John who was central to our Team was John Larcombe. Like 'Hoof' he was a superb ex-RAF pilot and, as a Qualified Flying Instructor on Gnats, had been Officer i/c Standards for 4 FTS at RAF Valley, where he polished the performances of many 'Red Arrows' pilots. He instructed on Canberras at Bassingbourn and was awarded the Air Force Cross for his distinguished flying in them. He was a naturally gifted pilot and had wide experience on 'warbirds', flying Robs Lamplough's aircraft amongst others. He joined British Airways and became a Trident Captain, and later a Tristar Captain, then Training Captain on Boeing 747 'Jumbos'.

We appointed him as Chief Pilot to BAM in 1980, and he not only performed many immaculate air displays, but also all of our flight testing. He carried out the first flight, and all the flight testing, of the restored Blenheim and flew some beautiful displays in it. 'Larks' – for that was John's nickname – also 'checked out' the pilots on all of our ex-military aircraft. He supervised and nurtured John Romain as a fledgling pilot and they often flew together. His thorough pre- and post-flight briefings set an excellent example, he encouraged us to adopt the correct attitude to making our flying both enjoyable and safe, and his readiness to explain to us the finer points of smooth and accurate flying were all invaluable contributions. We could not have wished for a better or more conscientious Chief Pilot, and he became like a father-figure to the Team – I know that he improved my own performance as a pilot, and I became a far safer one as a result of his helpful advice. That John Romain is today such a fine, safe, and smooth pilot is, I am sure, due largely to the excellent example set by, and the beneficial influence of, John Larcombe.

You will therefore understand that his loss in a fatal crash in June 1990 caused great grief to the Team, and left a void at the centre that was particularly hard to fill. He came down near La Ferte Allais airfield in France, in a Bell P63 'Kingcobra' of the Fighter Collection, shortly after take-off on a Monday morning following his usual superb displays there over the weekend. The fighter had a major engine problem, then caught fire. Although he had a parachute he did not bail out and it appears that – selfless to the end – he stayed in the cockpit to guide the doomed aircraft clear of a village at the cost of his own life. We consoled ourselves with the knowledge that he had died while doing what he loved best – flying a 'warbird'. At the very moment that he was laid to rest in Linton cemetery, after a moving memorial service, John Romain led overhead a fitting aerial salutation in the B25 Mitchell escorted by a Spitfire and Hurricane.

The tragic loss of John Larcombe caused another heavy burden to fall upon the young shoulders of John Romain, but they proved to be sufficiently broad and resilient, for he rose magnificently to the challenge of greatly increased responsibility, becoming our Chief Pilot and carrying on – I am pleased to say – in the same quietly efficient manner and the fine tradition of his mentor in ensuring that our flying is enjoyable but safe.

This was not the only distressing loss the Team had to bear. John Gullick, who had been the original Crew Chief in Ormond's day and led the expedition to India to rescue the Spitfire hulks, also passed away. He had moved with his job to Emsworth on the South Coast, but contracted cancer and died there. John was slightly older than the rest of the Team, but was much liked and respected by them; we went down to his funeral very dolefully.

He had become an aviation enthusiast through acting as a Flight Observer in Chipmunks and Austers while serving with the Army in Cyprus during the EOKA campaign, and his ambition was to fly his own Piper Cub. He was a solid and conscientious

Team Leader who put in a vast amount of work throughout the first Blenheim restoration and was a real 'salt of the earth' type who could – and did – turn his hand to almost any task on the rebuild. He accepted readily the reversal of roles that occurred when John Romain, who was a much younger volunteer helper, came to work at Duxford as our full-time engineer, and was soon made Team Leader. We all missed John Gullick and his input into the restoration, but mainly we missed his steadying, kindly, humorous guidance.

All who have visited 'Blenheim Palace' at Duxford, or been shown around the Blenheim in the hangar, cannot fail to have noticed the ever-cheerful features and friendly demeanour of jovial John Smith – the original 'laughing policeman'. They almost certainly will have heard his chuckles too, and may even have winced at some of his jokes! Known to all and sundry as 'Smudger' (from the universal nickname previously given to Smiths in the Forces), he is a great asset to the Team.

Following specialised RAF training, he saw service, mainly in Germany, as a skilled metal-worker and beer-swigger. He went on to do research work with the Ministry of Aviation, then joined the Hertfordshire Constabulary, firstly as a PC 'Plod', then on to detective and forensic work. Here he learned his skills as a photographer and developed a strong sense of humour to offset the demanding and often harrowing nature of his work. He has now retired from the Police Force and works full-time for the Aircraft Restoration Company, but still finds enough of his own time to help with the Blenheim.

Skilled 'panel bashers', especially those that can rework old and brittle alloy and are good welders, are hard to find. 'Smudge' has straightened and repaired numerous bent and battered parts of the aircraft structure, and has welded, panel-beaten, rolled, wheeled and planished panels, cowlings and fairings, only fabricating new ones if the originals were beyond repair. Thus he carried out innumerable but vital metal-working jobs, large and small, on the Blenheim restorations, and without his crucial contribu-

'Smudger' Smith (left) and Colin Swann, who did much of the work on the second airframe, with Ian Arnold, in front of the completed power plant built up by Nev and Cliff Gardner, who are standing proudly alongside it in 'Blenheim Palace'.

tion they would have taken very much longer to complete.

Over the years he has replaced tens of thousands of rivets by individually drilling out each of the old ones, re-drilling every hole, and fitting a new rivet – he says he knows most of them by name, and they all start with a 'B'! His convivial manner and fund of jokes hides a serious and hard-working man who is completely dedicated to the Blenheim restoration. His contribution to it has been – and still is – truly tremendous.

Two other long-serving stalwarts of the Team are brothers Colin and David Swann, who have both carried out an immense amount of Blenheim restoration work. They are highly skilled and very versatile aircraft engineers who originally came from Fowlmere, near to the Chequers Inn mentioned earlier. Colin is an ex-RAF Halton apprentice. Although known colloquially as the 'brats', their general aviation engineering training is acknowledged to be the best available. After RAF service, mainly in the Middle East, he worked on the 146 at British Aerospace at Hatfield. Usually working on night-shifts, he had most days free, which he spent at Duxford – we do not know when he slept! He is a very good 'troubleshooter' in sorting out snags on aircraft, particularly on the electrical side. He devised and installed the specially modified electrical system on the Blenheim, which is a clever mixture of the old 12-volt system and modern avionics. Made redundant when BAe closed the Hatfield site, he joined the Aircraft Restoration Company full-time, but – like 'Smudge' – he still makes enough of his own time available to help with the Blenheim maintenance.

David, too, is an ex-apprentice, although he trained with Marshalls at Cambridge Airport, and is a fully licensed aircraft engineer who has worked with Monarch at Luton Airport for over 15 years. He too is on shift work, so usually has sufficient spare time to work long hours at 'Blenheim Palace' as well.

Both Colin and David have turned their hands to many of the rebuilding tasks, from paint-stripping and metal working to making and riveting new skin panels, but their main speciality is the installation and 'plumbing in' of the various aircraft systems – fuel, oil, hydraulic, pneumatic, electric, engine and flying controls, instruments, etc. These form the very heart of any aircraft – without them it could not beat at all – and they take a great deal of care and meticulous attention to detail to get right. Each system has to be made up accurately, installed, checked, carefully adjusted, re-checked and rigor-ously tested and re-tested, until it functions correctly. That all of the systems did so perfectly when the time came for the Blenheim to fly once more demonstrates the high standards of workmanship achieved by the whole Team – but especially by 'plumbers' Colin and David.

Another key member of the Team is Bill Kelly, who has now been working at Duxford for 20 years. Starting in the free and easy days as a cheeky 13-year-old part-time helper in Ormond's original crew – when he was by reputation a tearaway – he has progressed to becoming the expert and highly experienced full-time aircraft restorer that he is today. For several years Bill was employed as a mobile air-conditioning and refrigeration engineer, all the time also working long hours at Duxford, where he increased his skills as a part-time Team member, joining full time in 1988.

Virtually single-handed he carried out the complete renovation of the complicated hydraulically operated Blenheim gun-turret to bring it back into full working order. Thus he naturally became our first airborne 'rear gunner'. Throughout the long restoration he kept his dry sense of humour very active, being very adept at bestowing suitably droll nicknames. He is an amusing companion and always very popular with the rest of the crew, especially in the pub after work!

Young Nick Goodwyn helped enthusiastically on the Blenheim. He was a slender, polite lad with long fair locks, until the RAF College at Cranwell transformed him!

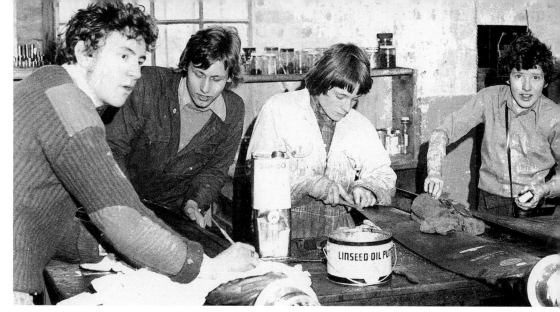

'Ormond gathered a team of volunteer enthusiasts' tweny years ago: including 'Beans' Smith, Robert Jackson, John Romain and Bill Kelly, cleaning down prop blades.

After gaining his pilot's 'wings' on Jet Provosts, and a tour instructing on BAe Hawks, he is now a Flight-Lieutenant operational Tornado pilot. How time flies!

Robert Sparkes is another personable young man who has helped with the Blenheim restoration for several years. Like David Swann he was trained as an apprentice at Marshalls of Cambridge, and later worked for BAe at Hatfield as a draughtsman, going freelance when Hatfield was closed down. His ability to produce proper engineering drawings has often been useful, and he is still a member of the Team. The connection with Marshalls continues to this day, as James Gilmour has just completed his apprenticeship there, and is a youthful but keen and hard-working Team member. The same description applies also to Chris Arberry; they both joined the Team only a few years ago and have fitted in very well, earning increasing respect from the others as they have gained practical experience.

Other Team members who played an important part in the Blenheim rebuild include Chris Hollyer, an aviation electrician whose work took him to Coventry, where 'Smudge' had often wished to send him anyway following some of their highly amusing verbal duels. Also taken away from Duxford by their jobs were Bob Hewitt, a gruff-speaking but hard-working Yorkshireman, and Hugh Smith who was particularly good at applying aircraft markings and now works for Histeric Flying at Audley End (sorry – I meant to say 'Historic Flying', but lapsed into one of Bill's nicknames). Young Mike Terry moved several years ago from doing restoration work at North Weald to becoming a freelance engineer, working conscientiously mainly for BAM and the Aircraft Restoration Company at Duxford – he is now excellent both at rebuilding and refinishing aircraft.

Ian Arnold, like Bill Kelly, has been working at Duxford for 20 years now, but, unlike Bill, always as a part-timer. Ian worked originally on Robs's aircraft – mainly the P51 Mustang – along with Barry Wright and Malcolm Chapman, but they joined our team when Robs moved his collection to North Weald, working mainly on the rebuild of 'Thumper', our now pristine T6-G Harvard.

Now that you have been introduced to the Team – apart from the engine specialists who will be presented later – let us look more closely at what they had to do to put a Blenheim back in the air.

Chapter Six

Evolution
of 'Britain First'

To help you to understand more readily the restoration process, I first need to describe briefly the genesis and design of the original Blenheim, as well as the methods of construction and the materials used by the Bristol Company during the 1930s, for that is what we had to deal with in the 1980s and '90s. If at the same time I sketch in some of the rapid developments in military and civil aviation in the context of the period, and the leading part played in them by the Blenheim, this may also help you to appreciate better its considerable historic importance.

The improbable origins of the Bristol Blenheim family of aircraft, and their progeny, the entire Beaufort, Beaufighter, Buckingham and Brigand ranges, is in itself a quite remarkable story.

The excellent reputation of the Bristol Aeroplane Company had been built up on a series of successful single-engined aircraft, from the famous Bristol Scout and F2B Fighter of the First World War (the latter still in service in 1928!), to the Bulldog, which served from 1929 to 1936. An early twin-engined monoplane design, the Bagshot of 1927, was a failure as the wings twisted when aileron was applied at more than 100 mph! This problem led to lengthy research into multi-sparred cantilever wings (those strong enough to withstand the loads without any external struts or braces), and to the Bristol Type 130 Bombay, which had no fewer than seven spars in each wing! The Bombay was first flown in 1935 and produced from March 1939 as a troop-transport by Short & Harland at Belfast.

But in 1935 Bristol was pinning all its hopes on being awarded a large production contract for its Type 133, a monoplane fighter of partially stressed-skin construction with retractable undercarriage and a Mercury engine. Those hopes were justifiably high, as the aircraft was highly advanced for the time, and testing showed that it very comfortably exceeded the demands of specification F.7/30. The company increased its production capacity in anticipation by building more construction 'sheds' and taking on extra employees. Alas, the sole prototype was destroyed in a needless spinning accident the evening before it was due to depart for the RAF Testing Centre at Martlesham Heath, and the contract went to rivals Gloster instead, with its conventional and much slower biplane, the Gauntlet.

Bristol persevered with single-engined aircraft, but to no avail. Only one Type 138, a high-altitude monoplane, was built, although with a supercharged Bristol Pegasus it did gain the prestige of a new world altitude record of almost 54,000 feet. Others were the Type 146, a fighter to F.5/34, but the single example was damaged in a landing accident and scrapped; the Type 147, a two-seater fighter to F.9/35, the contract for which went to the Boulton-Paul Defiant; and the Type 148 to A.39/34, an Army

Co-operation aircraft, the retractable undercarriage of which collapsed during a heavy landing, and the contract went to the Westland Lysander with its wide speed-range and strong fixed undercarriage.

These unadopted designs proved to be the last in a long line of single-engined machines constructed by Bristol, and the whole future of the company looked bleak. But this future became assured when the entire direction of the Bristol Aeroplane Company was changed irrevocably towards the design and manufacture of multi-engined aircraft instead. This sea-change, vital to the company's survival, and respons-ible for a great revival in its fortunes, came about in most unlikely and unexpected ways: through the confluence of chance meetings, working lunches, and the foresight and ambitions of a 'newspaper baron'!

In February 1934 Lord Rothermere, proprietor of the influential *Daily Mail* group of newspapers, previously the country's first Secretary of State for Air, and always cham-pion of the development of aviation, hosted a working lunch on this topic for his Editors, one of whom was Robert T. Lewis, editor of the group's Bristol paper. Earlier Lewis had covered for his paper a talk on aviation at a local function by Roy Fedden, Bristol's chief engine designer, where he mentioned a proposed civil twin-engined design using 'engines of advanced design' and 'revolutionary new construction methods', although adding that this was very much as a sideline to Bristol's single-engined aircraft activity.

Lewis, travelling to the meeting with his proprietor, met Fedden – quite by chance – on the London train, where they breakfasted together. Fedden expanded enthusiast-ically about the proposed design; he was convinced that his use of sleeve-valves in aircraft engines would be a great improvement, and praised the advantages of the novel monocoque form of airframe construction. He did not inform Lewis that these proposals had been turned down by the Bristol Directors.

Later that day, Lord Rothermere told his journalist guests that he wished them to encourage businessmen to make better use of rapid transport by civil aviation, saying that he would like the *Daily Mail* to set an example by being able to fly reporters and photographers to a news story that was 'breaking' anywhere in Europe. Lewis knew from Fedden that Bristol intended to exhibit at the Paris Salon a mock-up fuselage of the proposed small 'executive' all-metal low-wing civil monoplane, with two of the new Aquila sleeve-valve radial engines, as the Type 135. He believed that it would meet his proprietor's requirements, so drew his attention to the mooted project at Filton. Lord Rothermere expressed immediate interest, welcoming the opportunity to demonstrate that the British aviation industry could produce the fastest commercial aeroplane in Europe, and requested Lewis to provide full details within a week.

Lewis discussed the enquiry with Roy Fedden and Frank Barnwell, and obtained par-ticulars of their proposed new all-metal 'commercial twin-engined aeroplane' – com-mercial as opposed to military. When I say 'all-metal', the Bristol design was virtually an all-alloy aircraft, for only the engine and undercarriage frames and the spar booms were to be made in steel, and only the control surfaces were to be covered in fabric. This was to prove very fortunate for our restoration team some 50 years later!

The Type 135 had first been sketched by Captain Frank Barnwell, the Chief Designer, back in July 1933; he had merely outlined a neat four-passenger American-influenced light twin known in the company as 'the Captain's gig'. Fedden was keen to promote the idea within the company, as it was proposed to fit two of his pioneering new Aquila sleeve-valve engines, but the Bristol Board would not sanction the building of either the airframe or the engines, later authorising a 'mock-up' only.

Barnwell's ideas had been stimulated by the then emerging range of much larger all-metal American passenger planes, which used the new Alclad composite-alloy skins. Duralumin, an alloy with 4 per cent copper, was light yet strong (thus an excellent material), but corroded badly; thin external films of pure aluminium and a new heat-treating process cured this, so Alclad opened the way for aircraft construction methods that were a great improvement. Most of the main loads could now be dispersed over the aircraft skins, which were stressed to take them; these skins were held in place by light alloy frames and stringers as a semi-monocoque, resulting in far lighter and stronger structures. This replaced the earlier heavy warren-girder-type main frameworks of wooden or metal-tubing construction, usually rectangular in section, frequently wire-braced, and often with fabric-covered light outer frames of wooden formers and stringers curved to form the desired shapes.

The design advantages were confirmed during a visit to the United States by Frank Barnwell in 1934, where he studied the Douglas DC-1 and DC-2 (which had flown first in July '33 and March '34). These were of course the progenitors of the remarkable DC-3 Dakota series, as well as the Boeing 247 of 1933 and the Lockheed Electra of February 1934. All of these were low-wing cantilever monoplanes, of basic all-metal construction with the stressed-skins formed from the new Alclad material; all were fitted with twin radial air-cooled engines and retracting landing flaps and undercarriages.

I would like to mention here another American type with exactly the same layout – the excellent Beech Model 18 – as this has close links with the Blenheim Team, and we still operate one today! Although it was designed in 1935, and flew for the first time in January 1937, it was produced continually – mainly as the wartime C45 – until 1973, even longer than its famous contemporary the C47 Dakota!

By contrast, most European aircraft were still of fabric-covered all-wood, or mixed wood and steel-tubing, construction. De Havilland, which had been in the light-twin market for some years with the DH84 Dragon, produced two new all-wood fixed-undercarriage passenger biplanes festooned with bracing struts and wires: the four-engine DH86 and two-engine DH89 Rapide, both of which flew for the first time in 1934. De Havilland's first all-metal aircraft, the DH95 Flamingo – a high-wing mono-plane with twin Bristol Perseus engines – did not fly until 1938, and none were delivered until 1940. De Havilland was developing an alternative wooden stressed-skin structure via its DH88 Comet racer of 1934, which, through the DH91 Albatross four-engined airliner of composite wood construction in 1938, led to the outstanding wartime DH98 Mosquito, with its wooden 'sandwich' monocoque. But back in 1933, Frank Barnwell's sleek all-metal design for the Bristol Type 135 was, as we might say today, 'right at the cutting edge of technology'.

However, the Directors at Bristol were unimpressed initially by the proposal put forward by Lewis, fearing that the Air Ministry – by far the company's best customer – would be upset by Lord Rothermere's penchant for publicity, and particularly his declared aim to demonstrate that the state of aeronautical art had progressed far beyond that employed in the then current RAF fighters and bombers. But Lewis convinced them that the advantages outweighed this fear, and Barnwell and Fedden remained very keen to see their pet project adopted. They proposed replacing the 500 hp Aquilas with more powerful 650 hp Mercury engines, which they estimated would give a top speed of 250 mph, slimming down the fuselage to reduce drag, as well as providing the two extra seats Lord Rothermere required; this revised version became the Bristol Type 142.

A lunch was therefore arranged at Stratton House in London on 29 March 1934 with Sir Stanley White, Chairman of the Bristol Company, Frank Barnwell and Roy Fedden, plus Robert Lewis – who had worked hard behind the scenes. Lord

Rothermere was most impressed by the particulars of the Type 142, especially as it met his requirement of being 'the fastest commercial aeroplane in Europe', and agreed to finance the construction of a prototype to this specification, if the range could be increased for use in travelling between the capital cities of Europe. But he wanted to take delivery in one year's time, which was a tall order. He may have been influenced by the fact that his great business rival, Lord Beaverbrook, the Canadian owner of the Daily Express Newspaper Group, had just ordered an American Lockheed Electra of similar design – but 100 mph slower!

However, one of Lord Rothermere's most trusted advisers, Brigadier General P. R. C. Groves, formerly Secretary-General of the Air League of the British Empire, spoke out strongly against the intended order, stating in a memo that 'the proposed plane – if it ever flew' would be 'the joke of the technical press', although he overstated his case by adding that 'it would certainly kill any passengers foolish enough to fly in it'. Now it seemed that the project that so fired the imagination of Robert Lewis would be cancelled, so he briefed Roy Fedden carefully, and managed to persuade his boss to allow a meeting to permit the Bristol designer to justify the claims technically. Fortunately Fedden was a lucid and persuasive advocate and convinced an initially sceptical Lord Rothermere that the design was indeed sound, and that the estimated performance figures had been carefully calculated. The order was duly confirmed and a cheque for 50 per cent of the cost sent – but it had been a close run thing.

Had Lord Rothermere not been persuaded to continue, the history of the Bristol Aeroplane Company and of the Royal Air Force would have been very different, and the course of the Second Word War would have been changed. For there would have been no Blenheim, no Beaufort and no Beaufighter; post-war there would have been no Brigand, no Freighter, no Britannia, no Brabazon, and no Concorde – which was based on the Bristol Type 223 SST. It is most unlikely that the range of Bristol engines

The Bristol Type 143 and 142 'commercial monoplane' prototypes being built at Filton in 1934, showing clearly the semi-monocoque stressed-skin construction, highly innovative in those days.

would have been developed through the Mercury, Hercules and Centaurus to the Olympus that powers the Concorde and Vulcan, and the vectored-thrust Pegasus that lifts today's VTOL Harrier.

Once Lord Rothermere's order was confirmed, Bristol decided to develop the aircraft in two parallel versions, with a 70 per cent commonality of airframe components: the six-passenger Type 142 with twin Bristol Mercury 650 hp engines, designed mainly for speed; and the more economical Type 143, an eight-passenger version with twin Bristol Aquila 500 hp engines. A prototype of each Type was constructed purely as a private venture, for there was no Air Ministry interest or prospect of large production contracts. However, the Directors at Bristol were relieved to find that the Air Ministry did not object, but actively encouraged the project. Thus what had been up to then a low-priority 'back-burner' project while the company concentrated on single-engined aircraft, became its main undertaking, and was thrust suddenly into the limelight – and Lord Rothermere made sure that the light shone brightly! With patriotic pride he named his new aircraft 'Britain First'.

He also expressed concern at the growing might of Germany and the creation of the Luftwaffe, which highlighted the shortcomings of the RAF's equipment. The country was awaking from its peacetime slumbers and could no longer ignore the rapid rise of Nazi militarism. British rearmament commenced. 'Britain First' had appeared at a most opportune time.

The 142 first flew on 12 April 1935 and became an immediate sensation, greatly aided by the enthusiasm of the *Daily Mail*'s chauvinistic flag-waving. It had a very sleek and ultra-modern appearance, finished all over in polished alloy, and was aesthetically pleasing, with an attractive profile from the streamlined nose and straight top of the cabin leading into the elegantly shaped fin-and-rudder and curving below to rejoin the nose. Even with the original fixed-pitch four-bladed wooden propellers it was very fast; when fitted with two-position three-bladed metal props it went even faster.

The Type 142 that became 'Britain First' at a more advanced stage, with nose and rear fuselage sections mounted on the centre-section. What looks like the tailwheel is in fact a main wheel in the distance, as the tail wheel fork is resting on a jack!

The ultra-modern Bristol Type 142, commissioned by Lord Rothermere and named 'Britain First', created a sensation. It first flew at Filton on 12 April 1935, with fixed-pitch four-bladed propellers.

Incidentally, these were the advanced American Hamilton-Standard 'bracket' units, which could be changed from fine to coarse pitch during flight, and were soon being licence-built in England by de Havilland, later developed into the constant-speed variable-pitch propellers used on many British wartime aircraft. In 1937, Rolls-Royce and the Bristol Aeroplane Company jointly formed Rotol Ltd to create an alternative source of supply of similar propellers.

As a further footnote to history, Fedden was the prime and most vociferous mover in persuading the Air Ministry (and the British Aircraft Industry!) that the adoption of

'Britain First' at RAF Hendon: holding one of the new Hamilton-Standard propellers is a young RAF Armourer, Ian Blair. He went on to fly operations in Blenheims both as a WOp/AG and Observer, and won the DFM after removing his dead Pilot from the controls and landing the Blenheim Mk I. Ian later qualified as an RAF Pilot, and appears in the video 'Spirit of Britain First'.

variable-pitch constant-speed propellers and the use of 100-octane fuel were both essential factors in improving aircraft performance. They were both adopted, but only in the nick of time to save the nation in the Battle of Britain. Early Hurricanes and Spitfires had wooden fixed-pitch propellers, then the two-position Blenheim-type metal props, until a crash programme to convert the fighters to constant-speed units started on 22 June 1940! The Mercury, and its longer-stroked brother the Pegasus, were the first British engines to be cleared to run on 100-octane fuel, compared with the 87-octane then in use. They and other wartime engines, such as the Merlin, gave considerably more power when thus converted, as the better fuel permitted higher compression ratios and boost pressures.

However, back in 1935 the Air Ministry sat up and took notice, realising immediately the potential of the Type 142 as a fast medium-bomber. The Chief of the Air Staff wrote to Bristol inviting a 'proposal to supply the Bristol twin in reasonable numbers' and offering 'to test the aircraft made for Lord Rothermere at Martlesham free of charge in order to ascertain its performance and characteristics'. Note that this was before, not after as often stated, the sensational test results achieved at the AAEE at RAF Martlesham Heath. On being informed of the Air Ministry interest, Lord Rothermere, in a most patriotic and generous gesture, presented 'Britain First' to the Air Ministry 'for the Nation'. He had made his point, but at a cost in today's terms of several million pounds.

Sent to Martlesham Heath in June 1935, the Type 142 'Britain First' with 640 hp Mercury VI engines proved to handle beautifully and created a furore when it reached 307 mph with a light load, and 285 mph when fully laden. This was some 70 mph faster than the RAF's then standard fighter, the Gauntlet, and 50 mph faster than the Gladiator – which had only just been placed on order as the new front-line fighter.

In the Bristol drawing office Frank Barnwell, assisted by Leslie Frise and Archie Russell, commenced the design work – construction layout, stress calculations, perform-

Two views of the sleek prototype Bristol 142M (for Military), which first flew on 25 June 1936; it was soon named Blenheim and given the serial K7033. Large-scale production was already under way, and it was the first type to be produced in the new 'shadow' factories.

ance estimates, and so forth – involved in turning the Type 142 light civil transport into the 142M (for Military) medium bomber to carry a 1,000 lb bomb-load over a range of 1,000 miles. The wing was raised to the mid-position, allowing a bomb bay beneath the centre-section; a semi-retracting dorsal gun-turret, a forward-firing gun, and other military equipment were added; the cabin door and windows were deleted, and the nose re-configured to accommodate an observer; the tailplane was enlarged and raised; and the whole structure was strengthened. Unfortunately, this led to an increase in weight from 9,800 lbs to 12,250 lbs, which, with the extra drag of the turret, meant a drop in performance, even though the Mercury engines were uprated to 840 hp.

At a design conference called at the Air Ministry on 9 July 1935, Barnwell presented his proposals for the 142M, which were accepted without alteration. Instructions to commence detailed design work were given, and in August the specification 28/35 was issued to cover this. By September a firm contract for the production of 150 of the new 142M machines, by then named 'Blenheim', was placed. They were ordered 'straight off the drawing board' without waiting for the usual prototype to be built, with satisfactory completion of acceptance trials, before production orders were placed; it was felt that the outstanding performance of 'Britain First' had rendered these normal procedures unnecessary.

The Blenheim family of aircraft had thus been both conceived and born in most unusual circumstances. These were far removed from the standard method of the Air Ministry drawing up and issuing a specification, inviting tenders from selected companies, authorising the construction of a prototype by the favoured few, testing this extensively at Martlesham Heath, resolving any shortcomings revealed in the testing by agreeing modifications (which often had to be re-tested), before finally awarding a production contract. This procedure often took five or six years, with a further delay of three or four more before the new aircraft was ready to enter service.

New Mk I Blenheims K7036 and K7097 with 30 Squadron in Iraq in 1938, one being refuelled from drums; the contrasting Westland Wapiti illustrates the quantum leap forward in design. Two Squadrons of the similar Vickers Vildebeest biplanes fought alongside Blenheims against the Japanese invading Malaya in December 1941.

Further large orders to Filton for over 650 Blenheims quickly followed. The Blenheim thus became the first all-metal monocoque monoplane with retractable undercarriage, landing flaps and variable-pitch propellers ever produced for the Royal Air Force. The new government-sponsored 'shadow' factories, created to increase air-craft production capacity by car manufacturers such as Rootes, makers of the Humber, Hillman and Sunbeam-Talbot ranges, were also awarded large contracts to produce Blenheims, as were other aircraft manufacturers such as A. V. Roe, which built 250 at Chadderton.

At that time Avro was still constructing its Ansons by the 'old' methods, and study of the Blenheim's structure influenced the design of its own first all-metal stressed-skin aircraft, the Manchester, which with four Merlin engines replacing two unsatisfactory Vultures, became the famous Lancaster! The Manchester, though a much larger and more powerful aircraft, has the same basic layout as the Bristol aircraft: a mid-wing monoplane with a twin-spar straight centre-section carrying the bomb-load under the centre and the engines and retractable undercarriage units at the outer ends, passing through the centre of an alloy semi-monocoque three-section fuselage, but with gun-turrets nose and tail as well as the dorsal position, and with multiple fins and rudders. The two Manchester prototypes, to specification P.13/36, were ordered in September 1936 and the first one flew in July 1939.

By that time Bristol had become the largest aircraft manufacturer in the world; thousands of Blenheims were on order, with over 1,000 already in RAF service, and more than 6,000 were to be produced over the next few years. The Blenheim had saved the Bristol Aeroplane Company, and before long would play a vital part in saving our country too.

By that time also the Bristol Type 142M Blenheim Mk I – known colloquially as the 'short-nose' Blenheim – had been replaced on the production lines by the Type 149 Blenheim Mk IV – known rather unimaginatively as the 'long-nose' Blenheim.

Left *Blenheim Mk IV nose sections in quantity production at Filton in 1938. I wonder how many epic operational flights these units were involved in during the next two or three desperate years!*

Right *One of my favourite pictures: Bristol's test-pilot Bill Pegg shows clearly the clean lines of the Blenheim in this 1938 publicity photograph of a brand new Mk IV – L4842 – which was shot down on 17 May 1940 while serving with 53 Squadron.*

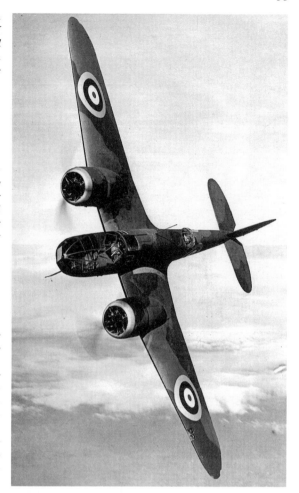

Below *This Mk IV was specially assembled to show the construction for the visit of the King and Queen to Filton in 1940. It reveals how the Blenheim is built around the wing centre-section, the front spar running between the engine frames and through the fuselage. The fuselage frames are revealed, as only the port side is skinned; the egg-shaped port inner-cowling is in place; and the rods on the face of the starboard outer wing spar are the aileron controls.*

Although delighted with the performance and fine handling of their Blenheims, the RAF was not happy with the cramped cockpit of the Mk I, especially regarding the Observer who barely had room to open his maps, and felt that the aircraft had insufficient range, particularly for Coastal Command use.

Bristol extended the nose by some 3 feet to provide a proper navigation position and table, and tried various nose configurations – for the view of the pilot had been spoiled – until arriving at the familiar asymmetrical scalloped nose shape we now know. More powerful Mercury Mk XVs of 920 hp were also fitted in place of the 840 hp Mercury VIIIs, plus extra fuel tanks in the outer wings, but the undercarriage had to be strengthened and fuel dump pipes fitted to keep the landing weight within limits.

The Mk II was a short-nosed version with the fuel tank and landing-gear modifications, but like the Mk III, which was a long-nosed version without these other additions, did not go into production. Many aircraft started off on the line as Mk Is and came off the other end as Mk IVs.

Most unfortunately, Captain Frank Barnwell OBE AFC BSc, designer since 1912 of many famous Bristol aircraft, was killed in his own light aircraft on 2 August 1938. A brilliant designer, he had been responsible for (amongst others) the Scout, F2B Fighter, Bulldog, Bombay, 'Britain First', Blenheim and Beaufort. In addition, following suggestions from Leslie Frise, he did the initial design work on the Beaufighter, originally a slim-fuselage Beaufort-Fighter using the same wings, rear fuselage, tail assemblies, and undercarriage. The Type 152 Beaufort first flew in October 1938, and the Type 156 Beaufighter in July 1939. See Appendix 2 for details of these types.

Blenheim Mk IVs had been coming out of the factories for a couple of months by the time of Barnwell's death, and the rate of production increased steadily to 24 a month through the Munich crisis as war looked more and more likely. Further development design work on airframes during that critical and hectic period was carried out by Leslie Frise and Archie Russell, while Roy Fedden continued to develop the range of Bristol engines and became overall Chief Engineer.

The first Mk I Blenheim to enter Squadron service joined 114 Squadron on 17 March 1937 and was written off on its initial landing through being inverted by the poor pilot who applied the brakes a little too enthusiastically. I imagine that he crept red-faced away from the wrecked Blenheim, avoiding the assembled 'top brass', to the airfield boundary where he lit up a Hamlet cigar to the strains of a Bach air!

The first Whitley also entered Squadron service that month, and the Fairey Battle a couple of months later; the Hampden and Wellington followed late in 1938.

Squadron service soon revealed that the Blenheim could carry 1,000 lbs of bombs 1,000 miles, was far faster than the RAF's front-line biplane fighters, and could readily evade or outpace them on exercises. This ability to avoid interception confirmed the faith of the influential 'the bomber will always get through' faction in the Air Ministry. It was indeed a 'hot ship' in those days, but the inevitable increase in weight caused by extra service equipment degraded the performance considerably and Squadron aircraft could only reach some 270 mph. Even the Mk IV, with 1,840 hp (using 100-octane petrol and +9 lbs boost) available from its two engines, was some 40 mph slower than 'Britain First' with only 1,300 hp, demonstrating the severe penalty of increases in weight and drag. Coincident with this degradation of the Blenheim's performance from 1937 to 1939 came the quantum leap forward in the performance of the new breed of single-engined fighters then appearing.

A far more meaningful comparison would have been with the eight-gun Hurricane and Spitfire monoplanes, both built as private ventures to the Specifications F36 and F37 issued back in 1934, and ordered into full production in 1936. It was evident that

Over 100 Blenheims were lost in accidents prior to the outbreak of war. The propellers of this 82 Squadron aircraft, L1112, were stationary when it crashed near Derby on 8 August 1939, as it had run out of fuel!

they possessed a performance far superior to that of the Blenheim and clearly out-gunned it by a factor of eight to one, for they were designed specifically to gain air superiority and ensure that the bomber did not 'always get through'.

In 1936 the Air Ministry, under Expansion Scheme F, called for 20 Squadrons of Heavy Bombers (Wellingtons and Whitleys) and 48 Squadrons of Medium Bombers (as Blenheims were then classified). That they anticipated heavy losses among the Blenheim Squadrons is shown by their requirement for the Original Equipment issue of 16 aircraft per Squadron to be backed up by 75 per cent extra (12 aircraft) in 'immediate reserve' and no fewer than 150 per cent (a further 24 aircraft) in 'reserve'. The significance of these figures did not percolate to RAF Command level; Fighter Command and Bomber Command seemed to inhabit separate ivory towers anyway, and the officially encouraged belief of the pre-war bomber-crews in the virtual invulnerability of their equipment was shown to be gravely misplaced once the war started in earnest.

Even more importantly, the most valid comparison would have been with the Messerschmitt Bf109E, already in widespread service with our potential enemy. It was far faster and more manoeuvrable than the Blenheim, and armed with 7.92 mm machine guns and 20 mm cannon, so that not only could it intercept the bombers easily, but also attack while still out of range of the Blenheim's totally inadequate rear-defence armament. Hundreds of Blenheim crews, plus those of many other RAF bombers, were to pay with their lives for this blinkered outlook of the Air Ministry in failing to recognise the realities of the comparative performance and armament of the aircraft in service with the prospective protagonists.

The airframe
takes shape

The first major section of the airframe upon which we concentrated our resurgent rebuilding efforts was the centre-section, in 1979. We moved it from its long-standing resting place in the corner of the hangar, transporting it by trailer to the work-shops adjoining Building 66, via the large double entrance at the rear, and placing it – inverted – on low trestles. As it is very large, being over 20 feet wide, we had to move most of the engines and piles of other airframe parts previously kept there out into storage to make room for it.

Meanwhile, in the main workshop several Team members carried on working steadily on the fuselage and nose sections, but the main effort was put into the centre-section. This was because we wanted to make it ready to move into 'Blenheim Palace' at an early stage, partly to free the adjacent workshop, which we intended to turn into our engine shop, and partly so we could start making 'trial fittings' of the other main airframe sections on to the centre-section in good time. We were planning well ahead, even if it did not always look like it!

The centre-section is the largest single portion of the entire aircraft. It has to be very strong as it carries the principal structural loads, and forms the central core of the Blenheim to which all the other main sections of the airframe are attached. The main fuselage fits right over the middle of it, with a large keel-plate joined to it below, and the nose-section fits on to both and to the front spar. The engines and undercarriage units are mounted on the outer ends.

The basic centre-section structure is built around the two full-depth main wing spars that run straight and parallel from end to end. The main undercarriage frames bolt between the outer ends of these wing spars, feeding their loads straight into them. These spars also carry the outer wings; the engine frames bolt on to the front spar; the fuel-tanks are carried between the spars, the oil-tanks over the front spars; and in wartime the bomb-load was suspended under the centre of them. Alloy chord-wise flanged ribs with span-wise 'top-hat' section stringers form the wing profile between the fuselage and the undercarriage bays, the whole assembly being stiffened by the stress-carrying alloy skin panels.

So, apart from the above considerations, it was clearly the most sensible section on which to start work. The tubular metal frames that formed the strong undercarriage bay and the engine mounting bays were removed, and these areas stripped right out. The flaps and their operating mechanism at the rear, and the mountings for the control runs at the front, were dismantled and removed, as were the inner fuel-tanks and all the pipework, cables and wiring. The skin panels were numbered then removed by drilling out the rivets individually. The entire interior of the centre-section was paint-stripped by hand, a long and laborious process, then inspected in minute detail.

However, the basic structure, built around the main spars, was not dismantled, although it was all paint-stripped and most carefully inspected, as were of course the spars themselves. As a jig to prevent any relative movement prior to removing the skin panels, we bolted a heavy steel frame to each end of the centre-section, using the lugs at the spar extremities to which the outer wings were attached.

The central 'well' between the spars, which forms the roof of the bomb bay, was separated out, repaired as necessary and replaced. Any of the alloy wing ribs, stringers, brackets or other parts found to be damaged were removed and carefully repaired, or used as patterns for the fabrication of their identical replacements, back-drilling all rivet holes to ensure correct alignment. We renewed the wood strengthening strips mounted internally beneath the walkways to the crew positions.

The only serious problem we found was slight surface corrosion on a few small areas of the steel booms of the main spars; the vertical spar webs and stiffeners were made of alloy and in good condition. We removed this superficial pitting by hand and treated the affected areas. We made up steel capping-strips and had them rolled to fit on top of the spars and heat-treated before they were bonded and riveted in place – this improved the overall strength beyond that of the original spar. The rest of the basic structure was quite sound, as it had been fairly well protected from the elements, so after the repairs and replacements mentioned above, it was all etch-primed and painted green.

Below left *The root-end of the outer port wing in the jig, showing the two main spars; rebuilt or new trailing- and leading-edge ribs are being fitted, plus the root- and tank-bay ribs.*

Below right *A close-up of the rebuilt trailing-edge ribs, with the recesses for the flaps at the top; the first two bays have new upper skins.*

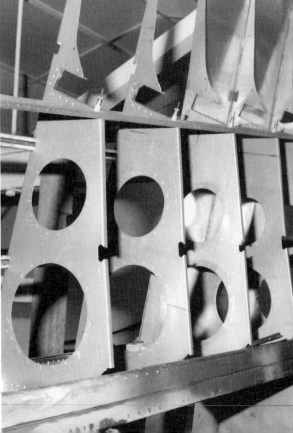

Re-skinning the exterior could then commence; we made up new panels using the old removed and numbered panels as patterns, having decided to go up a gauge in the thickness of the alloy and one size up in the rivets to improve the overall strength and longevity of this major structure. The new panels were made by placing the old numbered skin panel on a sheet of new alloy, marking it off with a scribe and cutting it to size, then back-drilling through each of the original rivet holes, securing the two sheets together with rivet pins as we worked along.

The new panel was then offered up to the airframe and held in position accurately by rivet pins of the size of the original rivets placed in alternate holes. The remaining holes were then re-drilled with a drill one size up from the original rivet, and secured by rivet pins of the larger size; the other rivet pins were then removed and the process repeated.

When all was checked, the new panel was removed, etch-primed all over and the internal side painted. It was then placed in position on the airframe and held again by rivet pins, so that it could be re-riveted in exactly the same location as the original, using the new oversize rivets to suit the freshly drilled holes.

This complete procedure does not take long to describe, but took very much longer to carry out in practice! In fact, more than two years of painstaking work was needed before we could move the rebuilt centre-section into the main workshop. There it was reunited with the fuselage, made entirely of alloy, which had been dismounted into its three main components: the main, nose/cockpit, and tail sections.

Each of these sections was then subjected to a similar methodical restoration process of stripping down, repairing or replacing, and rebuilding – and continued to be so for several more years to come! This involved countless hours of laborious paint-stripping by hand, right into the thousands of hard-to-get-at corners and crevices; cleaning down, using only non-metallic scouring pads such as Scotchbrite, so that we did not

The rebuilt centre-section, fitted with undercarriage units and oil-tanks, is moved from 'Blenheim Palace' to the hangar.

scratch or contaminate the surface; inch-by-inch minute inspection using magnifying glasses under strong lights, and dye-penetrants where needed; careful removal of any panel, stringer or part thus discovered to be damaged, cracked or corroded; the conscientious repair or making up of new replacements for any such items; replacing them, using the back-drilling method described above to ensure correct alignment; then etch-priming and repainting the myriad internal surfaces of the three main fuselage sections. Again, this process needs but moments to write about, but took several years of dedicated and very hard work to complete to the high standards required.

The pair of tubular steel frames that form the engine mounting and undercarriage bays, plus the engine bearers themselves, as removed from each side of the centre-section when work recommenced, had all been stripped right down and inspected particularly diligently – including crack-testing and X-ray examination of both the tubes and the welded joints – before being treated internally, shot-peened (with fine plastic 'shot'), etch-primed and stove-enamelled externally, then re-assembled as complete units. Over a year passed before these four substantial frames were ready. Looking just like brand-new assemblies, they were then bolted back into their position at the ends of the centre-section, using all new bolts and nuts.

At this stage we tried several trial mountings of the fuselage on to the centre section; this was satisfying as the airframe was growing visibly month by month.

John Gullick was mainly responsible for carrying out a similar process on the pilot's seat chassis assembly. This is another hefty tubular steel frame, but it bolts on to the forward face of the front spar and includes the control column and flying controls as well as the seat itself. This gave a rigid mounting and avoided any 'lost motion' in the controls that would have arisen if the assembly had been mounted on the slightly flexible light-alloy nose structure itself. Many other aircraft of the period, such as the Wellington, suffered from this handicap of 'vague' controls.

The very high degree of accuracy required can be illustrated by a couple of examples: the diameter of the shafts bearing the control-cable pulleys in the rear fuselage have to be within limits of +0.0001 inch to −.0004 inch (that is one half of one thousand parts of an inch), and a 5/15 inch steel pin in the engine controls has permitted tolerances of only two ten-thousandths of an inch!

John also overhauled the chains, the sprockets and their bearings (all duplicated) that transmit the inputs from the controls; rotational controls from the 'spectacles' forming the actual 'wheel' become outputs to the ailerons for roll control, while fore-and-aft movement of the column (pivoting on its base) becomes outputs to the elevators for pitch control. These outputs travel rearwards via more chains and sprockets in an enclosed section under the seat chassis to what is termed 'a suitable system of levers and torque tubes' mounted on the leading edge of the centre-section, then to the ailerons and, via cables and pulleys (again duplicated) that run the length of the fuselage, to more levers and the elevators. The crisp response of the Blenheim to control inputs from the pilot is due not only to the quality of the original detail design of the control systems, but also to the equally high standards attained in their rebuild.

A considerable amount of work also went into the nose-section over the years, and it too was restored using the same methods as were used on the centre-section. No longer just a bare shell, new floors of marine ply had been made and fitted; this material was also used for the numerous strengthening plates riveted on to the skin panels in the plane of the propellers, to prevent pieces of ice thrown from them from piercing the thin skins. The navigator's table was reinstated, and his circular folding seat was refurbished and recovered in the correct green leather.

Various panels surrounding the instrument panel were put back in, although there

Left *The bare nose section completely stripped out and with all the paint removed for its intense inch-by-inch inspection – most of the original skin panels seen here were found to be serviceable.*

Below *The rear fuselage undergoing the same process; damaged panels have been removed for replacement, while a temporary jury-strut stiffens the front that mates with the centre and nose sections.*

Above right *Work continues on the main fuselage, awaiting the now etch-primed nose section. Two tailplanes are in the foreground.*

Below right *John Romain working on the nose; the rudder pedals and nav table have been remounted.*

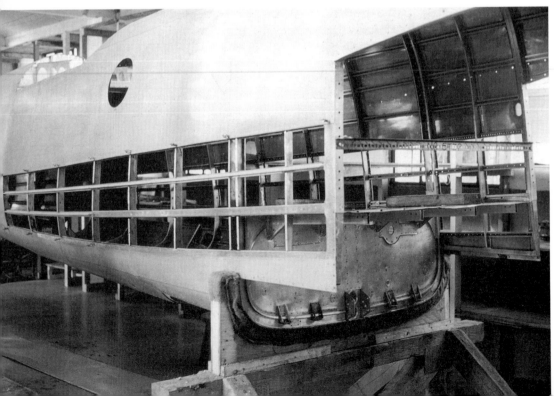

were no instruments as yet, and there was no cockpit or nose glazing at all. The under-nose escape hatch was also refurbished and fitted. The rebuilt pilot's seat chassis assembly was then mounted in the nose section – at least we could now sit in it and dream!

'Smudger' Smith constructed two beautiful examples of the new circular 'firewalls' that are mounted between the engine bearers and the engine mounting frames. In our only major departure from employing the original construction materials throughout, these were made up from stainless-steel – a very difficult material to work with – rather than the alloy/asbestos/alloy sandwich of the initial manufacture. This was a demanding task that took 'Smudge' many months and many curses, but the new 'firewalls' were much admired when completed and mounted on the engine mounting frames, marking a large step forwards – visually as well as practically.

The complete main undercarriage assemblies, including the Vickers oleo suspension units – rather like giant oil-filled shock absorbers – with their retraction mechanism and

The new stainless-steel firewall, fabricated by 'Smudger' Smith, and the rebuilt engine mounting frame are fitted.

linkages, all actuated by a powerful hydraulic ram, were dismantled and stripped right down. After the most thorough measuring and inspection procedures on the bare metal, they were overhauled (using some parts cannibalised from other undercarriage units that we had), polished, stove-enamelled silver, and re-assembled. We rebuilt the powerful hydraulic ram, and after overcoming a little trouble with leaking seals, it was tested satisfactorily.

We dismantled the main oleo legs too, after carefully releasing the high internal working pressure – which was still present even after 50 years! After scrupulous reconditioning these were pressure-tested for us by British Aerospace at Hatfield and certified correct. After many months we could then re-assemble the completed undercarriage units, which certainly looked 'better than new', and were delighted to be able to mount them back into their frames on the aircraft – another major step forward.

We also rebuilt and fitted the large fairings that attach to the front of the main oleos and cover the front part of the wheel bay when the wheels are retracted. In the air they act as air-brakes when the wheels are lowered; on the ground they help to give the Blenheim its characteristic 'sit'. The former feature is undesirable, as it increases the difficulties of the pilot if an engine is lost while the wheels are down, and on the later Mk V Blenheims they were replaced with more conventional inward-retracting undercarriage doors hinged on the outer edges of the wheel bay.

Bill Kelly, in the meantime, had been beavering away for a couple of years on returning the gun turret to full working order. He chose the one from the 'slice' of rear fuselage that had been used for many years as a plaything for children, as it had been stored mainly in sheds and barns so was more complete and less corroded than the other partial turrets we had. This he stripped totally, overhauling each component separately, using parts from one of the other turrets if needed, and gradually re-assembled the restored parts, using some new lengths of hydraulic pipe and all new fittings, into a completely functional turret. We had been fortunate to purchase two of the correct Browning .303-inch machine guns, which we de-activated and mounted in the finished turret. The final result was a magnificent tribute to Bill's workmanship.

The Bristol B1 turret is rotated through 90 degrees on either side of the dead-astern position by hydraulic power, and the gun mounting itself can then be moved a further 5 degrees, enabling coverage from wing-tip to wing-tip. The guns are elevated or

The Team, photographed on 31 May 1987, just after their first success in putting a Blenheim back into the skies. From the left: Colin Swann, John Larcombe, Graham Warner, John Romain, Christian Hollyer, John 'Smudger' Smith, John Gullick, Bob Sparkes, Nick Goodwyn and Bill Kelly.

The first restoration

The derelict airframes discovered in Canada had stood out in all weathers for decades after the war.

Above *John Romain gives scale to the outer port wing in the jig as he works on it. The two main spars and many ribs are shown.*

Right *A close-up of the worst area of corrosion on the steel spar boom flanges. Clearly renewal of these sections was essential, but how could this be done to satisfy strict airworthiness requirements?*

Left *The completed gun turret with its pair of .303-inch Brownings. The ammunition containers are fixed to the black columns that raise and lower the cupola; it is seen here in the fully lowered position.*

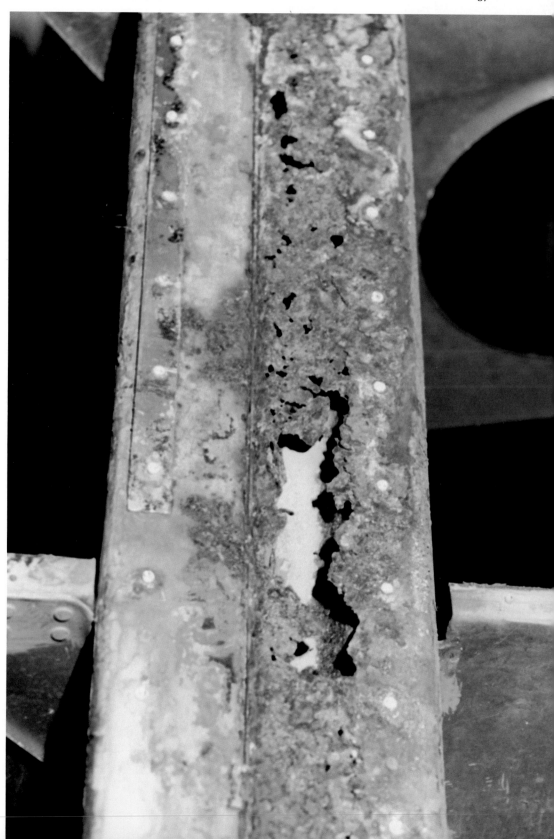

Left *Bob Sparkes tensioning one of the 12 control cables that run under the turret to the rear; the rear spar is behind his head and the open entry hatch hanging above it.*

Below *A virtually complete power plant, with the exhaust collector ring and one of its two exhaust outlets, the two oil-cooler intakes, and the ring of controllable cooling gills. The red glow is from a heat lamp used to combat condensation.*

Right *We decided to mark our Blenheim as V6028 GB-D – 'D-Dog' of 105 Squadron, 2 Group, RAF Bomber Command in the summer of 1941.*

Below right *The 'Happiness is Big Bristols' T-shirt says it all! The girl posing with a wartime motorcycle in front of the only airworthy Blenheim certainly put a smile on our faces!*

Left *John Larcombe brings the Blenheim over the runway threshold at Duxford for a beautiful three-point landing in May 1987.*

Below left *After the crash on 21 June 1987 the emergency services were on the scene very quickly and covered the wreckage in foam.*

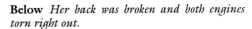

Below *Her back was broken and both engines torn right out.*

The nose was completely smashed, and this picture reveals just how very fortunate the crew were to escape with only minor injuries.

The wreckage on a low-loader at Denham for the ignominious return journey to Duxford.

depressed hydraulically by twisting the motorcycle-like hand controls; the gunner's seat is pivoted so that as the guns rise the seat lowers, and vice versa.

The transparent turret cupola was made to be semi-retractable in conditions when it was not likely to be required, to reduce the amount of drag created when it was raised to the operational position. All in all it was a very complicated device for what it did, which was to protect the gunner from the slipstream; up until then the gunner usually had to stand up in a cockpit open to the elements, manually moving and aiming his gun, which was mounted on a swivelling steel ring. His actual firepower, however, was not increased from that available to his First World War predecessors!

The stern section of the fuselage was also completely rebuilt. The central frame of this section is the only one in the entire fuselage to be made up from sheet steel rather than alloy. It needs to be very strong as the tailplane is bolted to the top of it, the fin post with the rudder pivots fastens to the rear, and the elevator control cross-shafts and the complete tailwheel assembly are mounted on it too. We were worried that we might find some internal corrosion in this important frame, but it turned out to be sound, so was treated, painted and re-assembled. The rest of the stern section was all alloy, so was rebuilt and partially re-skinned using the methods previously described.

The sturdy box-section fin post runs vertically all the way from the base of the stern fuselage to the top of the fin. It was reconditioned, primed and repainted, and the rudder pivot bearings were renewed. The damaged fin itself was stripped and rebuilt with several new skins; the curving panels that fair the base of the fin to the top of the fuselage were very difficult to shape and demonstrated 'Smudge's' panel-beating skills. Then the fin and fin-post were re-united permanently once again.

The one-piece alloy tailplane was bolted on to a steel frame by its spars – smaller versions of the wing spars – and the skin panels removed. The spars, ribs, stringers and elevator mountings were then inspected, and any items found requiring attention were

Left *The rebuilt stern fuselage section; the tailplane bolts to the central (steel) frame, the fin post to the rear frame, and the elevator control arms to the cross-shafts on the front frame.*

Below *The tailplane in the jig awaiting the upper skins; the lower skins have been replaced and the curved tips were added later.*

'Trial fit' of the nose and main fuselage sections, both still bare of internal fittings, in 'Blenheim Palace'. 'Visual Progress'!

removed to be repaired or replaced with a newly made item. The tailplane was then etch-primed and painted internally and the skin-panels replaced or renewed. Surprisingly, the curved tips of the tailplane, and the long pieces that fair the gap where

Another 'trial fit' of the nose to the centre-section; note the rebuilt undercarriage frames bolted to the front spar.

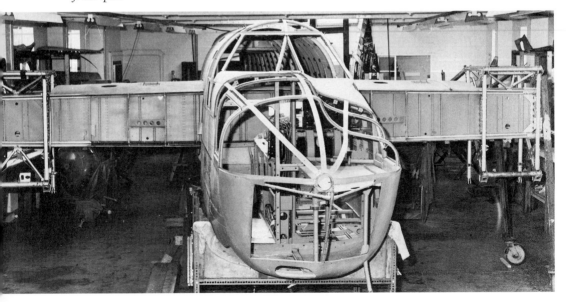

the elevators mount on the rear, are made of wood, and new pieces had to be made.

The tailwheel assembly itself was reconditioned, new leather seals were needed for the oleo, and a new tyre fitted. The completed tailplane and fin assembly, all etch-primed externally, was then bolted into place on the top of the fuselage stern section, with the fin post bolted to the rear of it, and the tailwheel unit mounted inside. The whole tail assembly was then offered up to the main fuselage and bolted to it on a temporary basis.

We needed to position the growing airframe very carefully in the workshops, as the fin poked up into a gap between the rafters! At least the workshop now contained the majority of what had become a recognisable Blenheim airframe: the fuselage extended from nose to tail and was mated with the centre-section in a 'trial fit'; the tailplane and fin were set upon it temporarily; and the undercarriage, 'firewalls' and engine mountings were all attached too.

It all sounds so easy, but it was far from it, even though it was all quite straightforward and used normal renovation procedures and practices. I have covered only briefly the considerable accomplishments of the Blenheim Team in rebuilding these major airframe sections, and have condensed the descriptions of the methods used, but I would remind you that the Team carried out these repetitive restoration processes continuously over a period of several years. They might be straightforward and standard procedures, but they form the backbone of any major restoration project, are messy and particularly time-consuming, requiring countless hours of sheer hard work, which was always carried out with scrupulous care and attention to detail.

That the bulk of this drearily repetitive work was carried out mainly in the spare time of the predominantly volunteer Blenheim Team is truly remarkable and demonstrates the depth of their dedication to the Blenheim. They are a wonderful bunch, who are acknowledged to be the best restoration Team at Duxford – and therefore probably in Europe, if not the world! I am very proud of their great achievements, and am honoured to count them as my friends.

The main and rear fuselage sections, now mounted on the centre-section in the hangar. Note the row of D-brackets for the control systems on the front spar.

One of the factors that almost grounded the Blenheim was the lack of tyres for the main-wheels – this view shows their retracted position. The four attachment points for the outer wings on the main-spars are protected by white tape.

However, some of the more unusual and intransigent problems with the restoration – although half-expected – were starting to rear their ugly heads. Also, one other major – and totally unexpected – problem arose. This was not connected with the actual restoration work, but it was one that undermined its very foundations. These problems, unless we could overcome or circumvent them, seemed bound to prevent completion of the rebuild to airworthy status. Was all the hard work we had carried out and the heavy expenses incurred to bring us to this point well along the road to making her fit to fly again going to be wasted?

Chapter Eight

Restoration dramas

One problem that definitely would have kept the Blenheim out of the skies and rooted to the ground was the lack of suitable main wheel tyres. Although the original tyres still held their wartime air, over the years the rubber outer casings had hardened and cracked, making them potentially unsafe, so unusable on any airworthy aircraft. We contacted all the tyre stockists, both in Europe and the United States, that might hold such old and odd sizes, or suggest where we could find them, but we drew a complete blank. Various manufacturers were approached to see if they produced any tyre in a similar size, or could modify a production tyre so that we could use it, but nothing at all suitable was available. Unfortunately Dunlop, which made the original tyres, and who had a department producing small 'runs' of vintage car tyres, had long ago done away with the moulds. We enquired about the possibility of having a few new tyres specially manufactured to our requirements, but the astronomical costs quoted for making the new moulds and so on for such a limited production made it impossible for us to adopt this solution.

Just when we were at our wits' end, Shorts in Belfast, which during the war had manufactured Sunderland Flying Boats (and Bombay Transports for Bristol, which was too busy producing Blenheims!), showed its small 360 'Feeder' airliner at the Farnborough SBAC Show. The tyres made for it were exactly the right size to fit the Blenheim rims, were the correct rating and were therefore strong enough, and only a quarter of an inch larger in radius. Although they were tubeless tyres, the makers agreed to modify them to accept our inner tubes. Eureka! We had been saved, but only by the fortuitous intervention of benign good fortune.

By the time the tyre problem had been resolved we were over five years into the restoration since I had rescued it through my garage company, The Chequered Flag. We had employed our first full-time aircraft engineer, a German recommended by Personal Plane Services, and supplied him with a car, which he promptly damaged, as he did the next one too! We also paid him the money to take his CAA engineering licence exams, but he appeared to spend that in the public house. Bill had nicknamed him 'Herman the German', and when he attacked the engines, causing more damage, Bill said he was merely carrying on where his compatriots had left off! However, he only lasted a few months. Fred Hanson had left him clear instructions and remonstrated with him when he did not follow them, but he did not mend his ways so was sacked. He left a vitriolic screed, which I have just re-read, saying that 'he wasn't going to work on piles of rubbish' and that 'it was all a waste of time as this heap of scrap would never fly anyway'.

At that time, and most providentially, John Romain had just completed his engineering training, and we took him on full-time. This turned out to be the best thing that ever happened to the Blenheim. Fortunately it took place at a very early stage in the rebuild; the improvement was immediately noticeable as he knew what he was doing and soon got to grips with the task. A large proportion of all the restoration work on the major airframe sections during that five-year period, as described in the previous chapter, was actually carried out by John personally. He also organised the rest of the team properly; the part-time volunteers were delighted to see the steady progress and knuckled down to their own work even harder.

Throughout this period, inspired by the steady progress on the Blenheim, I had become drawn progressively deeper into the vintage and 'warbird' aircraft scene, devoting more of my time and energy to it, and taking my eye from the 'ball' that was The Chequered Flag. Robs had been right – I did find my further involvement in the scene both interesting and enjoyable.

The company purchased one of Ormond's Chipmunks from his estate. It was very scruffy, but the Team refurbished it beautifully in the RAF training colours of silver with yellow bands, and I used it to renew my Private Pilot's Licence. I bought a French licence-built Fieseler Storch in Belgium; we painted this in Luftwaffe markings and I enjoyed displaying it at many airshows, as I did a Max Holste Broussard, which was like a French Beaver. The actual Auster AOP9 that had been flown single-handed in a race to Australia by a foolhardy Army Air Corps Major was also added to the growing BAM collection. Then I purchased a partially completed Lysander restoration project from Canada, seeing this as an ideal subject to follow on after completion of the Blenheim. 'Lizzies' are very rare pre-war Army Co-operation machines, full of character, that share the same Bristol Mercury engine and DH prop with the Blenheim, and are best known for their nocturnal agent dropping and retrieving operations.

The last aircraft acquired by BAM during this period were a pair of ex-RCAF Beech 18 Expeditors, which had been decaying quietly at Prestwick for several years, left there by a defunct Canadian survey company. We sold one to Anthony Hutton, and fully renovated the other, finishing it in an attractive 1943 US Navy blue and grey colour scheme, obtaining a Certificate of Airworthiness and showing it at air displays. We did this so that we, as a Team, could gain experience of operating a 'medium piston-twin' aircraft while we were completing the Blenheim.

Apart from the flying training aspect – and I wanted to obtain my own 'twin' rating – we needed to master all the maintenance, ground-handling and general operational aspects too, well in advance of the time when we would need to apply these lessons to ensure the safe operation of the Blenheim. The Beech 18 was ideal for this purpose as it was used by the US Forces as an advanced trainer throughout the war. It is rather like a twin-engined Harvard, being quite demanding to fly properly and therefore an excellent training aircraft.

However, back to the nascent Blenheim restoration, and soon after we had mated the fuselage and tail assembly to the centre-section in the hangar, a devastating, indeed almost terminal, blow fell on the project; a blow that was very traumatic for me and which completely demoralised the Team. Once more the future of the project was thrown into doubt and confusion, and it seemed that the rebuild was destined not to be completed.

At the end of 1984 The Chequered Flag, my privately owned garage company, became the subject of an unwelcome and enforced take-over. This came about as we had put our General Motors franchise on the market, with the consent of the Luton HQ; although we sold hundreds of new cars each year, the company's system of target-related bonuses (whereby they raised the target each time we reached it!), and without which the dealership could not be run at a profit, made the franchise a barely viable treadmill. We had superb sales and servicing facilities operating from separate show-rooms and specially built modern workshop premises, but the new car dealership had not, alas, been formed into a separate limited company. A potential buyer of the GM part of our business enquired about purchasing the well-known sportscar side as well, as this had its own dedicated showrooms and workshops, but we said, 'Sorry, it is not for sale'.

Then the finance company, whose 'Stocking Plan' we were obliged to use to carry the high level of stocks required, demanded instant repayment – as the small print of the agreement revealed that they were entitled to do. As we were unable to pay off the large sum concerned, they appointed a Receiver/Manager to find a buyer for the com-pany. Thus the entire 'Flag enterprise, including the main sportscar business that we did not wish to sell, was sold over our heads to the company that had been interested in the GM dealership and wished to buy the sportscar business too.

Although I had founded the 'Flag and run it for 28 years, I was out in the cold; I lost the capital I had put in the company, and, after staying on for a short period as General Manager for the new owners, I lost my sense of identity with it, so left to 'dabble' in a few classic cars from home. I felt sad at losing the 'Flag, for it had been my life's work, but even as that door was closed in my face, another one was being opened on to a more satisfying future.

The Blenheim project by then stood in the company's books at some £250,000; the new owners were not at all interested in the aircraft and instructed that the partly com-pleted project be sold. As I was unable to raise the book figure that they required, the accountants concerned put it out to Public Tender, seeking far more than the sum I had been able to offer. This action further prolonged the terrible uncertainty over the future of the project, and unsettled the Team even more, for it was a full five months before the twice extended closing date for the tender was reached in April 1985. The accountants claimed to have received 'strong interest from overseas' and the thought that our beloved Blenheim – into which we had all put so much that we regarded it as 'ours' – might be going to some unknown foreign land was galling.

Fortunately the other aircraft operated by BAM were owned by me and not the com-pany, so were not affected by this dreadful uncertainty. The Team rallied round magni-ficently, but felt disillusioned and frustrated as they were unable to do anything to avert the threat that hung over the Blenheim. The IWM was also concerned that the partially completed project might well be taken away from Duxford. Had it been removed, the prospects for completion to flying condition looked bleak indeed. We did not know if another, probably overseas, buyer would possess the commitment, tenacity and deter-mination, the extensive engineering facilities, plus the ability to provide continuous financial support, all of which would be required in considerable amounts to see this ambitious and long-term restoration project through to completion. We did know that they would suffer from the lack of the essential elements of the unrivalled accumulated expertise and dedicated steadfastness of our Blenheim Team.

This dreadful uncertainty was deeply depressing, and it was a nail-biting period. I had already submitted a tender in my own name at the highest sum that I felt I could afford, but they knew I was most anxious to retain the Blenheim and 'twisted my arm' with hints that they had received other bids that were superior to mine. As the final closing date due near, and after many sleepless nights, I put in another, larger tender, this time as BAM.

You can imagine the enormous wave of relief that washed over me when I was informed that this last-minute tender proved to be high enough – but they led me to understand only just high enough – to be accepted. The Team were delighted and relieved that the stalled Blenheim project had been rescued once more from an unknown destiny, and I was delighted and relieved that I had managed to save it from that obscure fate so that the restoration work could be re-started, and continued to completion, in their most capable hands. Although euphoric at this news, I had to dig uncomfortably deep into my own resources to purchase the project, and was soon brought down to earth with the realisation that from then on I would have to finance the vast amount of work still required from my own pocket directly, rather than indirectly as before.

So we had to start seeking more effective ways of containing the costs, for example by badgering suppliers so that we could buy our materials very selectively, and by doing all the work ourselves, rather than placing some items with outside contractors. In this we were successful; for instance, we had been quoted a large sum for repairing the oil-tanks, and an even greater one for the main fuel-tanks, so we did them all ourselves! We purged them very thoroughly, removed all dents and welded up any splits or leaks in the alloy, renewed the filler-cap gaskets, pressure-tested them, and finally re-painted them – the oil-tanks yellow and the fuel-tanks green. Indeed, I am proud to say that the entire Blenheim restoration was carried out by the Team 'in house' – with but one major exception.

We had tried hard to obtain commercial sponsorship, and achieved one notable success, for John Romain and John Larcombe persuaded the Propeller Division of British Aerospace at Lostock to rebuild, as a training exercise, our Blenheim propellers; the commercial cost of such work would have been prohibitive. They rebuilt and certified three Blenheim props for us, so that we would have a spare; their workmanship was superb and the props looked brand new when we collected them. Lostock had previously been a factory for de Havilland (Propellers) Ltd, and they were able to establish, from the stamped numbers, that the props had in fact originally been manufactured there in 1940, and shipped by wartime convoy to Canada. So, after being shipped back to the UK by Ormond over 30 years later, they had been almost around the world before being returned to their birthplace at Lostock after some 45 years. Indeed, a young apprentice who had actually worked on one of these props back in 1940 had risen to become Director of Production at BAe Lostock when the props returned in the 1980s!

John Romain became a self-employed aircraft engineer, and did work for other 'warbird' owners at Duxford, charging BAM only for the hours he spent on the Blenheim – although he still spent most of his time on it. I found a partner who purchased a half-share in the Westland Lysander project, we took on some outside work to help offset the overheads, and we looked more actively for film, photographic and air display work for BAM's other aircraft. All the income from these various activities was put straight into the Blenheim.

Leaving aside the constant struggle to supply financial support for the restoration, one critical problem arose concerning the actual rebuilding work. This, which at more than one stage appeared to be completely insuperable, was the problem of the repairs needed to the steel portions of the main wing spars. Each outer wing has two full-depth one-piece spars, picking up from the centre-section spars and extending right to the wing-tips, tapering accordingly. The main vertical webs of the spars are made in a heavy alloy with light alloy stiffeners, and these webs presented no problems. But they are supported structurally by load-bearing angled spar-booms that form a 'T' shape to the top and bottom of each web, together with their curved stiffening cornices. These were made from a special high-tensile spring steel, parts of which had suffered from the years

The outer-wing mounted in the jig and de-skinned, showing areas of severe corrosion on the flanges to the rear spar booms.

of exposure to the elements. One or two areas of surface corrosion were apparent, and stripping them down revealed other and more serious areas of internal corrosion, so repairs were needed.

This raised the question of obtaining some of this very special steel. A series of discussions with specialised steel experts and stockists convinced us not only that none was available anywhere, but also that no modern equivalent was being made that was close to its unusual and obsolete specification.

We were therefore overjoyed when, after extensive enquiries at BAe, they managed to locate a few short lengths of this original steel for us in some remote corner at Filton. But the CAA insisted that we could only repair any of the small affected areas on each of the 20-foot boom or cornice sections by means of a one-piece replacement of the entire section, and then only with steel exactly to the manufacturer's specification. These sections were not obtainable in 20-foot lengths – and no modern equivalent was available. Despite all our entreaties, the much shorter lengths that we did have ready to be shaped to fit were ruled out as unacceptable.

This did seem like the end of the road towards an airworthy Blenheim, but John Romain's persistence and ingenuity were rewarded when a Good Samaritan at Filton discovered an old wartime Bristol Aeroplane Company 'Battle Damage Repair Manual', which illustrated with a series of line drawings exactly the type of localised splicing repairs to the booms and cornices that we required, and gave details of the official methods to effect them, showing that we could carry them out with the lengths of the material that were available. The CAA accepted this repair scheme as it had been issued by the original 'Design Authority', and we were allowed to proceed in accordance with it. The Blenheim had been saved again!

But we were not out of the wood yet on the repairs to the upper and lower booms and cornices of the front and rear spars. Due to the curvature of the wing profile, none of the 'T'-shaped steel booms are at right-angles to the webs! In fact, all eight have a different angle, and have to be rolled exactly to these differing profiles, as do the curved supporting cornices, no two of which are alike. The shaped steel then has to be heat-treated and hardened, and there we hit another major problem.

We had these new sections already annealed, cut and shaped to the complex profiles as needed; but only one company in the country had an oven large enough to accept our 6-foot sections for the heat treatment. These carefully shaped sections had to be heated up to 860°C and oil-quenched, then air-quenched at 460°C; most unfortu-

Eventually the corroded sections of the wings were renewed satisfactorily, and the spars capped, as detailed in the text. Here, several years later, with all the ribs and stringers also rebuilt, John Romain – with a mouthful of rivets – is riveting the new outer skin panels in place.

nately for us, while cooling down after this process sufficient distortion took place on several of the sections to render them unusable. We just had sufficient to carry out the approved repair to the starboard wing, but we had used up the very last of our limited supply of the original steel! Back to square one.

We went through the rounds of searching at steel stockists again. I was referred to Rheinmetall, near Essen in the Ruhr and a target for many an RAF raid during the war, and rang them up. After being shunted around a bit, I was put on to a man who knew what he was talking about, for when I quoted the lengthy specification number, he looked it up in their records and came back with, 'Ah yes, zis steel was used in ze Blenheim, ze Beaufort and ze Beaufighter!' (Just imagine a German telephoning a major British steel company, quoting a specification number well over 40 years out of date, and being informed that it was used on, say, the Junkers Ju 88!) To my delight they confirmed that they would be able to manufacture some for us to that spec, but to my dismay they said that their minimum order was for 30 tons, and they would not deviate from that!

Upon hearing this tale, the Chairman of the British Steel Corporation, to his great credit, arranged for a small batch to be made at one of his mills in 6-foot lengths. Thus we could commence going through the process of shaping, heat treating and hardening some new sections all over again, before – a couple of years later – splicing them into the spar booms and cornices of the port wing.

Even when the spars had been rebuilt, we still had to rebuild and re-skin the rest of the wings, fabricating many new ribs as most of the trailing-edge ribs were missing. We could not obtain any of the original 'fir-tree' section extruded alloy that formed the

The port wing is finally completed; this view shows the gaps where the outer tank-bay and inspection covers are fitted. The wing-tip, flaps, aileron and landing lamps still remain to be fitted.

The port wing finally being mounted on to the airframe in the hangar; this was well over a year after the starboard wing had been fitted.

actual trailing-edge, so we obtained a quotation to have some manufactured, but it proved prohibitive. Assiduous enquiries revealed that the Canberra used trailing-edge strips with the same angles, and we were able to obtain sufficient to replace the missing or damaged Blenheim trailing-edges.

To draft this brief description of how the Team overcame this whole series of critical problems that arose during the crucial repairs to the wing spars has taken but a few minutes. To actually surmount them in practice, and to the satisfaction of the CAA surveyors, took several years of persistence and perseverance. The primary responsibility for resolving them lay with John Romain, and it was only his dogged determination over the years that enabled us to conquer these decisive difficulties. I say decisive, for if, at any stage, we had not been able to overcome each one of them satisfactorily, then – like it or not – the Blenheim would have been forced to stay on the ground for ever.

Chapter Nine

Vital systems

Having described how the Team overcame some of the intractable and most obdurate of the problems that beset the rebuild – indeed, came close to defeating it – I can now turn my scrutiny back to the mainstream restoration work, for this had been continuing steadily in the background, over the months and years, while we were tackling the especially crucial difficulties.

While the centre-section was in the workshops, 'trial fits' of the main and nose fuselage sections to it had been made. They revealed difficulties with the 5-foot-long double-skinned keel-plate that links the main and nose sections, dividing the bomb bay longitudinally. Clearly these vital structural members were not jig-built originally and had been fitted individually; as our centre-section was from RCAF 9893, and the fuselage sections were from RCAF 10038, we had to do a considerable amount of re-fitting by hand to ensure that everything aligned properly. The stern section and complete tail assembly were from the 10038 fuselage, so they all fitted to it, and to each other, readily.

The centre-section was then moved to the hangar and placed on trestles; soon afterwards the main and rear fuselage sections were mated to it permanently, and a few weeks later the fin and tailplane assemblies were also joined to it. The rebuilt under-carriage units, still without their main wheels at this stage, were in place, and we soon repaired the long lower nacelles that fair in the wheel well, and refitted them too. As the new 'firewalls' and the renovated engine bearers, plus the yellow oil-tanks, were added to the centre-section, at last she started to look like an aircraft that might – one day – fly again!

What was left of the rudder formed the basis for a rebuild in the workshops. We had to make eight out of ten new ribs for it, plus a new alloy leading-edge, all attached to the vertical tubular spar; we also reshaped the entire trailing edge. It was then recovered in Ceconite fabric, which was sewn and taped in place before being shrunk to a drum-like tautness by several coats of silver dope. (Incidentally, we used Ceconite rather than the original Irish linen as it is a much longer-lasting fabric.) Both the elevators were also in a terrible state; they too are built on to a tubular spar and required a similar reconstruction, with nearly all the ribs needing renewing, and new wooden curved tips making up, before they were recovered and doped. The controllable trimming tabs, and their operating screw-jacks, in both rudder and elevators were also renovated, and all the bearings upon which the control surfaces pivot were renewed. The rebuilt rudder was then mounted on the fin, and the elevators on the tailplane. This was all substantial, and readily apparent, progress.

Another long, but very necessary, task was the fabrication of a complete set of the extensive and complicated glazing for the nose and cockpit, which forms one of the Blenheim's major characteristics. This was done by renovating all the alloy supporting

The hydraulic jack and hoses for operating the landing flaps; the actuating arm is at the top, with the heavy cable that runs via pulleys and levers to operate the flaps on the other wing.

tubes – mainly curved – and glazing bars on the other unrestored nose section from RCAF 9073, taking great care to establish exactly the correct profiles in all three planes. Then we filled the entire nose above the navigator's table, and those parts of the cockpit that had curved windows, with expanding polystyrene foam. When set hard, this was most carefully and accurately shaped to all the desired profiles, especially the double-curved ones, and cut into sections of two or three individual glazed panels, though each of the more complex panels was treated individually, each section being mounted on an 'L'-shaped wooden base and back. Male and female moulds in fibreglass were then taken from these and mounted in wooden frames; the internal surfaces of the moulds were finely polished to a high degree as any imperfections whatsoever would be reproduced in the final perspex panels. This painstaking work was carried out, mainly by Roy Pullan, our reserve pilot, over a period of some three years.

Sheets of one-eighth-inch aviation perspex were then heated and clamped between the matching pairs of moulds, removed when cured, and trimmed. Those panels that were completely flat, such as some of the side windows in the cockpit, we simply measured up and cut to fit. The other flat panels originally made from toughened glass, such as the windscreens and bomb-aimer's panels in the nose, we also had cut from glass to the appropriate sizes. They were all fitted, sealed and held in place by small bolts or screws to the inner and outer glazing bars. Thus we had created a replacement set of optically perfect glazing panels, mainly double-curved, and capable of withstanding the considerable aerodynamic forces involved. We made a further set of glazing panels from these moulds and sold them to another museum, which was restoring a static Blenheim, to help defray our costs.

The complete nose section, with its new glazing gleaming proudly through the plastic film with which we had covered it for protection, was wheeled to the hangar and re-united with the main fuselage and centre-section, including being bolted on to the keel-plate. Now both the Team and the many visitors could view and admire a complete Blenheim fuselage, readily recognisable all the way from the distinctive scalloped nose to the gracefully curved tail. This represented another significant step forward in the restoration.

Rapid progress was maintained over the next two years: the restored gun turret was winched into position; the repaired main fuel-tanks were fitted and new fuel pipes made; the 'D'-shaped mounting brackets on the leading edge of the centre-section wings (which carry the various control runs) were positioned, with the torque tubes for the aileron and main engine controls soon located on them with new bearings; and the large wing-root fairings were repaired and attached. The landing flaps that extend right across the trailing-edge of the centre-section were refitted after repair, and reconnected to the rebuilt hydraulic ram, torque tubes, linkages and cables that operate them. The large sliding hatch over the cockpit, plus its stainless-steel runners, were fitted and adjusted; the lower escape hatches for nose and rear crew positions were rebuilt and put in place, as was the entry hatch forward of the turret; and the tall wooden aerial mast was installed.

The brake drums had been de-rusted by dry-blasting, re-machined, trued and repainted externally. We had found sufficient serviceable sets of the rubber bags that are expanded by pneumatic pressure to press the brake shoes against the inside of the drums, plus enough of the multiple shoes themselves with uncontaminated linings, to re-assemble the complete wheel/brake units on to the overhauled axles and bearings. These wheels were initially re-fitted with the original tyres so that, once mounted on

Right *Work on the engine controls that run along the front spar face. The oil-tank is mounted on the top of the cross-braced undercarriage frame; the flange accepts the 'beetle-back' rear cowlings.*

Below *The fuel cocks in the fuel transfer system, mounted on the front spar and awaiting their links to controls in the cockpit.*

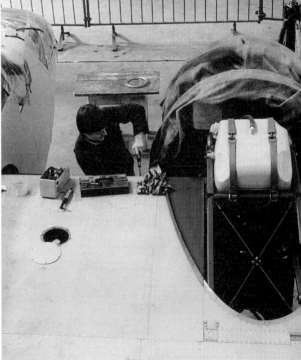

the undercarriage oleos, we could check clearances in the retracted position. When the new tyres were eventually obtained and fitted, the complete wheel assemblies could then be mounted permanently, and the completed undercarriages looked very impressive.

The entire retracting mechanism for the undercarriages had been meticulously overhauled, and was now adjusted and tested, using an external source of hydraulic pressure. The large wheel assemblies retracted and locked in the 'up' position with a resounding 'clunk'; they extended and locked 'down' with an equally reassuring 'clunk'. It was great to see, hear and feel the airframe becoming 'live' at last: we took it in turns to sit in the cockpit and select undercarriage 'up' or 'down'!

Of course, to make the undercarriage and flaps operational we had first to install, connect up, test and adjust the complete hydraulic system, each part of which was first overhauled and tested separately. This was the first of the vital aircraft systems that were virtually redesigned – for they had long since gone – then re-installed and, as each was made to function, were responsible for bringing the dead aircraft gradually back to life.

When I described the Blenheim Team members I said that Colin and David Swann were our main 'plumbers' – for that is the term applied to those engineers who work on aircraft systems – and the amount of meticulous work they put into each of the aircraft systems was enormous. John Romain too spent hundreds of hours deciding on the correct pipe and hose runs, then installing, checking and testing these essential systems along with Colin and David.

The Blenheim was one of the first British aircraft to have a hydraulic system, which may explain some of its idiosyncrasies. In the contemporary Avro Anson the undercarriage was wound up and down mechanically, and both aircraft had wheel brakes operated by air pressure. Hydraulic power in the Blenheim was supplied from a single pump on the port engine, via filters, pressure-relief and non-return valves to a reservoir. The pressure available was indicated by a gauge on the instrument panel, and its distribution was controlled by three vertical 'T'-handled plungers set alongside the pilot's seat. The lower position of the first diverted the hydraulic power to the circuit for the undercarriage and flaps, the upper position sent it to the gun turret only, and the central 'neutral' position released the pressure by recirculating it. So it was no good trying to select 'undercarriage up' after take-off if the main plunger was not fully down, as nothing would happen!

The actual undercarriage and flap selector levers were two more similar vertical plungers, with handles showing the function by small letters engraved on them. They were thus hard to tell apart without looking hard, and were responsible for many an inadvertent selection and resultant accident, so it was not long before the undercarriage selector was protected by a spring-loaded alloy flap, which skinned the knuckles of most Blenheim pilots even though they wore gloves!

The term 'good ergonomics' (even if it had been coined in those days) certainly could not be applied to the layout of the Blenheim controls. A further glaring example of this was the two sets of identical push-pull plungers with circular knobs that were set just below two levers for the air-intake controls, most awkwardly behind the pilot's left elbow. One pair operated the propeller pitch-change, the other the carburettor cut-outs! The latter were also later protected by a spring-loaded flap.

Although these knobs were painted red for the port engine or propeller and green for the starboard ones, this was not much help in the dark. Normally these controls would be operated together as a pair, but in many emergencies only one would be needed and it became vitally important to select the correct one!

If a Blenheim pilot lost his port engine, he lost hydraulic power too, once any pressure remaining in the reservoir was exhausted. He had a hand-pump, with its own filter and valves, for use in such a situation, so apart from the difficulties of flying the aircraft on one engine, he was kept pretty busy if he wanted to lower the wheels or flaps. In the event of a severe hydraulic leak when the hand-pump was unable to build up pressure and was thus rendered ineffective, an emergency 'blow-down' system was provided to lower the undercarriage. A pressurised CO_2 bottle in each wheel bay was connected by a shuttle valve first to the 'unlock' side of the radius-rod jack, then to the 'down' side of the main undercarriage jacks. These were operated by an emergency 'pull-ring' located behind the pilot's left shoulder. These bottles would lower the wheels once only, but had no effect on the flaps, so the poor pilot while struggling to maintain control during his single-engined circuit – with no hope of 'going round again' if he misjudged his approach – had to make a flapless landing, which added to his difficulties.

The poor layout of the Blenheim minor controls, coupled with the great leap in performance and complexity compared with the simple biplanes with which most RAF pilots of the time were accustomed, was undoubtedly a factor in the large number of accidents to Blenheims that occurred in the early days. Before the outbreak of war, over 10 per cent of the aircraft in use were lost in this fashion, so the RAF entered the war with only 1,089 Blenheims of the 1,200 plus that had entered service.

I feel that it is fair to comment that this haphazard arrangement of the Blenheim's controls, other than the excellent main flying controls, was only a contributory factor to this high rate of flying accidents. The main cause was the introduction of such advanced features as the retractable undercarriage, propeller pitch change, powerful flaps, and supercharged engines, which needed sensitive handling, plus the quantum increase in overall performance. Most pilots came from unsophisticated fixed-undercarriage, fixed-pitch, flapless biplanes such as the Hawker Hind, Demon or Fury, or even the then new Gloster Gauntlet. Further, the RAF conversion training at the time was equally haphazard and was usually left to the Squadrons. Essentials such as Pilot's Notes, cockpit drills

An interesting shot showing some of the 'plumbing' on the firewall behind the port engine. The oil-tank is mounted on the top of the undercarriage frame, and the white CO_2 bottle for emergency undercarriage lowering is on the rear of the front spar.

with 'vital actions', single-engine handling techniques in twin-engined aircraft, proper instrument- or night-flying instruction, and dedicated Operational Training Units for advanced aircraft, were only introduced later as the need for them became all too apparent. Unfortunately the Blenheim was at the forefront of this steep and painful 'learning curve'. Later in the war – and certainly post-war – RAF pilot training became recognised as the finest and most thorough in the world.

Fortunately, we could benefit from these improvements, and in any event the minor controls were arranged very much better in the Canadian-built Mk IVs and the British-built Mk Vs. The propeller controls were moved and set alongside the throttles, and the master control to direct the hydraulic power, with the two levers to select under-carriage or flaps operation protruding from it, was mounted prominently in the centre of the panel. Thus we avoided both the 'plunger problem' and the skinned knuckles!

Therefore the Team had to overhaul or fabricate (then install, adjust and test) each component of these systems until every part, and then the entire layout, responded to the controls correctly, and each of the three complete systems functioned perfectly: the normal hydraulic system for lowering and raising both the undercarriage and flaps, and

Below left *A wartime photo of a single-Browning turret in service showing the central hydraulic ram and pivoted arms that raise and lower the gun mountings and the seat, the lower rams that rotate the turret, and the arms to the mounting tubes (inside the alloy sleeves), which raise and lower the cupola.*

Below right *The central pivot and part of the hydraulic system for rotating the turret on our Blenheim; the lower arm is the one shown in the foreground of the picture to the left.*

Some of the hydraulic and pneumatic lines behind the central instrument console; the rudder pedals can be seen lower right, with the brake balance valve at the end of the three copper pipes above them.

operating the gun-turret; the manually operated back-up method supplied for performing these functions; and the provision made for lowering the wheels once only in an emergency.

I mentioned above that the Anson and Blenheim both had braking systems operated by air rather than hydraulic pressure, as indeed did most of the new breed of RAF aircraft produced during the pre-war re-armament period. In the original Blenheims the wing-mounted machine-gun, the fuel jettison valves and the nose-mounted camera function were also operated pneumatically, but we deleted those parts of the system as superfluous to our intended operations! The air pressure is supplied by a compressor, driven by the starboard engine, and its circuit feeds, via an oil-trap and reservoir, to a large storage bottle in the centre of the fuselage; an air-filter and ground charging point are sited here too. All had to refurbished, pressure-tested and certified.

The pressure in the system is controlled by a complicated valve (which required very careful overhaul and testing), and is shown to the pilot by a triple-gauge instrument that displays the overall pressure and that available at the port and starboard brakes. Air pressure is distributed between the brakes by a large Dunlop multiple-valve contraption linked to the rudder pedals – another item requiring a scrupulous strip and rebuild. When the pedals are level, pressure is distributed evenly; when either pedal is pushed forward, more pressure is diverted to the side in question until, at full rudder, it is all applied to the brake on that side. This enables the pilot to apply differential braking and steer the aircraft on the ground, and can be especially useful in keeping it straight during the landing run.

The amount of pressure released to the braking circuit, and therefore the degree of braking effect obtained, is controlled by a small hand lever mounted on the left-hand side of the control column 'spectacles' and linked by cable to the multi-valve distribution device mentioned above. This brass lever needs a delicate squeeze to avoid over-braking, so is not easy to apply gently when the aircraft is bucking over a rough grass airfield. A small catch can be set to lock the brake lever in the 'fully on' position, and so act as a parking brake, but this should only be applied when the brakes have cooled down after use, or heat transfer can cause the expanding rubber bags that force the shoes on to the drums to over-heat and burst in protest!

There is one other system on the Blenheim operated by air, or rather the lack of it – the vacuum system needed to drive the gyroscopic flight instruments. This is served from a vacuum pump on the port engine, and the circuit includes an oil-separator and

Part of the new electrical system, with wiring installed in the original trunking, showing the main electrical control panel, with the electric master-switch above and the fuses below, mounted in the rear fuselage.

pressure-relief valve. There is an alternative vacuum source, with its own relief valve, drawn from a venturi-tube mounted on the port side of the cockpit; this is selected by the pilot in case of engine or vacuum pump failure, and the negative pressure is shown on an indicator, tapped into the circuit downstream of the control valve. Clearly both the pneumatic and vacuum systems have to be completely airtight and free of leaks throughout if they are to function properly, and it is a tribute to the patience and skills of the Team that both systems were trouble-free when they were put to the test.

On our restored Blenheim, the entire electrical system had to be redesigned, keeping the appearance as original as possible while taking into account present-day require-ments, especially those pertaining to the safety aspects of operating this old aircraft. The obsolete 12-volt system and all the associated wiring was ripped out completely and all reworked and rewired, using modern electrical cables, relays and connectors through-out, hidden inside the original alloy trunking. We deleted the circuits for the original radios, bomb-arming, signalling, and other redundant items, and fitted modern avi-onics equipment, including a transponder, to facilitate operations in today's controlled airspace. This compact kit was partly concealed on a shelf low on the left of the pilot's seat, which was previously used for the bomb-arming and selection switches. The small modern aerials used were also hidden as far as possible.

Electrical power is supplied by a 500-watt DC generator, driven by the port engine, to the 12-volt 25-ampere/hour general service battery in the rear fuselage. There is also a similar battery specially for engine-starting set beneath the observer's seat. Remember that in those days cars and aeroplanes had old-fashioned dynamos, not modern alternators! We replaced both batteries with new 35-ampere/hour units and adapted the new circuits to suit. The generator was sent away for rewinding and overhaul.

The main electrical panel, master switch and fuses – for there were no pop-out cir-cuit-breakers in those days – are mounted on the port side of the rear fuselage, in the care of the Wireless Operator/Gunner. The master switch isolates the batteries from the power; the main panel includes charging rate controls and cut-outs, voltage regula-tors, ammeters and voltmeter as well as rows of fuses. We retained this crew position as completely as possible for the sake of originality. In the old Blenheims the bulky radio equipment – a 1082 Transmitter and a 1083 Receiver – was mounted to the rear of the turret; frequency could only be changed by removing one coil and plugging in another, taken from the wooden drawer below the shelf that supported the old-fashioned valve radios. One long aerial ran from the mast behind the cockpit to the tip of the fin, while another 50-foot-long trailing aerial was wound in and out via a fairlead by a wheel with a knob on it! Back in those days there were no instant push-button changes to pre-set very high frequencies, or 'self-searching' for others, on small black transistorised boxes complete with visual read-outs!

The modified electrical system, a clever mix of old and new, was devised by Colin Swann, cleared by the CAA, and installed and checked by him, helped by Chris Hollyer (who, to the amusement of the Team, was over-fond of using plastic tie-wraps) and Hugh Smith. The whole complicated process took well over two years to complete, and was a magnificent achievement.

I have deviated from the chronological order of the restoration work in order to talk about the installation of the aircraft systems, as they played such an important role in bringing the inert airframe back to life. I have also described various pumps and the generator as being 'driven from the port or starboard engine'. So what was happening regarding the rebuilding of the two principal components that were absolutely indispensable – the original Bristol 'Mercury' engines?

Chapter Ten

The beating hearts

The engine is the very heart of any aircraft. It is required to beat strongly and steadily, but above all to continue beating for long periods – often in highly adverse conditions – with absolute reliability. The weight of an aircraft engine has to be kept as low as possible, yet it must deliver as much power as is attainable for that weight. The Bristol Mercury engines in the Blenheim were indeed steadfast, sound and dependable; they run as sweetly now as they did many decades ago, and are so beautifully engineered that they can be considered as technical works of art.

The Mercury can be traced right back to the First World War. In 1910 Roy Fedden was Chief Engineer at Straker Squire, manufacturers of fine cars at Fishponds, Bristol. During the early part of the War the RFC obtained its airframes and engines from the Royal Aircraft Factory (later Establishment) at Farnborough, but the Admiralty obtained its from a variety of sources – for no aviation industry then existed – including Straker, which was awarded a contract in 1915 to build and repair aero engines for the RNAS. Rolls-Royce had developed its Eagle, Hawk, and Falcon aero engines from the pre-war Mercedes Grand Prix racing engine, and Straker was instructed by Their Lordships to build hundreds of the latter types, plus Renault V8 aero engines.

In 1917 the Admiralty issued a specification for a 300 hp air-cooled engine of no more than 3 ft 6 in diameter. Fedden's design was chosen – a 14-cylinder 20-litre rotary that he called Mercury. However, this is not the Mercury that later powered the Blenheim, although it shows Fedden's penchant for names from mythology. It gave 315 hp and first flew in a Bristol F1 Scout in 1918, but had overheating problems. Fedden also designed a 400 hp single-row nine-cylinder radial (not rotary) of 28 litres called Jupiter, which was flown first in a Bristol Badger in 1919, and did lead directly to the Blenheim's Mercury. He also laid out a 1,000 hp twin-row radial (effectively a doubled-up Jupiter) called the Hercules – more of these famous names later!

Early in 1918 Straker was taken over by the Cosmos Engineering Company, but due to cancellation of aero engine contracts at the end of the war, the company went out of business in 1920. Fedden had an order for six Jupiters, but Cosmos had only delivered two; he nonetheless managed to complete the new 50-hour type-test successfully, and this helped the Air Ministry to persuade the Bristol Aeroplane Company to purchase the assets of Cosmos and set up its own Aero Engine Department headed by Roy Fedden, assisted by 'Bunny' Butler, a meticulous design engineer.

They developed the Jupiter over the next decade, with a reliable 550 hp for widespread civil as well as military use, and it was produced under licence by Gnome et le Rhone in France, by Alfa Romeo in Italy, by PZL in Poland, by Siemens in Germany, and by Nakajima in Japan. The excellence of Bristol engines was acknowledged throughout the world.

For the 1927 Schneider Trophy Race the Air Ministry contracted Bristol to develop a special version of the Jupiter to be fitted in a Short Crusader. This had a shorter stroke to permit higher rpm (dropping the mean piston speed at 2,400 rpm from 3,000 ft/min to 2,600), a reduced overall diameter and thus drag, plus – for the first time – cylinder heads made of alloy, with four valves, and supercharging; it was called the Mercury. The Crusader crashed (not due to engine problems!), but the engine delivered over 800 hp for short periods from a weight of only 684 lbs – a truly remarkable achievement for 1927.

Over the next decade Fedden and the Bristol team continued to develop the 23.6-litre Mercury and its long-stroke version, the 28.7-litre Pegasus, intended for heavier, slower aircraft where the slight increase to the original diameter was not so important. This need to increase capacity and power without increasing diameter, and the difficulties of providing overhead camshafts to radial cylinders, were two of the factors that lead Fedden to develop the sleeve-valve range of Bristol radial engines – Aquila, Perseus, Taurus, Hercules (the earlier name revived!) and Centaurus – which continued

Right *The very centre of the Mercury engine, showing the short built-up crankshaft, the slim connecting-rods, the counter-weight and the alloy crankcase, which is split at the bore centres.*

Below *An 'exploded' view of the core components: the reduction-gear housing, front cover, camshaft-drum housing with paired mountings for the push-rods, the alloy crankcase split at the cylinder bore centres, the steel engine-mounting ring, the supercharger housing and volute casing with outlets, rear cover, and 'tower' of drives for the magnetos, various pumps and other ancillaries.*

in widespread use until the mid-1950s, when piston aero engines were overtaken by gas turbines. Remarkably, the cylinder bore and piston size of $5^3/4$ inches chosen by Fedden in 1917 for the Cosmos Jupiter was carried right through the entire range of Bristol Jupiter, Mercury, Pegasus, Perseus, Hercules and Centaurus engines for well over 40 years!

To digress for a moment, all Bristol engines were air-cooled radials, whereas Rolls-Royce engines were liquid-cooled in-line units. The merits of these rival cooling methods were fiercely contested throughout the 1930s and '40s. In Germany Daimler-Benz and Junkers Jumo favoured liquid cooling, while BMW with Bramo chose air cooling; in America air cooling was predominant with Pratt & Whitney and Curtiss-Wright's radials, while only Allison used liquid cooling. Although an in-line V-12 could be cowled very neatly, as on the Spitfire, the extra weight and drag of the radiators had to be taken into account. The 448 mph Tempest Mk II with a Centaurus was faster than the 434 mph Mk V with a Sabre and its huge 'chin' radiator. In wartime the increased vulnerability of liquid cooling systems was a further factor – many an aircraft was forced down by loss of coolant from pressurised systems, often through only a tiny puncture or leak.

In the mid-1930s the almost empty Bristol airframe works was searching for orders, but the Bristol engine works was kept busy – even the Gauntlet and Gladiator from its Gloster rivals used the Bristol Mercury, as did aircraft built by other competing manufacturers such as Vickers, Handley-Page, Blackburn, Westland, Shorts, Fairey, Hawker and Supermarine. (See Appendix 4 for brief particulars of Bristol piston engines and a list of some aircraft to use them.)

For the restoration project we were faced with a pile of old Mercury engines, nearly all seized solid and all far from complete, which had been laying out in all weathers for over four decades. Four were just cores that turned out to be useless. Therefore the first, and momentous, task was to strip them all right down for a detailed examination, and a careful selection of potentially serviceable components.

As soon as the centre-section was moved into Building 66, we turned the adjacent workshop into an engine shop so that we could start this lengthy and most demanding process. Fred Hanson had recommended Edgar White – known of course as 'Chalky' – a retired highly skilled and fully licensed aircraft engineer, as being suitable to take on this awesome task. He had become bored with sitting at home and rose to the challenge of rescuing the Blenheim engines magnificently. We took him on part-time initially, then virtually full-time, and the job provided the interest and sense of purpose that he had found lacking in his retirement – in fact, it gave him a new lease of life. He helped John to organise the engine shop with benches, pressure-cleaning baths, engine hoists, sets of steel shelving, surface plates, compressed air and electricity points, and so on. He and 'Smudge' made up some stands and two special engine-building frames from unwanted engine mountings.

Engines were 'humped' into the workshops half a dozen at a time for stripping, and the shelves soon started to fill with engine components, all removed, cleaned, inspected, and tagged. Most were found to be unserviceable and sadly were beyond redemption, but the number of items that had been examined, measured and found fit for possible use grew steadily as the months, then years, went by.

The main difficulty had been removing the cylinder barrels from the crankcases, for often the cast-iron piston rings and the steel cylinder bores had rusted together, although sometimes the presence of a slight film of old oil reduced or prevented this. Even if, all those years ago, some cylinders had stopped on the compression or firing stroke with the four valves closed, others would be on the inlet or exhaust strokes with a pair of valves open. In most engines the platinum-tipped spark plugs had been removed, which let in the elements anyway.

We applied penetrating oil and/or de-rusting fluid above and below the seized rings and left them to soak; we filled cylinders with it and left the engine suspended on that barrel with the retaining bolts loosened. If that failed to separate them we removed the rocker-gear so that all four valves were closed, and pressurised the cylinder by pumping in hydraulic oil via an adaptor in a spark plug hole, and left the full engine weight hanging on it while still under pressure. Sometimes they 'let go' with quite a bang! Usually

Above *Remains of a dozen Canadian mice recovered from inside a couple of Mercury cylinders, which they had entered via an open valve and, being unable to climb out again, had perished.*

Right *The start of the oft-repeated stripping process; the inter-cylinder baffles, exhaust and inlet manifolds, valve-gear covers, push-rods and their tubes have all been removed. Now the difficult task of trying to remove the cylinders can commence!*

Left *On this engine we managed to remove all nine cylinders and their pistons. Now it can be stripped down completely.*

Above *Over the months reclaimed cylinders appeared on the shelves. On the lower shelf is a rear volute cover with the twin inlets from the carburettor, to its left a camshaft drum, and above it some pistons.*

we had to make many attempts using several methods in sequence before we could free some of them.

Often a promising-looking engine would have to be abandoned if one particular cylinder proved impossible to separate even after prolonged and determined efforts. Frequently a cylinder barrel, finally freed from its piston after the greatest difficulty, would turn out to be too corroded to be of any use – the air then turned blue with oaths and curses!

'Chalky', helped by John, beavered away at this for many, many months, until there were neat rows of cylinders, each cleaned, numbered and tagged along with its own piston, sitting on the shelves ready for more detailed inspection and measurement to ascertain if they were capable of reclamation.

The pistons and their gudgeon pins were all cleaned and examined minutely, including crack-testing, so that potentially useable examples could be marked as such. They then joined the other engine components that had been subject to the same process.

'Chalky' was a wiry little man, of Welsh extraction and thus prone to bursting into song. The trouble was that he knew only the chorus and not the verses of his favourite, the old music hall song 'It's a great big shame', so we heard this rendered hundreds of times. It was something about 'nagging at a fella what is six foot four and 'er only five foot two'. Sometimes he would emphasise the last two words of the line 'if she belonged to me I'd let her know who's who' with resounding hammer blows!

The alloy crankcases were made in two halves, joined at the bore centres, and are beautifully machined; after a thorough cleaning and inspection, several sets were found to be well within the manufacturer's own tolerance figures, so Chalky could select the best ones to use. Sufficient of the large alloy castings that form the front and rear engine covers, plus the casings for the supercharger, auxiliary drives and reduction gears, all machine-finished internally, proved to be completely serviceable too. The oil collection sumps (from where the scavenge pump returns the oil via the coolers and filters to the oil-tank in the dry-sump lubrication system) were made in magnesium, which suffered much more from surface corrosion than the hard alloy of the other engine castings, and many had to be discarded before we could pick two sound examples.

We selected four excellent crankshafts from the engines that had been stripped down; no measurable wear or run-out at all was discovered during intense inspection, including X-rays and crack-testing, and the most careful measurement to thousandths of an inch. They are magnificent examples of technically pleasing design and superb workmanship, and are machined all over to a mirror finish. These remarks also apply to the forged steel connecting-rods, or the master and eight articulated rods to give them their correct description; the accurate machining of the varying radii in the fillets to the webs of the slender 'H'-section rods is quite outstanding.

The large main roller-bearings, and the plain bearings for the big- and small-ends of each connecting-rod, were also found to be well within manufacturer's tolerances. Similarly, the gear-driven camshaft drums that acted on the roller tappets to the exhaust and inlet push-rods were inspected minutely; the lift and dwell of each camshaft lobe was measured most carefully, and found to be in excellent condition. These rotary cams are gear-driven from the crankshaft (with a vernier adjustment for setting the timing accurately) and run concentric to it, but in the reverse direction and at one-eighth engine speed, just to complicate matters!

To produce these magnificent cranks, connecting-rods and camshafts to such exceptionally high standards must have required hundreds of man-hours per item from the

The reclaimed cylinders, now complete with their overhauled valve-gear, are fitted to the crankcase by 'Chalky' and John. The top piston can be seen below the cylinder that they are carefully lowering into place, with a piston-ring clamp in position. The cylinder to the left has the rebuilt rocker-assembly mounted.

skilled workforce, whose abilities were of an equally high standard, so the costs of production must have been very high too. Certainly, such labour-intensive and expensive methods of production could not be employed nowadays. These impressive Bristol engines are themselves a fine tribute to the excellence of design and manufacture that demonstrate British engineering skills at their very best.

'Chalky's' next task was to lap in the pistons to the matching cylinders. He made a jig on which to mount a cylinder, and a tool using an old piston with a wooden 'T'-handle, and spent countless hours polishing out any surface irregularities, using 'engineer's blue' to make sure that all the high-spots were smoothed away. We had new sets of piston rings specially manufactured to the original specification, using salvaged rings as patterns – these were the only new parts (apart from some gaskets, nuts and bolts) used in rebuilding the engines. This fact alone demonstrates the very high standards of the original construction, for these engines, uninhibited and unprotected, had lain out in all weathers for several decades.

When each piston and cylinder was honed to a perfect fit they were weighed and balanced to fractions of an ounce. 'Chalky' next rebuilt the overhead valve gear. The triple valve springs for each valve were measured and checked before re-assembly. The rocker arms are machined all over and pivot in roller-bearings – further examples of what today would be called 'over-engineering' – and all were scrupulously checked, as were the roller-tappet and push-rod assemblies, which incorporate a cunning device to cater for the differing rates of expansion of the push-rods and the cylinders to maintain the correct tappet clearances. Every one of the 36 valves in each engine was meticulously lapped in to ensure a perfect seal, and tested by the time-honoured method of pouring some petrol into the inverted cylinder with the four valves closed, and leaving it to soak overnight – any slight leak thus revealed could be rectified by lapping in the offending valve further, and re-testing, until perfect.

Many, many months were to pass before we could admire the rows of completed and tagged matching cylinder and piston assemblies, with their barrels bead-blasted and painted, and their overhauled valve-gear assemblies back in situ, sitting on the shelves looking like brand-new items. This marked the passing of another most important hurdle, for during all of these months, if not years, we had been kept in suspense as to whether or not it would be possible to reclaim sufficient serviceable cylinders to rebuild two engines. So we were very relieved when, finally, sufficient components had been accumulated so that we were in the position of being able to start the lengthy process of actually building up the engines on their special stands.

In the meantime all of the various ancillary engine components and their gear and shaft spring drives were individually stripped down, cleaned, inspected, measured and serviced or overhauled as necessary, then re-assembled, checked and tested. These items included the oil-pumps – both scavenge and pressure – and the hydraulic, fuel and vacuum pumps, plus the compressors. The inlet and exhaust manifolds, plus the exhaust collector rings that form the front of the cowlings, all with their expansion joints, and the cooling baffles and oil-cooler ducts, were repaired and replaced. The Serck cylindrical oil-coolers were flushed out under pressure in different positions for weeks at a time, then filled with oil and pressure tested; when all was well they were mounted and connected up. The magnetos were rewound, new ignition harnesses made up from the special braided high-tension leads, and the starter motors and generators overhauled. The reduction gear assemblies, a train of epicyclic gears that run between the crankshaft and the propeller shaft, were stripped, most carefully inspected, measured for truth and run-out, and meticulously rebuilt to the original clearances and tolerances.

Another of the excellent skilled engineers who helped with the Blenheim restoration in their spare time was Neville Gardner, known to us as 'Nev'. He worked in the early days while he was a lanky apprentice at RAF Halton, but on completing his training he was posted to RAF Leuchars, so we did not see him so often. Later on, by then promoted to Sergeant and based at RAF Wattisham, he was able to put in many hours of first-class work on rebuilding the engines. But more about Nev – a vital member of the present team – anon.

Ten of the complicated Claudel-Hobson compound carburettors were stripped right down so that we could repair and renovate three complete units – one as a spare. They contain delicate devices that provide automatic boost and mixture control; these maintain constant supercharger pressure (at the level selected by the pilot) from the variable data produced as the aircraft climbs into the lower-pressure air, and ensure that the fuel/air mixture is always correct for the rpm and boost in the thinner air. These are operated by a series of paper-thin brass bellows-type airtight capsules that expand in their float chambers as the aircraft gains altitude, and through a multiplicity of links, levers and needle-valves meter the output of the fuel jets, and also control the boost pressure.

We had to build our own fuel-flow rig, to pass measured quantities of fuel at specified pressures in given periods, to set the various float levels accurately, to calibrate the carburettors against the figures in the manual, and to test the correct operation of these automatic controls, which were very advanced for their day. On other contemporary aircraft the pilot needed to 'lean off' or enrich the mixture control constantly, and adjust the throttle settings continually as the aircraft climbed or descended.

Each of the twin chokes has powerful accelerator pumps that squirt over 3 pints of neat fuel directly into the chokes to cater for the increased demand as the engine accelerates. They are supplemented by two more delayed-action pumps that continue this temporary enrichment $1^{1}/2$ seconds later to help the engine 'pick up' cleanly. This was to overcome the difficulties of persuading a 25-litre engine with updraught carburettors to accelerate without backfiring due to a momentarily too-lean mixture, as it would if opened up fully on the normal mixture. However, conversely, care has to be taken to open the throttles smoothly and progressively to allow this process to take place, for if the throttles are opened too suddenly the accelerator pumps produce too rich a mixture and a 'rich cut' occurs. Modern fuel-injection systems cater for this varying fuel demand automatically, but although in the 1930s the carburettors on the Mercury were the most advanced available, they required handling with understanding and care. The venturis are heated by circulating hot oil from the engine within the bodies to help prevent ice forming.

So, all in all, restoring the carburettors properly presented a considerable challenge to the skills and ingenuity of 'Chalky' and John. That the carburettors performed their complex functions so well when they were called upon to do so is the best tribute to their excellent workmanship.

The supercharger impeller, driven by triple epicyclic spring clutches from the rear of the crankshaft, and their roller-bearings, required the most careful assembly and balancing. They are geared up to run at several times the engine speed – at 2,650 rpm they rotate at 24,800 rpm! Minor works of technical art, they accept mixture from the carburettor into their central 'eye' and expel it centrifugally into expanding-curved volutes that are beautifully machined into the two-piece alloy supercharger casing, and thence via the similarly curved inlet manifolds into the cylinders. Wartime Mercurys had a rated supercharger pressure of 9 psi over atmospheric pressure ('Plus 9' boost) for 5 minutes or emergency use, but normally used 'Plus 5'. Our engines are restricted to 'Plus $4^{1}/2$' in the interests of longevity.

'Chalky' simply revelled in the beautifully made engines and conveyed his enthusiasm

The two halves of the beautifully machined alloy supercharger casing with the steel impeller and vanes to deflect the mixture into the volutes that lead to the inlet manifolds.

to the Team, delighting in pointing out the matchless machining, the accurate mating of components, and many other examples of the superlative standards of manufacture, reminding us that they originated from the period of the First World War. His vast engineering experience and depth of knowledge on early piston engines were prodigious, and he transferred much of this expertise to John Romain, who proved a very apt

Both engines mounted on to the airframe, awaiting their exhaust manifolds and collector rings and 'plumbing' into the various systems. The machined fins on the cylinders give each engine a total cooling area of over 650 square feet!

A completed and 'zero-houred' Bristol Mercury engine, showing the baffles between the cylinders, the push-rod tubes and valve gear covers, the blanked-off exhaust outlets, the oil collection sump (lower centre) and the flexible oil hose to the VP prop on the reduction-gear casing. Twin reproductions of this photo by 'Smudger' were used for his popular 'Happiness is Big Bristols' T-shirts!

and receptive student, absorbing from his mentor much invaluable information, plus many practical hints and tips, over the years they worked together.

'Chalky' then started to build up the first engine, starting from an empty crankcase and the bare crankshaft, ably assisted by young John, to whom he explained and demonstrated each step. John later built up the second engine himself, under 'Chalky's' close supervision, thus gaining the most thorough 'hands-on' experience of engine building.

Little did we realise just how soon this experience would be put to the test, for the Team suffered a great blow when poor 'Chalky' went into hospital with an eye infection but developed other complications and sadly passed away. We missed him very much, but feel that he is still part of the Team as he passed on so much of his skill and expertise to John Romain. In his memory we erected an oak bench with an engraved plaque

The most rewarding day when both the Bristol Mercuries were run up together for the first time.

opposite 'Blenheim Palace'; this was the first of several memorial benches that have been installed at Duxford.

'Chalky', alas, did not live long enough to see and hear his beloved Mercurys actually running, but the Team all knew that he was with us in spirit when the rebuilt engines fired up for the first time and ran perfectly.

In July 1986 the aircraft was towed out for the initial run of the starboard engine. It was still finished in yellow etch-primer, riding proudly on its undercarriage, although without its outer wings or bomb doors, with the engines mounted but lacking their cowlings and nacelles.

Feverish activity had preceded this proud moment. The fuel system had been connected up from the main tanks in the centre-section and tested under pressure; the dry-sump lubrication system had been installed, connected up, tested and primed with warmed oil; all the engine controls had been fitted, tested and adjusted; the engine instruments had been plumbed or wired in and checked; and the engine fire-exting-uishers had been serviced, certified and fitted. Chocks were placed under the wheels and the 'trolley-acc' plugged in. The starboard engine was hand-turned to make sure that it did not hydraulic on any oil that had drained into the lower cylinders; it was fuel-primed from the hand priming-pump in the undercarriage bay, and the engine was turned over by hand to 'suck in' the mixture.

A small crowd of well-wishers had gathered, including Norman Chapman, Fred Hanson and Pearl White, 'Chalky's' widow, plus photographers from the aviation press, to witness the Blenheim burst into life at last.

The starter motor was engaged, the engine turned for the customary 'three blades', then John switched the magnetos on. The Mercury fired instantly, for the first time in over 45 years, and ran beautifully, to the cheers of the Team and the band of supporters. I'm sure that 'Chalky' White, too, was with us – and cheering.

Chapter Eleven

Towards roll-out

A few months later we repeated this procedure for the initial runs of the starboard engine, but this turned out to be a great anti-climax – it only coughed and back-fired a few times and refused to start! There were no cheers this time, just some embar-rassed banter and a few red faces. The trouble was soon traced: both magnetos had

An interesting view of the rear of the starboard engine; the undercarriage is partially retracted owing to the height of the trestles. The four mounting points on the spars for the outer wings are protected by tape, and the inner cowling from the cylinders to the firewall deflects the airflow to the controllable cooling gill ring. The systems have yet to be installed on the firewall – compare with the picture in Chapter Nine.

been removed from the engine earlier to attend to some minor problem, and while they were being replaced the previously carefully set ignition timing had slipped. This was easily remedied and the starboard engine did then start instantly and run perfectly too.

It then followed the same programme of ground runs and tests as the port engine until it reached the same stage. We could then run them together, with the rear of the fuselage tethered; the airframe vibrated with the power and shook in the slipstream. Exciting days! Photographs of the Blenheim with both engines running appeared throughout the aviation press, and in some of the nationals too, and we started getting visits and letters from intrigued and delighted ex-Blenheim crews.

However, the aircraft could not fly without its outer wings, and the rebuilding of these was still far from complete. At that stage we had been deeply involved for a protracted period in the problems of locating the special steel needed for the wing spar booms and cornices, and when the material was found and the new sections had been formed into the eight different shapes required, we then had the difficulty of overcoming the severe distortion that took place during the heat treatment process, before we could proceed to remanufacture the mainplanes. The way in which John Romain led the Team so brilliantly in solving these potentially terminal problems was described in Chapter Eight – suffice to add here that overcoming them delayed for over a year completion of the restoration.

Even when the CAA-approved repair schemes to all four spars had been completed, we still had to rebuild or replace many of the ribs – 75 per cent were renewed – and span-wise stringers. After the entire skeleton was reconstructed and painted, we could then make anew all the upper and lower skin panels, from 22-gauge L72 alloy, thicker than the original 24-gauge material, and using rivets a size larger too, utilising the painstaking back-drilling techniques previously described.

Throughout this entire process, the wing sections remained bolted rigidly into the substantial steel jigs in order to retain their structural integrity even while partially dismantled. That these jigs needed to be both substantial and accurate is demonstrated when I explain that each wing has a slight built-in twist, known as 'washout', which reduces the angle of incidence by 1° over the span from root to tip. This twist, which is barely discernible to the eye, ensures that the outer portion of the wings will stall slightly later than the inner portion, and helps avoid sudden wing-drop at the stall. Our rebuilt wings, with their thicker skins and larger rivets, were stronger than the originals, and lighter too as we had deleted the outer fuel-tanks and quite a bit of other equipment.

While this work on the wing sections was proceeding steadily in 'Blenheim Palace', fitting out the interior of the aircraft, plus completing and testing the installation of the various controls, circuits, pipework and systems continued apace in the hangar.

We had been fortunate in purchasing, some years earlier, a complete 'blind flying' instrument panel fitted as standard to all RAF aircraft of the early 1940s. The flight instruments were individually overhauled, re-calibrated and certified by CAA-approved specialists, refitted into the panel – which is carried on shock-proof mountings – and plumbed into their appropriate systems. This meant connecting up with the pitot tube and static vents for the Airspeed Indicator, Altimeter and Climb or Descent instruments, and with the vacuum system for the gyroscopically controlled Artificial Horizon, Turn and Bank, and Direction Indicators. We had found a correct P11 compass and fitted this to the original mounting.

Much of the original operational equipment was deleted as superfluous to our needs. This included the complete oxygen system; 'George', the rudimentary automatic control system; the bomb-arming, selection, fusing, release and jettison systems and circuits (although we reinstated some of the bombing controls into the cockpit and bomb-aiming position for the sake of authenticity); the F24 camera and its mounting frame; the downward-signalling switchboxes and lamps; the emergency 'boost over-ride' lever and its linkages; the heating system for the cockpit and for the fixed gun in the port wing; the pneumatic gun-firing and flare-release systems; the ancient and heavy radios and IFF box; the additional instruments in the navigator's and wireless operator's positions; and the pneumatically operated fuel jettison system. The absence of all this equipment (and the fact that we did not need to carry any armour-plating, bombs, flares or ammunition either!) helped to reduce the laden weight by over 3,000 lbs. This was to enable us to restore, or exceed, the original Blenheim performance, even though we run the engines at significantly lower boost pressures, thus providing in turn greater reliability and longevity from them. We had adjusted the linkages to the automatic boost control to allow a maximum supercharger pressure of 'Plus $4^1/2$' (psi) at 2,400 rpm, half the 'Plus 9' allowed on wartime aircraft.

Work meanwhile continued on rebuilding and fitting the lower nacelles, and the main engine cowlings, mainly by 'Smudge'. He and David Swann made wooden bucks for the large upper nacelles – known as 'beetle-backs' – so that new ones could be manufactured. Canadian-built aircraft had bulkier beetle-backs, made to suit their larger oil-tanks and a dinghy, but we reverted to the British type. When completed and a good fit, only achieved after many trial fittings, the nacelles and cowlings were etch-primed inside and out, and the interiors painted green.

The flying control runs – all duplicated – were fabricated and connected up, with new cables and bearings throughout for the elevators and rudder, plus the controllable trimming tabs on each. These cables run through a system of pulleys and guides from the cockpit controls, over the roof of the bomb bay, and right down the floor of the rear fuselage to cross-shafts and levers in the stern frame. Each length has to be made up, installed, carefully tensioned and adjusted with great accuracy, keeping friction to the minimum. The rod, lever and torque tube aileron-actuating controls had been rebuilt with new bearings and completed up to the outer ends of the centre-section.

The engine controls for the throttles, mixture levers, hot or cold air intakes, cooling gills, carburettor cut-outs, fuel cocks and cross-feed controls, fuel-priming pumps, ignition switches, and the propeller pitch controls had all been installed, adjusted and conscientiously tested before the initial engine runs. Similarly the individually checked and calibrated engine instruments: boost pressure gauges, rpm indicators, cylinder-head temperature gauges, oil pressure and temperature gauges, and fuel pressure and contents indicators. When the other systems were installed their gauges were also checked and connected up: vacuum pressure, hydraulic pressure, the triple gauge for pneumatic and brake pressures, plus the mechanical flap position and trimming tab position indicators. The undercarriage locked/unlocked, 'up' or 'down', indicators and warning lights had been installed earlier, together with the emergency system for lowering the wheels, when we had tested the retraction and extension of the units.

Colin Swann, helped by Hugh Smith and Chris 'Tie-Wrap' Hollyer, continued to make up and install the completely new wiring loom for the modified electrical system, supplied by the 500-watt generator and two 12-volt 35-ampere/hour batteries, one of which is for engine-starting only. Colin and Co connected up and tested in turn the many electrical items and services, including several instruments and a revised intercom system that extended to the undercarriage bays so that the pilot could speak to the engineer who operated the priming pumps from there. As previously mentioned, the modern Nav/Comm radio kit with a transponder was fitted discretely below the left-hand side of the pilot's seat, on the shelf previously used for the bomb-arming switches,

The engines now have their exhaust collector rings fitted as well as the cooling gills. The glazing is in place, the turret cupola is in the retracted position, the rudder and elevators are fitted and the controls connected. Now it looks like a Blenheim that might even fly again!

and the small aerials required for them were also hidden as far as possible. We fitted an accelerometer to record the maximum positive or negative 'G' experienced on each flight; this was mounted in the bomb bay so that the pilot could not reset it in flight and conceal his misbehaviour!

Both the engines had been inhibited over the autumn and winter of 1986 while all this fitting out and other work was going on in the hangar, as we realised that there would be a long delay before the wings could be completed. However, noticeably and progressively, the Blenheim was becoming more and more a 'live' and functional air-craft as these various systems were installed, meticulously checked, adjusted and tested for their correct operation.

We fitted Avimo couplings into the hydraulic system so that we could check the operation of the undercarriage, flaps and turret from an external source of hydraulic pressure. Similarly, we had fitted a ground charging point, extra filter and non-return valve into the pneumatic system near the main reservoir in the fuselage, so that this system too could be tested. The engine fire-extinguisher system had also been rebuilt, installed and tested before the engine runs. It comprises a large CO_2 reservoir in the fuselage, with the outlet controlled by a selector, which directs the discharge via pipes and nozzles to the engine compartment and carburettor intake of whichever engine is selected when the 'red knob' in the cockpit is pulled.

The whole Team worked harder, and for longer hours, throughout this demanding but exciting period, for they could see the triumphant end result of their efforts approaching. Holidays, long weekends, and all the time off the volunteers could manage were devoted to completing the restoration; John Romain worked with the Team right through these weekends and late into many a night. No other restoration project at Duxford received such consistent and dedicated effort as the Blenheim – the

Team were demonstrating to the world some of that spirit of 'Britain First' shown by the original 'Blenheim Boys' all those years before.

Finally, first the starboard outer wing, and several months later the port one, were completed, removed from the jig in the workshops, etch-primed, painted internally, and bolted into place on the centre-section. The mounting lugs on each spar had been re-bushed and, with the forked eye fittings, were examined by radiograph at Quest Inspection Ltd at Luton Airport and cleared. The new main attachment bolts were specially made, and the triple-link heavy-gauge mounting and web-joint plates, which set the dihedral angle of the outer wings, were cross-bolted into position with all new nuts and bolts. We had deleted the long-range fuel-tanks, together with their associated plumbing and the fuel dumping system, from the outer wings to reduce the laden weight.

The rebuilt and recovered ailerons were attached and the rod and torque tube aileron-actuating runs, which provide for Frise-designed differential aileron operation by means of an off-centre pivot in a link, were overhauled, fitted with new bearings throughout and reinstated, as were the outer sections of the refurbished flaps. Strangely, there is only one hydraulic jack for the operation of the four flap sections; this acts directly on the port inner flap, which is connected by a heavy cable via pulleys and levers to the starboard inner flap, and both are joined to their outer flaps by torque tubes and links. This all had to be set up, adjusted and tested to ensure that the four flaps lowered and retracted exactly together.

The rounded alloy wing-tips, with their curved wooden outer formers and perspex inserts for navigation and station-keeping lamps, were rebuilt and fixed into position. We replaced the retractable landing-light used on Canadian-produced aircraft with the original fixed lamps behind a perspex cover in the leading-edge of the port wing, as originally fitted to British-produced Blenheims.

When the outer wings had been attached and the mounting bolts all locked in place, we could carry out a full rigging and dimension check, during which the entire airframe is measured carefully from specified points to ensure complete symmetry of construction and assembly, and the range of movement of the flying control surfaces adjusted and set. Measurements from datum points on the fin to each wing-tip were within a quarter of an inch of each other, as they were from the wing-tips to the tailplane datum points, and from the latter to a point on the fuselage and to one at the rear of each wheel bay; measurements from a datum point on the nose to each propeller-boss were also identical. The fin was truly vertical and the tailplane at exactly 90° to it; the 1° incidence angle of the wing, and the 6.5° dihedral of the outer wings were also 'spot on'.

The achievement of this exceptionally high standard of accuracy in the reconstruction of the airframe and flying controls is the finest possible tribute to the skills of the restoration team. This is especially so considering not only the long-derelict state of the original hulks, but also that the major components – main fuselage, centre-section, keel-plate, and outer wings – all originated from different airframes.

The range of movement of the control surfaces was adjusted to give the correct number of degrees travel in each direction. The rudder was set to move 17.5° on either side of the centre-line; the elevators to move up through 33° and down through 26°, and the ailerons through 31° and 14° respectively.

Everything was checked, tightened, locked or split-pinned, and signed off. The volume of the paperwork increased continually. Some wag had said, at an early stage of the restoration, that when the weight of the paperwork equalled that of the aircraft, it would be ready to fly!

The 'nuts and bolts' side of the physical restoration was by then almost completed. It had been a long and hard slog, although I have had to condense my description of it into a few short chapters. Mention of nuts and bolts reminds me that these mundane items proved to be a source of frustration and difficulty throughout the restoration. The Blenheim, designed in the 1930s, naturally used Imperial measures throughout: weight was expressed in pounds, dimensions in feet, inches and fractions of an inch (indeed thousandths of an inch in engine measurements), and the aircraft was built to the British Standards (BS) of the day, using AGS (Aircraft General Stores) sizes for nuts, bolts, rivets, fittings, connectors, etc. These consisted of the BA (British Association) range, which had metric threads; the BSF (British Standard Fine) range; and some of the Whitworth range – none of which were mutually compatible.

When the Canadians built these aircraft under licence during the war they caused further complications by mixing these AGS sizes with some American UNF (United National Fine) and UNC (United National Coarse) sizes, so it became a right hotchpotch of obsolete sizes. Since in the intervening years most of these had become virtually unobtainable anyway, we tried to regularise the position during the restoration by using British AN sizes where we could and American UNF sizes where this was not possible. Some of the smaller fittings use BA sizes and threads, and the pipes and connectors used a complete variety of all these sizes.

The thickness of the alloy sheets used for the skins and fairings, and the steel used for the spar repairs and capping, was measured under the old SWG (Standard Wire Gauge) system, but now millimetres or thousandths of an inch are used – although 20 gauge is not anything as simple as 20-thousandths of an inch! Further inconsistencies arise as rivet

Rolled out for the first time! Still lacking her outer wings, cowlings, nacelles, bomb doors and some systems, but ready to run.

Getting ready for the very first engine runs, when she would no longer be merely an inert and lifeless airframe.

sizes are still measured in fractions of an inch. The many sizes of alloy tubing needed, as in the flying and engine controls for example, possessed a wide variety of different diameters, wall thicknesses, lengths and end fittings. The telephone bills grew as the difficult search for some of the more obscure sizes of tubing became more time-consuming.

At long last we had created a virtually complete Blenheim, and we towed her out proudly on to the flight line one Sunday evening in February 1987, so that we could admire her and take photographs. Only the bomb doors and some of the internal fittings were missing. She was still finished in the all-over dull yellow etch-primer with the fabric control surfaces in their silver dope. She looked graceful yet purposeful, and – to our eyes at least – quite beautiful.

The great day when the Blenheim finally became alive.

The finally completed aircraft towed out for the first time by 'Terence the Tug'.

The Team were still together late that night, although not working on this occasion, but celebrating in the John Barleycorn Inn at Duxford – a well-earned celebration!

Talking of the Blenheim's 'graceful yet purposeful' appearance, I would like to observe that, although they were machines designed to wage war – to bomb and to strafe, to kill and to maim – many aircraft of that period did have lines that were aesthetically pleasing. Prime examples are the Spitfire and Mosquito; lesser-known ones are, for instance, the Westland Whirlwind and Hawker Tempest, with the American Lockheed Lightning and Douglas Boston, plus – later on – the de Havilland Hornet and Hawker Hunter.

At that time our Blenheim carried her UK registration letters G-MKIV, which of course was needed for all the CAA paperwork, although we had been granted exemp-

We admired her sleek but purposeful lines, although she looked most odd with the civil registration and finished in yellow etch-prime with silver-doped fabric control surfaces.

Masked up and being sprayed all over with a grey filler primer.

tion from displaying those markings. For the time had arrived for us to select the exact colour scheme and markings of a specific wartime Blenheim, so that our resurrected aircraft would become truly representative of all the hard-pressed examples, and would in particular exemplify their outstandingly courageous crews – the famed 'Blenheim Boys'.

We felt that they, above all, deserved this special tribute, as we had discovered during our researches that their exceptional bravery and distinctive, dashing devotion to duty had been overlooked or understated for far too long.

Chapter Twelve

The forgotten bomber

While working away on the rebuild over the preceding years we had carried out a considerable amount of research, studying all of the published material on Blenheims that we could find, in order to ensure the complete accuracy and authenticity of our restoration. This research had revealed that Blenheims played a major and valiant part in Royal Air Force operations for the first few years of the war; indeed, far more major and far more valiant than we, and I'm sure many other people, had ever realised.

We discovered that the RAF had more Blenheims – 1,089 – on charge at the outbreak of war than any other type of aircraft; for example, they had less than 200 each of the Wellington and Whitley bombers. We found that Blenheims enjoyed the unique distinction of being the only aircraft to serve in all of the RAF Commands then existing – Bomber, Fighter, Coastal, Army Co-operation and Training (the pedants must excuse me

A pleasing shot of a Mk IF Blenheim of 25 Squadron, with toned-down roundels, taken during the last pre-war exercises on 11 August 1939. RX-M was L1426, which crashed shortly afterwards when taking off from Northolt on 17 December 1939.

Blenheim Mk IV TE-A of 53 Army Co-Operation Squadron in May 1939, a few months before they were re-coded PZ and sent to France, there to suffer heavy casualties.

for not including Balloon Command!) – and in every Theatre of War – European, Middle East and Far East. The Hurricane did not serve with Bomber Command, nor did the Wellington make it into Fighter Command; Maintenance Command of course worked on all types of RAF aircraft, and Transport Command was not formed until 1943.

We learned that the Blenheim had served as a bomber by day and night, at low, medium and high level; as a long-range day fighter; as a night fighter; as a ground attack and tactical support aircraft; in the armed reconnaissance role both for strategic and tactical purposes; as a night intruder against enemy airfields; in low-level anti-shipping sorties; in convoy protection patrols and on anti-submarine operations; for radar development and calibration; for laying smoke-screens; and as an operational crew trainer. Indeed, it was the RAF's first 'Multi Combat Role Aircraft' long before that term was even coined!

In the course of our research we came across many examples of historically notable 'firsts' achieved by Blenheims. For example, they were the first RAF aircraft to take offensive action against all three Axis powers – Germany, Italy and Japan – in the three Theatres of War, and they were used to pioneer and develop many new techniques such as low-level anti-shipping attacks, night 'intruder' operations, and the use of airborne radar. Indeed, the world's first ever successful radar-guided interception of an attacking enemy bomber at night was achieved by a Blenheim from the Fighter Interception Unit using AI. To give an idea of the importance of the Blenheim in the development of the wartime Royal Air Force I have listed some of these 'firsts' in Appendix 3.

Given these impressive antecedents, it is quite natural to assume that the Blenheim would be renowned for the extensive and widespread part it played in the war effort, that it would be famous for the heroic deeds performed by its crews, that it would stand alongside other well-known wartime RAF aircraft in public appreciation, and that it would be remembered with pride. But, alas, it was none of these things. Far from being renowned, it was largely reviled. Its great wartime efforts were overlooked, and the heroism of the crews had not received the recognition that was rightfully due; indeed, the Blenheim had almost slipped from the public memory altogether.

Why had this been allowed to happen? Why had it simply faded away to become 'the forgotten bomber'? Surely it deserved far better?

We began to realise that the poor Blenheim, being associated with that period of the war when this country stood alone and was very much on the defensive, had just not been given the credit it deserved for constantly being 'thrown in at the deep end'. The British and their Allies had suffered a series of major defeats, being ejected by the Germans from the whole of Continental Europe and Norway, plus Greece, Crete and the Western Desert, and by the Japanese from Burma, Malaya and Singapore – and Blenheims had been heavily involved in desperate holding operations in the fighting at all of these locations.

Blenheims had to be deployed on these highly dangerous, sometimes almost suicidal, attacks simply because there were no other aircraft available in any numbers to the RAF at that time. Often Blenheims were not at all suitable for such operations, which although carried out with great courage and without regard to the immense risks involved, alas frequently proved to be quite futile. As a result, the Blenheims suffered very high losses during this period of desperate fighting and earned themselves a poor reputation.

On 17 May 1940 12 Blenheims from 82 Squadron at Watton set out on a low-level daylight attack on a German Panzer column advancing through Belgium near Gembloux. All were shot down bar one, which staggered back, badly damaged and on one engine, to collapse at the end of the runway and be written off. The entire Squadron had been wiped out, and the Air Ministry moved to disband it, but the CO, the Earl of Bandon (an inspired leader, known affectionately as 'Paddy, the Abandoned Earl'), reformed it instantly and it was back in action three days later. Indeed, on 13 August 12 replacement Blenheims from the same Squadron manned by fresh crews set out on a medium-level attack on the German-held airfield at Aarborg in Northern Denmark. One turned back – all of the remaining 11 were shot down. The Squadron had been decimated twice in less than three months. Yet Aarborg was but one of over 70 German-held airfields that were attacked by Blenheims of 2 Group.

This Blenheim IV of 18 Squadron at Great Massingham in 1941 is unusual in that the duck-egg blue is carried further up the sides of the fuselage than usual; it is also fitted with spinners, probably in an attempt to gain a little speed, and the light-bomb-carriers are armed. WV-F of 18 Squadron dropped a spare 'tin leg' for Douglas Bader on to St Omer airfield on 19 August 1941.

This Blenheim Mk IV, RT-O of 114 Squadron at West Raynham, took part in the first '1,000 Bomber Raid' on 30 May 1942. Note the matt black lower surfaces and the flame-damper on the exhaust.

The Staff at Command, Group and Wing Headquarters were not heartless, and found this severe wastage of skilled men and valuable machines very disturbing. But they had no alternative. The Blenheim was the most suitable of the types of aircraft then to hand – indeed, often the only aircraft available – so the brave Squadrons were ordered into action again and again, frequently in the face of the most daunting odds.

These casualties to Blenheim crews clearly disturbed the Prime Minister, Winston Churchill, who sent two ambivalent messages at the end of August 1941 – 36 Blenheims had been lost that month. On the 29th he sent an 'Action this Day' minute to the Chief of the Air Staff: 'The loss of 7 Blenheims out of 17 in the daylight attack on merchant shipping and the docks at Rotterdam is most severe. Such losses might be accepted in attacking Scharnhorst, Gneisenau or Tirpitz . . . but they seem disproportionate to an attack on merchant shipping not engaged in vital supply work . . . While I greatly admire the bravery of the pilots I do not want them pressed too hard. Easier targets giving a higher damage return compared to casualties may be more often selected.'

On the 30th he sent to the Headquarters of 2 Group a personal message to the Blenheim crews: 'The devotion shown in the attacks on Rotterdam and other objectives is beyond all praise. The "Charge of the Light Brigade" at Balaclava is eclipsed in brightness by these almost daily deeds of fame.'

The wartime 'Ministry of Information' (or should I say 'Ministry of Propaganda') needed to make the most of any success. The Spitfire, for example, was glamorised for its role in the Battle of Britain – at the expense of the Hurricane, incidentally, which shot down far more enemy aircraft. The valiant efforts of the Blenheims hardly got a look in, yet during the Battles of France and Britain, Bomber and Coastal Commands suffered more casualties – the majority Blenheim crews – than did Fighter Command.

During the four months of July to October 1940 inclusive, the height of the Battle of Britain, Fighter Command suffered 1,002 casualties on operations, Bomber Command 2,134 and Coastal Command 600. If aircrew losses in operational accidents of 276, 584 and 145 respectively are added, the totals become Fighter Command 1,278, Bomber Command 2,718, and Coastal Command 745. This represents 1,278 fighter crewmen lost against 3,463 bomber crew members – almost three times as many – and the number of Fighter Command casualties includes crew members from the six Fighter Command Blenheim Squadrons who lost 22 aircraft in the period.

The figure for pilot casualties are more even, at 1,095 in Fighter Command and 1,369 in the other two Commands, as most fighters are of course single-seat aircraft; but they exclude the many Blenheim and Lysander crews lost while operating with Army Co-Operation Command.

It was not only the Luftwaffe's failure to gain supremacy in the air over the United Kingdom in the autumn of 1940, but also the constant RAF attacks – mainly by Blenheims – on enemy shipping and on the invasion barges being gathered in the Channel Ports, that created the doubts in the minds of the German Naval Command as to the wisdom of the proposed seaborne invasion of these islands. For example, in the last two weeks of September there were 121 attacks by Bomber Command Blenheims on invasion shipping at Dunkirk, 70 at Calais, 58 at Ostend and 33 at Boulogne. These were in addition to the attacks on enemy-held airfields mentioned above, and were carried out by the 13 Blenheim Squadrons of 2 Group; the further six Blenheim Squadrons of Coastal Command carried out many similar attacks. Admiral Raeder persuaded his Fuhrer and the Wermacht High Command initially to postpone and then to cancel Operation

A photo from 1941, showing Sgt WOp/AG Ken Whittle of 139 Squadron stepping from the hatch. This Blenheim still has the hopelessly inadequate single Vickers .303-inch gas-operated magazine-loaded machine-gun with First World War ring-and-bead sight.

A typical all-NCO crew in April 1941: Pilot Ted Inman between Observer Ken Collins and Tommy Cooke. Their Blenheim, R3B03 UX-A of 82 Squadron, has the later twin-Browning turret.

Sealion – the planned invasion of the UK. Hitler then cast his covetous eyes eastwards upon Russia, and the history of the world was changed for ever. The gallant and significant contribution made by the Blenheims in sparing this country from the necessity to defend itself against a full-scale invasion has never been adequately acknowledged.

Similarly, it became clear to us that the valiant role that Blenheims played in attempting to stem the tide on a dozen other fronts all over the world had been 'swept under the carpet' too. The Spitfire became world-famous, the Mosquito was hailed as the 'Wooden Wonder'. Both possess that purity of line that conveys so well the combination of power, grace, and deadly efficiency. Both were very successful and were also most aptly named; in fact, perfect material for the Air Ministry Press Department and the Ministry of Information. The Lancaster, too, has that menacing but graceful appearance, and by the sheer weight of numbers employed by Bomber Command, and the enormous tonnage of bombs they dropped on the enemy, they became world-famous as well.

This publicity is to a degree understandable in view of the need in wartime to minimise ineffectiveness or defeats on the one hand, and to make the most of any successes to bolster morale on the other. But it becomes far less understandable to find that most post-war historians also failed to give the Blenheims proper credit for the many tasks – mainly dangerous low-level daylight attacks – that they were called upon to execute time and time again. Bomber Command Blenheims carried out 12,214 operational sorties, over 8,000 in daylight, and Coastal Command Blenheims nearly half that number.

So we became determined to restore and rehabilitate not just the physical aircraft but also its very reputation. Both had been neglected and overlooked, indeed virtually ignored, for far too long. We felt that the Blenheims – and more especially their cour-

The interior of a Blenheim with the twin-Browning B.Mk IV turret, showing the two ammunition containers and feeds with the chutes for the ejected cartridge cases on either side of the seat (fully down as the guns are raised and pointing aft), and the twist-grip controls and small pedals that moved the gun further to cover from wing-tip to wing-tip when the turret reached the 90-degree either-side limit of rotation.

ageous crews – deserved better recognition for the major part that they had played in our war effort all over the world. The attitude of those – like the visitor mentioned in the Prologue – who believed that 'they didn't do much in the war' had to be changed. This aim did not come to us in a sudden flash of inspiration, but dawned gradually as our researches continued.

Another factor that has perpetuated the fame of the Spitfire, Hurricane and Lancaster is their constant appearances at hundreds of air displays, over many years now, in the hands of the RAF 'Battle of Britain Flight'. This also applies to a lesser degree to the British Aerospace Mosquito. Many millions of spectators from several generations have admired them in the air and been reminded of the great part they played in the war. Films such as *The Dam Busters, Battle of Britain, 633 Squadron, Reach for the Sky*, etc, have also helped to keep them in the public eye. We made up our minds to attempt to redress the balance of this public awareness by putting our Blenheim up there in the air right alongside the Spitfire, Hurricane, Lancaster and Mosquito at as many Air Displays as we could, and to keep it up there for as long as possible.

To this end, we intended to change the colour scheme and markings of our Blenheim every few years to reflect some of the many different roles that Blenheims undertook during their wartime service. The choice of scheme and markings was important as it enabled us to focus attention on particular episodes in the Blenheim's long, varied and distinguished career; and by completely changing the appearance of the Blenheim at intervals we would be able to offer a 'fresh' aircraft to the organisers of air shows, which made it more attractive to them. We knew that as the only flying example in the world, our Blenheim would attract considerable attention from the media, and that photographs of it would appear throughout the aviation press. In addition the aircraft would be performing at air displays in front of literally millions of spectators in the course of each season, and would be on permanent public display as an exhibit at the Imperial War Museum, Duxford, so the choice of colours and markings had to made with great care.

An early wartime photo, with the turret removed, showing the obsolete T10B2/R1083 WT set mounted behind the turret. Frequencies were selected by changing coils – stored in the wooden drawer under the mounting shelf! The later T1154/R1155 sets at least had knobs that could be twiddled, but both were very difficult to reach and operate – especially with frozen fingers!

When our 'Blenheims didn't do much in the war' visitor saw it, our Blenheim was still finished in greeny-yellow etch-primer with silver dope on the fabric-covered control surfaces. Detailed research into the colours and markings that we were about to apply was being carried out to ensure that they were correct for the period in terms of size, position, colour, style of lettering and numbering, etc, for the 1941 aircraft of 2 Group, Bomber Command, that we had decided upon. It was fairly easy to reach that decision as 2 Group had been the main operators of Blenheims throughout the most difficult and dangerous period of the war, and we wished to pay particular tribute to them. So the aircraft would be finished in the appropriate dark-earth/dark-green temperate camouflage scheme on the upper surfaces, with 'sky' lower surfaces, Type B red and blue upper wing roundels, Type A1 fuselage roundels with the yellow outer ring, and the 'short' fin flash. The choice of the black individual aircraft serial number and the medium sea-grey Squadron Codes was not too difficult either – we chose the aircraft of the only Blenheim pilot who actually survived to receive his Victoria Cross, the highest award made for gallantry in the face of the enemy; the other two VCs won by Blenheim pilots had both been awarded posthumously.

During the last days of June 1941 there had been two completely unsuccessful attempts at Operation Wreckage, a daylight low-level raid by 2 Group Blenheim Mk IVs on the heavily defended German naval base at Bremen. They were intended to follow up immediately after night attacks on the same target and so demonstrate to the Germans that they could expect bombing 'round the clock'. For the third attempt, on 4 July, the orders were quite specific: they must get through to the target – no excuses would be tolerated. 2 Group HQ felt that the previous raids had failed as the leadership had not been sufficiently forceful, so Acting Wing Commander Hugh Edwards, awarded the DFC only days before, a dashing and very determined 26-year-old Australian who had recently been given command of 105 Squadron, was chosen to lead this most dangerous raid.

'Hughie' Edwards did so brilliantly. Although the formation was spotted well out

A photograph showing the devastating result on the lightly constructed Blenheim rear fuselage of a single explosive shell from a captured German cannon during a test-firing – in the air the whole tail would have separated instantly, leaving the crew with virtually no chance of escaping.

over the North Sea by German 'squealer' ships, which alerted the defences, he led his men in at very low level to attack the docks from the landward side, and they scored several hits on the targets. All the 12 attacking Blenheim Mk IVs were damaged by AA fire, four were shot down and destroyed, and three returned with wounded crew on board, including Hughie's own Wireless Operator/Air Gunner, Sgt Quinn. Several – again including Hughie's own aircraft – had telephone wires wrapped around their tail-wheels.

In late 1942 he was awarded the DSO for leading the Mosquito wing on the famous daylight raid on the Philips factory at Eindhoven – 105 at Swanton Morley was the first Blenheim Squadron to re-equip with the new Mosquito. He went on to become the most highly decorated Australian in the war, and, as Sir Hugh Idwall Edwards VC, KCMG, CB, DSO, DFC and two bars, OBE, served as Governor General of Western Australia.

Only the two prototypes of the Mark V Blenheim, which Bristol wished to call Bisley, were built at Filton: AD 657, a ground attack version shown here, and AD 661, a bomber version with a glazed nose. All other Mk Vs were produced at Rootes, as Filton was busy with Beauforts and Beaufighters.

A Blenheim Mk V bomber in North Africa in 1943. Hugh Malcolm won his posthumous VC for leading a formation of Mk Vs, which was completely destroyed. Note how the different nose and the change from the undercarriage 'apron' fairings to side-hinged doors completely change the ground 'sit' of the Blenheim.

During the Second World War only three RAF pilots were awarded the VC, DSO and DFC, the other two being Guy Gibson and Leonard Cheshire, who, of course, became living legends throughout the land. We wanted to help place Hugh Edwards alongside the other two in this trio of great RAF wartime leaders, to be held in equally high public esteem that all three so richly deserved. We hoped that the publicity surrounding the only flying Blenheim being in the markings of his own aircraft would assist this aim. Not only had the Blenheim become 'the forgotten bomber' of the war, but also the extreme bravery of the Blenheim crews was fast becoming forgotten too.

As already mentioned, Hughie Edwards was the only Blenheim pilot to survive the operation that led to the award of the Victoria Cross; the other two had to be granted posthumously, for the recipients (to use the wartime phrase) 'had made the supreme sacrifice'. Most appropriately, one VC went to each of the three marks of Blenheim, and one to each Theatre of War. Squadron Leader Arthur Stewart Scarf flew a Mk I Blenheim from Butterworth, Malaya, in the Far East, and Wing Commander Hugh Gordon Malcolm was CO of 18 Squadron of Mk V Blenheims in the Middle East; both operations had seen the entire attacking force of Blenheims wiped out. The citations for these three well-deserved Victoria Crosses 'for valour' are included as Appendix 5. So you can understand how their wartime RAF peers, aircrews on other aircraft and in other Commands, recognised the outstanding courage of the 'Blenheim Boys', and see how this recognition needed to be extended to present, and future, generations.

Thus our Blenheim Mk IV would be marked as V6028, with the Squadron Codes GB-D – 'D-Dog' – of 105 Squadron, 2 Group, RAF Bomber Command in the summer of 1941, the aircraft flown by Hughie Edwards as Commanding Officer of 105 on the Bremen raid. We chose these markings for the reasons given and as our own special tribute to this very courageous man who in our view personifies and exemplifies perfectly all of the brave 'Blenheim Boys'. 105 Squadron's badge features a 'Battle Axe', and its most apposite motto is 'Fortis in Proeliis' ('Valiant in Battle'). It was indeed.

Chapter Thirteen

Take-off!

So, with the selection of our colour scheme and markings made, in the spring of 1987 the Blenheim was thoroughly degreased and carefully 'masked off' to protect those areas that were to remain unpainted. The bomb doors, in eight separate sections – four hinged on to the keel-plate and two on to each outer side of the bomb bay – were the last items to be fitted. Two coats of a grey filler-primer were applied over the entire aircraft. The upper surfaces were then masked completely and the lower surfaces painted in the shade officially known as 'sky' but known colloquially as 'duck-egg blue'. When dry the lower surfaces were masked in turn, and the correct shades of 'dark earth' and 'dark green' sprayed in the 'camouflage pattern A' of 1941. When this was dry, we applied the RAF roundels and fin flashes, then our chosen markings of V6028, GB-D, Hughie Edwards's 105 Squadron aircraft. As mentioned in the previous Chapter, the scheme and markings had been researched carefully to make sure that they were entirely authentic and accurate.

The programme of engine runs continues: here the starboard engine is being run up without its cowlings to improve both cooling and access.

The inhibited engines were prepared for use once more, and a further series of engine runs took place, up to and including the first full-power tests. These were most impressive to watch and hear – the Blenheim writhed, roared and strained at its tie-downs, and there was no doubt that it was well and truly 'alive' at last. Details of these tests were recorded in our own records, and the main points entered in the engine log-books.

The great day for which we had waited so many years was fast approaching, when the world would once more be able to see a Blenheim back where it belonged – up in the air. The Team worked even harder, their dedication became more evident, their antici-patory enthusiasm was palpable, the increasing excitement infectious.

During this period a touching incident occurred that brought home to us the strong evocative appeal of the Blenheim. An ex-Blenheim Observer and Gunner had met up again with their wartime skipper, who was on a rare visit to the UK from his native New Zealand. They visited the RAF Museum at Hendon and gazed nostalgically at the static Blenheim there, then they brought him to Duxford without telling him what was in store. The trio walked round a corner that sunny spring day and there was a Blenheim being worked on in the open between the hangars – a familiar sight in their service days – the engines tinkling as they cooled down, the smell of hot oil lingering. This unex-pected scene brought back such vivid memories of shared wartime experiences that the pilot was overcome with emotion and wept quite freely and openly. Clearly the Blenheim could still arouse deep feelings among those who had risked their young lives flying in them those many years ago.

The complete aircraft, resplendent in its freshly applied colours and markings as GB-D, and complete with oil and all equipment, was jacked up into the flying position and weighed. She came out at 9,430 lbs, over 5,000 lbs lighter than the maximum permiss-ible wartime all-up weight. The exact centre of gravity was measured and the allowable limits of its fore and aft movement calculated, so that we could prepare a weight and balance schedule.

John Larcombe, our chief pilot, was entrusted with the task of making the initial post-restoration flight and carrying out the demanding flight-testing programme. He visited the Civil Aviation Authority's Airworthiness Department at Redhill and drew up a special flight test schedule with them. Roy Pullan, our reserve pilot, compiled operat-ing notes from the original RAF and RCAF Pilot's Notes, taking into account the modi-fications to the aircraft systems that we had incorporated. He needed to be 'checked out' on the aircraft too. I should add that these two were the only pilots considered by our insurers to be, at that stage, sufficiently mature and experienced to fly the aircraft; neither John Romain nor myself were approved by them. That their criteria, which appeared to be based solely on age and how many tens of thousands of hours were in the Pilot's Logbooks, were inappropriate was soon to be demonstrated most forcefully. The reasoning behind our selection of pilots for the onerous but prestigious duty of flying the one and only Blenheim is given later.

The CAA surveyors carefully inspected the aircraft and the pile of documentation that John Romain and Fred Hanson had been preparing assiduously for years, declared themselves satisfied and issued a 'Permit to carry out Test Flights to obtain a Permit to Fly'. We could now see with clarity the light at the end of the long and often dark tunnel; indeed, we were almost dazzled by it!

Taxying trials were then carried out. It was marvellous to see and hear the Blenheim moving across the airfield under its own motive power at last. The speeds were increased progressively, the aircraft and the engines behaved well, and the tail was allowed to rise a couple of times. I watched this stirring sight with joy and pride, but even at that late stage failed to grasp the true significance of our tremendous achievement – for she was about to become the only flying Blenheim in the world.

As the brakes bedded in they developed a weird wailing sound when applied, and this mournful wail, combined with the hissing of the pneumatic valves, was described delightfully by 'Roger Bacon' (nom de plume of Mike Ramsden) in *Flight International* magazine as 'a passable imitation of peacocks in the mating season'!

Everything was carefully checked and re-checked, all the systems were systematically re-tested and cleared, each item on the final batch of job sheets was signed and counter-signed, until all the paperwork was completed so that, at last, the aircraft could be signed off as 'fit for flight'.

John Larcombe took a short leave from his job as a Training Captain with British Airways. The usually cheerful John Romain looked more and more worried as he – more than anyone else – felt the weight of the heavy engineering responsibility that he bore for his 'baby'. He racked his brain to see if he had overlooked anything that might cause a problem, for he was conscious that he was to sit alongside 'Larks' in the right-hand seat as co-pilot and flight engineer on the first flight and throughout the flight-test programme; his young shoulders carried a heavy burden. The insurance cover for ground risks, which we had increased steadily as the aircraft neared completion, was extended to include flight risks. Our broker found this difficult as there is a very limited market for such specialised aircraft.

The Blenheim was all ready to go, both the Johns were ready to go, the CAA and the insurers were ready to let us go, the Team were ready to go – only the British weather was holding us back. May 1987 was particularly dull and damp. Many weather forecasts were studied, many worried telephone calls to the Met Office were made. Several times, to be ready for a forecast fair period, the Blenheim was prepared for flight, towed to the flight-line, started and warmed up, only for the drizzle to return or the visibility to deteriorate sufficiently to cause the two Johns to call off the first flight. The deep disappointment, tension, and sense of being badly let down by these anti-climaxes was most nerve-racking for everyone on the Team, but must have been especially so for the Johns.

Then, late in the afternoon of 22 May, a 'window' in the unseasonably inclement weather opened just wide enough to allow the first flight. Once more the Team went

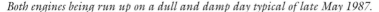

Both engines being run up on a dull and damp day typical of late May 1987.

Twice the two Johns taxied out, only for the weather to close in again and cause the first flight to be postponed.

through the sequence of starting up and warming up. The two Johns strapped themselves into the cockpit, taxied out, carried out engine tests and their pre-take-off cockpit drill; all pressures and temperatures were good, all systems 'go'. They lined up at the threshold of the 060 runway, and received permission from the Control Tower to take off.

John Larcombe opened the throttles smoothly and the Blenheim accelerated down the runway. The note of the engines rose, the tail came up, and we all held our breath as – at long last – the magical moment for which we had all been waiting had arrived. Then our hearts missed a beat for, just as she was about to become airborne, John throttled back and the aircraft slowed suddenly. The take-off had been abandoned. The tailwheel settled back down on the runway and our hearts sank with it as she rolled to a stop. Something must be wrong – we all wondered what the trouble was.

John called the Tower on his radio – it was nothing serious. The under-nose escape-hatch had not been secured properly and had partially opened, with a noisy rush of air, just as the airspeed had reached lift-off speed, so he quite correctly aborted the take-off.

John Romain went down into the nose and secured the hatch, then they taxied back to the other end of the runway to try again. Cockpit drills completed, and permission received from ATC, John opened the throttles once more, the Blenheim accelerated, the engine note rose, the tail came up, and this time she lifted off cleanly and was suddenly airborne. We all cheered, slapping each other on the back and shaking hands excitedly. We had done it!

The Blenheim really was flying. The undercarriage was coming up and the engine note was dropping as John changed to coarse pitch and climbed away. He set cruising power, and carried out a few simple manoeuvres. She flew beautifully and was rigged perfectly – he could trim her to fly 'hands off' straight away. John returned to Duxford and did a few fly-pasts and low passes to our great delight. We were so exhilarated that we did not notice that it had started to rain again.

Then, with wheels and flaps down, John turned on to his approach and did a beautiful three-point landing. He taxied back to an euphoric welcome and opened the champagne that had been carried on the first flight. Delighted, we drank toasts from plastic cups, and ignored the rain. A Bristol Blenheim had graced the skies over Duxford once more, to stir memories, and to fulfil our intention that she would become a fitting

For the first time, the speed is reached when the wings take the weight, the wheels leave the runway – and the Blenheim is airborne and climbing away!

aerial tribute to the original brave 'Blenheim Boys'.

The Blenheim was towed back to the hangar where she had been worked on for so long, and stood quietly dripping and gently ticking away as the engines cooled down.

At last the world had an airworthy Blenheim again! John Larcombe and John Romain over the Cambridge countryside at the end of May 1987.

The Team repaired to our favourite pub; we were tired, wet, grubby, hungry and thirsty, but still buoyant on the 'high' of our achievement. Yet I still found it hard to believe, for it all seemed strangely unreal, as if it were taking place in a dream world, and to someone else, but not to me.

But it was real enough, for over the next few days the two Johns successfully carried out the Blenheim's onerous flight test programme. The aircraft was remarkably 'snag-free'. There were just two minor problems – the batteries were becoming discharged so the charging rate had to be increased, and there was a discrepancy in the readings of the electric oil pressure gauges, cured when additional direct-reading gauges were fitted.

The tests included several timed single-engined climbs. These are difficult and demanding on both pilot and the 'live' engine as the non-feathering propeller of the 'dead' engine windmills, causing severe asymmetric drag that acts in the same yawing sense as the asymmetric thrust from the 'live' engine. Thus the aircraft, if uncorrected, turns itself ever more steeply against the 'dead' engine and rapidly becomes inverted as control is lost.

The 'safety speed' was also established; that is the minimum speed in the single-engine configuration at which directional control can be maintained by applying full rudder. Operating at our lighter weight, and with the boost on the good engine limited to 'Plus $4^{1}/2$', we were very fortunate in that the safety speed equalled the lift-off speed of our aircraft. This makes for much safer operation as it closes the dangerous window that exists when an aircraft loses an engine just after take-off and before it has reached its safety speed. Many were the heavily-laden wartime Blenheims that crashed, usually with fatal results, if they lost an engine below their 120 mph safety speed, due to the impossibility of maintaining directional control at the much higher all-up weights and greater engine outputs then in use. As the original Pilot's Notes warn, all that could be done was to throttle back the 'good' engine sufficiently to keep straight with 'instant and coarse application of rudder', select undercarriage 'up', and 'immediately land straight ahead' regardless of any obstructions that might be in the way!

The Flight Test Report was submitted to the CAA by John Larcombe, and accepted as satisfactory. The CAA's Surveyor sent his 12-page Airworthiness Approval 'Note', and the actual 'Permit to Fly' was issued on Friday 28 May 1987. This was just in time for our 'official first flight' ceremony and celebration that very afternoon. We had invited several friends and the aviation press to this, and the IWM invited several ex-Blenheim crews who had watched the aircraft taking shape over the years and had asked to be advised. We put up a marquee next to the Control Tower and provided refreshments and press-packs. These gave information on the Restoration Team and the British Aerial Museum, and listed some of the 'firsts' and other achievements of the Blenheim in RAF service (as shown as Appendix 3) as the start of our campaign to put the Blenheim itself 'back on the map'.

John Larcombe started up the Mercuries to applause, taxied out to much clicking of camera shutters, ran up the engines to excited chatter, took off to more cheers, and gave a beautiful short flying display to a chorus of 'oohs' and 'aahs'. John's dramatic initial approach was over the brow of the rise to the south of the airfield, right opposite the small crowd of well-wishers, and low towards them, pulling up into a beautifully judged wing-over. They were enchanted and enthralled by the stirring sights and the surprisingly soft sounds of the Blenheim in full flight. We too were equally enthusiastic, for this stimulating demonstration was the crowning consummation of our achievement.

To see the effect of this short private display lighting up the faces of the Blenheim veterans with elation was in itself a fine reward for our prolonged efforts. The ex-

Blenheim crewmen were tickled pink to be allowed to crawl over the aircraft. There were also many joyful reunions: one crew met up again for the first time since the war, one crew member had flown in the original V6028 and showed us his logbook, while another had been the fitter who was proud to have worked on GB-D for Wing Commander Hughie Edwards. We were glad to see that vivid memories of wartime days were being revived, and that our objective of presenting the Blenheim as a fitting aerial tribute to the Blenheim and its crews was beginning to be realised.

We were also delighted to win the 'Mike Twite Trophy' for the best aircraft restoration, voted to us by the readers of *FlyPast* magazine. It was presented to John Romain alongside the Blenheim by Mike's widow – he had been the founder-editor of *Flypast* but was killed in an accident to a Vickers Varsity while writing a feature for the magazine. We were glad to see that Pearl White, 'Chalky's' widow, was with us too – he would have been proud of us.

Later that evening, John flew a photo-sortie in the Blenheim, formating on John Romain in our Beech 18 for 'Smudge' and a few selected aviation photographers, then he checked out Roy Pullan on the Blenheim, and Roy did a solo sortie. We all rushed back to the workshops to watch the 'first flight of the Blenheim' during the main news bulletins on both BBC and ITV television. We sat out by the marquee late that fine evening, enjoying our drinks, replete with a glow of well-being, sharing with our wives and girlfriends a sense of satisfaction and justifiable pride in our achievement. We had ambitious plans for the Blenheim and were brimful of hope and optimism. That wonderful afternoon and memorable evening represented to me, and I believe to the rest of the Team, the very zenith of the whole Blenheim experience that we had shared together for so long.

We did not know then that – just three weeks later – we would share the absolute nadir of the experience too, as our beloved Blenheim crashed cruelly to the ground, and with it crashed all of our joy, our hopes, our plans, our ambitions. For Fate was rolling the dice and, having climbed the last long ladder in triumph, we were about to land on the large snake that was waiting, unsuspected and unseen, to send us sliding straight back to square one with a seering, shattering, suddenness.

Chapter Fourteen

Disaster at Denham

Although we were not quite ready to take part in the Air Fete at Mildenhall that same weekend, we were kept busy as it was my birthday on the Sunday 31 May, and John Larcombe took me and several Team members up for our first flights in the Blenheim – a thrilling and satisfying experience for all concerned. The Blenheim was due to make her public airshow debut at Biggin Hill the following weekend, and she was needed on the previous Wednesday as a Press Day centred on the Blenheim was being held at Biggin on the Thursday to publicise the event. This had been arranged by Richard Lucraft, an astute freelance PR man acting for 'Jock' Maitland, the Air Fair organiser. Richard had the bright idea of inviting the present Lord Rothermere, in view of the crucial role played in the birth of the Blenheim by the Harmsworth family and their Associated Newspapers Group. As this group includes the *Daily Mail*, the *Mail on Sunday* and the London *Evening Standard*, Richard was angling for good coverage of

The Blenheim 'basked in the sunshine and the glory' at the Press Day for the 1987 Biggin Hill Air Fair, the day that Roger Peacock went for his first flight in a Blenheim turret 47 years after being blown out of one, and wrote the moving poem rendered so effectively by Raymond Baxter in the video 'Spirit of Britain First'. It is reproduced as Appendix 11.

Lord Rothermere was most interested in the Blenheim and is pictured talking to Graham Warner and Roy Pullan – the pilot at Biggin and at Denham two weeks later.

the forthcoming event, and we were pleased for the opportunity to publicise the Blenheim.

I flew down in the Blenheim to Biggin that Wednesday; the Captain was our back-up pilot Roy Pullan, as John Larcombe was needed by British Airways. Roy flew it 'by the book' and gave a very good short display on the Thursday, which was much appreciated by Lord Rothermere and the other guests. The Blenheim revelled in being the centre of so much attention, positively basking in the sunshine and the glory. We found it rewarding to watch the years falling away from the faces of several ex-Blenheim crews, and could see the gleam in their eyes when the memories crowded back, as they inspected the Blenheim and witnessed the display.

One of these was Roger Peacock, who, under the nom de plume of Richard Passmore, had written very perceptively about his time as a young Wireless Operator/Air Gunner in his book *Blenheim Boy*. We took him up in the turret, the first time he had been in one since the harrowing experience of being blown out of an exploding Blenheim when his crew was shot down on a night-intruder mission in 1940. The *Evening Standard* published a very good feature about this poignant return to the skies, while Roger found his first flight in a Blenheim for nearly 50 years to be such an emotional experience that it inspired him to set down his thoughts and feelings on paper. He put this away in a drawer and forgot all about it, until some seven years later he found it and sent it to me. I found it moving and arranged publication in the Blenheim Society Journal. Raymond Baxter speaks it beautifully and effectively in our video *Spirit of Britain First*, and it is reproduced for you as Appendix 11.

Lord Rothermere spoke to several of these ex-crew members and was equally fascinated by the Blenheim. He climbed into the cockpit, asked many pertinent questions, was delighted to be presented with a brass model of GB-D mounted on an inscribed

Lord Rothermere shows his presentation brass model Blenheim to the ex-Blenheim crews who were delighted to see the Blenheim at Biggin Hill.

plaque that we had prepared, and stayed for far longer than his busy schedule really allowed. Roy flew several photo-sorties, formating on John Romain in the Beech 18 with press and TV cameramen on board. The media covered the event widely, telling the world that a Blenheim had been put back into the skies once more, and we were pleased to see that it featured well in both the midday and evening main television news programmes.

We put the Blenheim into a hangar at Biggin and went back to Duxford in the Beech 18, content with the way the day had gone. On the Saturday we returned to Biggin in the Beech with the two Johns and a crew from the Team; Roy brought the 'Broussard' down with some friends and returned later, as he had to display the French machine at Duxford on the Sunday.

Thus John Larcombe, with John Romain in the right-hand seat, performed the first public display by the Blenheim at the Biggin Hill Air Fair on 6 and 7 June 1987 to acclaim from the crowds. They also displayed at Brands Hatch and Weathersfield that same weekend, and were the star attraction at the big SSAFA Display at RAF Church Fenton the following weekend, 14 June. The weather was foul at the latter venue, but the Blenheim performed perfectly at all five events, and John said that it was a delight to fly.

A week later, on 21 June, she was due to appear both at the Duxford Military Display and at the Guild of Air Pilots and Air Navigators event at Denham. The following weekend she was booked at the 'Fighter Meet' at North Weald and at Filton, home of the Blenheim, for the British Aerospace and Rolls-Royce Aero Engines Open Day, a venue to which we were looking forward with particularly keen anticipation.

We had over a dozen other confirmed air display bookings for the rest of 1987, including the big International Air Tattoo at Fairford, and serious enquiries for the

The Blenheim takes off from Duxford on 21 June 1987 on her ill-fated flight to Denham. The Captain is Roy Pullan, with John Romain in the right-hand seat; 'Smudger' is in the rear jump seat as the turret was not occupied during take-off and landing.

1988 season were coming in fast now that organisers could see that the Blenheim was actually up and running – some of them did not believe that we would do it! The financial burden was easing, and that aspect of our future looked much brighter too, for the income generated by these events would start to repay BAM for the enormous investment sunk into the Blenheim over the years, and I informed our somewhat anxious bank manager that we would soon be able to commence reducing our sizeable overdraft.

After the Biggin Hill weekend we carried out a complete post-permit check on the Blenheim. The aircraft and engine logbooks show that all the filters were cleaned and inspected, the engine oil changed, oleo pressures set to 465 psi, brake pressure adjusted to 60 psi on each side, charging rate increased, and the engine idling set at 650 rpm. Everything was thoroughly inspected, checked and signed off as satisfactory. We were doing everything possible to ensure the reliable and safe operation of the aircraft; that we allowed one crucial exception to this policy was entirely my own fault, and is a cross that I carry to this day.

I have explained that only two pilots, John Larcombe and Roy Pullan, were allowed to fly the Blenheim, and I need to expand on how I arrived at this critical but deeply flawed choice. The responsibility for selecting the pilots who were to be entrusted with this unique and priceless aircraft rested solely with me, and I was aware of the pivotal nature of that selection; indeed, it had been exercising my mind for some time prior to the completion of the Blenheim restoration. I had watched hundreds of individual air displays over the years and fully realised that the correct choice of safety-conscious pilots with the necessary levels of skill, experience, mechanical understanding and sympathy, plus availability and compatibility with the Team, was absolutely vital to the safe and proper operation of the Blenheim.

A 'safe pairs of hands' is not in itself sufficient, as those hands need to be controlled by a brain that is in tune with an aircraft designed over half a century earlier, and does not become flustered or overloaded, however demanding the circumstances – for if it did those hands would no longer be safe. My choice was further restricted by the need for nominated pilots to be approved by our insurers. I considered that John Romain would be suitable, for he was a fine pilot and no one knew or understood the Blenheim better, and I would love to have flown the Blenheim myself, but at that time we were both held to be insufficiently experienced, although we were both covered to fly all of our other aircraft including the Beech 18.

Our Chief Pilot John Larcombe was the natural and obvious choice, certainly the correct one, as the principal Blenheim pilot, and he was readily approved by the insurers. He had thus been invited to make the first flight, complete the flight test schedule, and fly the first five displays. As British Airways then required his services as a Training Captain, our reserve pilot, Roy Pullan, was delighted to be asked to carry out the Biggin Hill Press Day and the five airshows that followed the one at Church Fenton. Roy, on paper at least, seemed an excellent choice for this role.

I mentioned earlier that John had checked out Roy on the Blenheim on the day of our first flight 'do'; a previous attempt to check him out had to be abandoned on the runway threshold when he found difficulty in releasing the brake lever, which he had put on 'park' while running up the engines, pulling the nipple off the end of the brake lever cable. I had taken John quietly to one side and asked him how the second check flight had gone. I became concerned when John told me that Roy had shown impatience while John was showing him the cockpit layout and drills, and had left the impression that he considered our check-out procedure to be an unnecessary formality. I pressed John on whether, in his opinion, Roy was safe to be entrusted with the aircraft.

He paused and answered, 'Yes, he is, providing that he doesn't get a rush of blood to the head.'

At the time I failed to recognise in John's answer the accuracy of this perceptive insight into Roy's temperament – his prophetic phrase would return to haunt me.

It is difficult, in view of subsequent events, for me to remain objective when talking about Roy Pullan, but I will try to do so, as it is important to maintain the accuracy of this narrative. Roy was a long-standing and dyed-in-the-wool aircraft enthusiast, who kept Chipmunk and Tiger Moth components in a large shed in his garden. He helped the Blenheim restoration conscientiously for four or five years, preparing the moulds for all the cockpit glazing, and fabricating the bomb doors in his own shed, both to very high standards of workmanship and accuracy. He was a charming family man, with a caring wife and daughters, and we enjoyed several sociable evenings together at theatres and restaurants. Far more important, he was a most experienced, entirely accident-free pilot, with some 15,500 P1 hours, who had just retired as a British Airways Senior Captain. He was current too on tailwheel piston-engined aircraft; he flew in the Harvard Formation Team, regularly displayed our Beech 18, and was being checked out on the B17 Fortress. I had observed from the ground many displays by Roy in various aircraft and they all had appeared to be performed well and safely. The final consideration was that he was welcomed by our insurers, so he appeared to meet all of our criteria as a suitable back-up pilot for the Blenheim.

However, while actually flying with Roy during the preceding years, several alarm bells had been rung, casting doubt on his temperamental suitability as a display pilot, although I failed to take heed of their message. A couple of years earlier he had asked to do the test flying on our Beech 18 at the end of a major overhaul; he felt that as he had more flying hours in his logbook than John, and was senior to him both in age and in the British Airways hierarchy, he was more qualified to be our Chief Pilot.

He was not pleased when I told him that I was not willing to alter the arrangements with John, and sulked for a while, then wrote to apologise and accept that the choice of pilots to fly my aircraft was my prerogative. Later, Roy asked rather half-heartedly if he could carry out the test flying on the Blenheim, but seemed to accept the position readily when I confirmed that John would do this and would be my first choice for displays, and that he (Roy) would be able to fly and display the Blenheim when opportunity arose.

Another warning bell had sounded the year before, but went unheeded – perhaps because I tend to forgive too readily a pilot who makes mistakes that I know I would probably have made myself in the same circumstances. At Goodwood in the Beech 18 Roy had to abandon a take-off when the aircraft developed a very nasty swing towards a nearby row of parked aircraft – including three of our own! He had failed to lock the tailwheel, the last vital action made after lining up on the runway. This alarming incident was partly my fault, as I was in the right-hand seat and should have monitored his correct compliance with the check-lists.

That same weekend there was another incident, potentially even more dangerous, for in the middle of Roy's display in the Beech 18, I noticed both oil pressures dropping right off the bottom of the gauges, and both oil temperatures climbing right off the top of them – all the indications were way out of limits. Roy called an emergency, throttled back, lowered the wheels and flaps as he turned straight in, and landed immediately. The starboard engine seized as we taxied in; most fortunately we had been above the into-wind end of the airfield when the problem was discovered – another few seconds and we would have suffered a disastrous double engine failure during the display.

Our display 'slot' had been moved forward unexpectedly, and Roy had become flustered and hurried through his cockpit drills while taxying out. To help the engines reach their working temperatures in time, he operated the oil bypass valves, but forgot to de-select them again. They permit only the oil in the engines to circulate, and cut off the flow to the oil-coolers and the dry-sump oil-tanks, to aid rapid warm-up in harsh Canadian winters; we had never used them before so they were not included in our check-lists, which Roy had compiled. Again, I must accept my share of responsibility for this oversight, as he had called out that he was selecting them while I was strapping myself in, and I should have checked that he de-selected them before take-off. They should, of course, have been wired up to prevent use, and labelled as 'inoperative' – they are now! He apologised profusely and offered to pay part of the costs if we had to remove the engines for overhaul, but fortunately when they had cooled down, we inspected the filters and found them free of debris, so we changed the oil and filters and no harm was done. But it had been a close call.

The warning bell gave another clang during a display by Roy at the 1986 'Great Warbirds' meeting at West Malling, but it too fell on deaf ears. For this incident also I was sitting alongside Roy during his display, this time in our Max-Holste 'Broussard' in foul weather conditions with fine rain, very low cloud, and atrocious visibility. In one of his low passes along the crowd line he actually flew right over the pilot's tent, and I said to him, 'We were too low that time. It's getting dodgy – let's scrub it.'

He was called to the Control Tower later and 'torn off a strip' by the Safety Officer, but he told me that 'they had ticked me off for being on the low side'. Some five years later, at an Air Display Safety Seminar, I learned that he had offered the feeble excuse that he 'could not see a thing in the awful visibility', and that he 'hadn't even noticed the pilot's tent', so it really had been the most frightful 'clanger'. I saw the enclosure and tent just below us on the starboard side as we were banking to port and did not

The Team, photographed on 28 May 1993, celebrating after putting a Blenheim back into the skies for the second time. From the left (standing): 'Smudger' Smith, Michael Terry, Andy Gilmour, Cliff and Neville Gardner, Colin Swann and Graham Warner; (kneeling): James Gilmour, Chris Arberry, John Romain and Bob Sparkes.

The second restoration

The major airframe components of 10201 and 9703 loaded up and ready for their journey to Duxford.

Left *Colin Swann stripping the centre-section. The corroded under-carriage frames are between the spars, the bomb rails are in the centre between the tank-bays, and the mounting for the main under-carriage pivot is by Colin's knees.*

Above right *New skin panels are made to pattern and fitted; the V-flange to the right mates up with the under nacelle, and the wooden strips visible in the tank-bay strengthen the wing-root walkway.*

Right *The nose section repaired and awaiting glazing.*

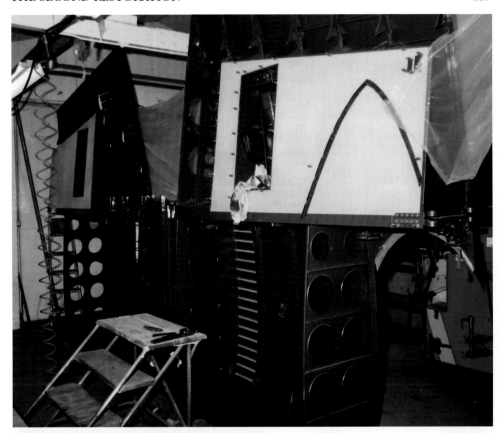

Above left *The airframe painted all black, with the port engine mounted and being connected up. The starboard wing is attached so that 'Smudger' can fabricate the rear nacelles to fit.*

Left *The name 'Spirit of Britain First' was sign-written below the cockpit before our official first flight and naming ceremony.*

Above *A small part of the large crowd, including some 500 Blenheim survivors, who witnessed the event. The vital fax from the CAA granting the Permit to Fly arrived only an hour before this first public flight!*

Right *'Smudge' had clearly been waiting for years for the champagne to be cracked open after the successful first flight. It did taste good!*

Above and below *Two fine studies by John Dibbs of WM-Z over the clouds while filming for the video 'Spirit of Britain First'.*

Right *A dramatic shot of the Blenheim running up in darkness – evocative of wartime night sorties – and showing the gun-pack.*

The Blenheim over Blenheim Palace. This brought back memories for the present Duke of Marlborough, who recalls seeing Blenheims from the OTU at Bicester 'beating up' the Palace when he was a boy.

realise that he had not; this later revelation that he couldn't even see it brought home to me just how lucky we were to have missed it! Several years later Robs told me that Roy had once made such a hash of flying his Staggerwing that he declined to allow him to fly his aircraft again; unfortunately I was not appraised of this at the time, and remained blissfully unaware.

However, it is easy to be wise after the event, and – even if I had not taken sufficient notice of some of the warning signs, and had not been ignorant of others – Roy had been chosen as our reserve pilot for the Blenheim. He was to fly the displays at the Duxford Military Show, the GAPAN event at Denham, the BAe day at Filton, and the 'Fighter Meet' at North Weald; the sorties at Biggin had given him more time to familiarise himself with handling the aircraft and the opportunity to rehearse his display sequence.

Being aware that the CAA required a qualified pilot to occupy the right-hand seat on the Blenheim during displays, and that normally (if John Larcombe was unavailable) this duty would be carried out by either myself or John Romain, I determined that I would monitor most scrupulously all of Roy's cockpit drills, and briefed John to do the same. I reminded Roy as tactfully as possible about the need to take sufficient time to carry out cockpit drills properly, admitting that I had made mistakes when I allowed myself to be hurried. These were extra precautions as, although Roy was generally a competent pilot, I had seen that very occasionally he could become forgetful or flustered. I thought that they, together with the onus being on him to take particular care when trusted with such a rare machine, would be sufficient to ensure that he flew it responsibly and safely.

However, that next weekend Roy Pullan did suffer from the very 'rush of blood to the head' that John Larcombe had intimated might be possible, and quite needlessly destroyed our beloved Blenheim. In the event his hands, and the brain that controlled them, turned out to be far from safe; in fact, they proved to be dangerous. He committed several serious lapses of good airmanship, made grave errors of judgement, recklessly placing this unique aircraft in a position of rapidly increasing danger, mishandled the engines, then 'froze' in fear and failed to retain any control whatsoever, so that the Blenheim crashed on Denham Golf Course. It was entirely 'in the lap of the Gods' that

The Beech 18 'Expiditor' operated by B.A.M. as an advanced trainer for the Blenheim, in which Roy Pullan had a couple of 'dicey' displays.

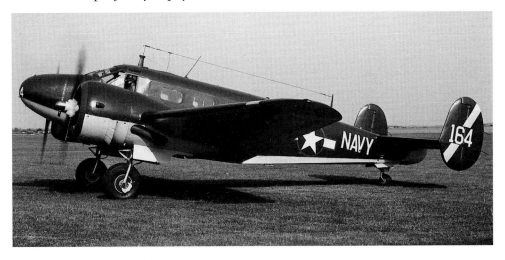

no one in the Blenheim or on the ground was maimed or killed in this terrible accident.

I set out the sequence of events and the series of misjudgments, the cumulative effect of which resulted in this tragedy, in a letter that I wrote to Pullan soon afterwards. Although drafted in the depths of my despair shortly after the disaster, *Log*, the Journal of the British Airline Pilots Association, when reviewing my book *The Forgotten Bomber*, referred to it as 'The most devastatingly accurate report and analysis of any aircraft accident that we have ever read'. It was reproduced in that book exactly as it was written at the time. I do not wish to dwell further on the causes of the crash, except to say that a pilot, well respected on the air display scene, told me later that it was summed up perfectly by the comment in the book that 'The Blenheim was needlessly sacrificed on the altar of Roy's ego'.

That fateful Sunday, 21 June 1987, I was waiting at Duxford with keen anticipation for the Blenheim to return from the display at Denham and perform the first public display at Duxford. It had been arranged with the organisers of both events that Roy would fly straight into his planned display 'slot' at the Duxford Military Show, and the timings of both shows were carefully co-ordinated to suit this. The promoters of the GAPAN event at Denham had asked originally if the Blenheim could land at Denham to be on static display, but Roy, quite rightly, had declined to do so. We had not had time to establish the performance parameters for normal take-offs and landings, yet alone 'short' ones; the length of the runway at Denham was pretty marginal, and he did not have sufficient time on the aircraft at that stage to attempt it in complete safety. John and I were relieved at the decision not to land there and supported it fully. I had intended to accompany Roy, but as Ted Inman asked me to stay at Duxford to show their Royal Guest of Honour over the Blenheim, I had to forgo the trip, to my disappointment.

As the appointed time for the appearance by the Blenheim came we scanned the skies anxiously, but to no avail; when the time passed by and a Harvard was substituted, our anxiety grew, but we thought that it must have landed at Denham after all with some minor problem. Then an announcement on the PA called me to the Tower. I walked along in front of the crowd line with a growing sense of foreboding. I was stunned to be told that the Blenheim had crashed badly and that the crew were all in hospital. My immediate concern was for the crew, as they were good friends, but it took many phone calls to establish their whereabouts, for they were not all in the same hospital, and then – thankfully – that their injuries were not critical.

I was shocked, but far from angry, concentrating on the positive fact that no one had been killed or seriously injured. I went straight down to Hillingdon Hospital to see John Romain and 'Smudger' Smith, and then on to High Wycombe to see Roy, but he had been sedated and I couldn't speak to him. I emphasised to their wives, and to all of the Team members, that by far the most important thing to focus on was that the crew had been spared from death or disablement; airframes could be replaced but human beings could not.

'Smudge' told me that Roy had been attempting a 'touch and go' at Denham, had 'got it all wrong' and that the Blenheim had hit a tree and cartwheeled across Denham Golf Course. Her back was broken, the nose completely smashed, and both engines had been torn right out. Most fortunately the wreckage did not catch fire, for there was petrol everywhere from ruptured fuel lines; the emergency services were on the scene very quickly and had smothered it in foam. He said that it was far too badly damaged to even think about rebuilding it.

Had Roy stated his intention of performing a 'touch and go' I would certainly have prohibited it, as being far too dangerous to attempt, especially at Denham with its short

'Blenheim bunkered' was typical of many headlines in the national press following the crash on to the golf course alongside Denham Airfield. The starboard engine is by the left-hand golfer's head; the port engine, torn from its mounting just above the head of the other golfer, lies behind the starboard wing.

runway, and particularly so without any practice or rehearsal. I should explain that it is a landing followed by an immediate take-off (or 'go round again') without allowing the aircraft to roll to a rest, and is used to save time during circuit training by avoiding the need for lengthy taxying back to the start of the runway; it is not a suitable manoeuvre to be performed at air displays. Roy's decision to attempt one was the fundamental cause of the accident.

I then went to the golf course. By then the evening had become dull and dismal, adding to the gloom of the grim scene. She lay there, twisted and torn, at the head of a scar in the earth, pieces of wreckage scattered over a hundred yards behind her. Members of the Team were there; all were devastated and in a state of shock, some were in tears. It was clear that she was wrecked beyond hope of rebuild.

The Team were grief-stricken. It was as if each had suffered from the personal loss of a loved one – but then I realised that they had. For it was their devoted dedication to the restoration, and the labour of love from their own skilled hands, applied over many years, that had returned the Blenheim to the skies. Now they, and everyone else, were to be denied the opportunity to see a Blenheim back in its natural element once more. For no longer did a single example of an airworthy Blenheim exist anywhere in the world.

All those years of unremitting hard work had been so needlessly thrown away, all our great efforts in overcoming so many difficulties throughout the restoration had been dissipated in a few fleeting seconds. All the joy and pride we felt at our unequalled achievement, all our bright hopes for the future and our ambitious plans, our endeavours to put the Blenheim itself 'back on the map' and to pay our special aerial tribute to the Blenheim crews, had been destroyed along with the actual airframe.

Chapter Fifteen

Aftermath

That disastrous roll of the dice at Denham had sent us sliding back way past square one – we had been pushed right off the board.

In the aftermath of the accident the whole Team were disconsolate and demoralised. The two key members in the aircraft at the time had seen the crash coming but had been helpless to prevent it; they were badly shaken and we all knew that they had been lucky indeed to escape from far more serious, possibly fatal, injuries. Had either John or 'Smudge' been killed or badly injured we would not have considered a further restoration and the Blenheim story would have ended there. The memory of a flying Blenheim would soon fade away to become 'the forgotten bomber' once more, so we should give thanks on both counts for their miraculous survival. John Romain and I in particular were devastated at the destruction of the Blenheim, for it had been the central focus of our lives. We had both lost our sense of purpose and direction, and felt initially that we couldn't face the prospect of climbing up on to that first square and starting the struggle all over again.

Our beloved Blenheim was a pile of inert wreckage, far too badly damaged to be capable of rebuilding to airworthy status. Once 'written off' it belonged to a disgruntled insurance company who were sifting through everything with a very fine toothcomb. Should they come across any contravention of proper operating procedures, any oversight in the paperwork, such as an out-of-date licence or medical certificate, any non-compliance with the strict terms of the Permit to Fly, or any failure to observe all of the myriad CAA rules and regulations, then it would probably have resulted in payment of the claim being denied. This would have bankrupted me personally and removed for ever any chance that a Blenheim might be made to fly again under my auspices. In addition, the Accident Investigation Branch of the Department of Transport, and both the Legal and the Airworthiness Departments of the Civil Aviation Authority, were scrutinising all aspects of our operation of the aircraft to establish the causes of the crash with a view to instigating prosecutions.

We did not have another airframe to restore, let alone the will or the money to restore one, for to help finance the first restoration the second ex-Haydon-Baillie Blenheim shell had been passed on to the IWM earlier (at cost corrected for inflation) for eventual rebuild as a static exhibit. Once more it looked as if all the surviving airframes were destined to remain firmly grounded, if not for ever, at least far into the foreseeable future. No longer would anyone be able to see and hear a Blenheim back in its true element – the skies. This prospect was galling to us and to all aircraft enthusiasts, and deeply disappointing to the dwindling band of wartime Blenheim survivors. It was hard to avoid negative thoughts in these depressing circumstances and even harder to think and plan positively for the future.

They say that 'Time is a great healer', but we were allowed scarcely any time at all to recover from the cruel destruction of the Blenheim. Over the next few days telephone calls flooded into Duxford, and into the major aviation magazines, wanting to know what had happened, how such a disaster had been allowed to happen, and nearly all hoping – some even demanding – that we would restore another Blenheim to fly. Some 1,200 letters in similar vein arrived too; many contained unsolicited cheques and postal orders for small amounts as contributions towards a second restoration. I received supportive hand-written letters from, amongst others, Lord Rothermere, Sir George White (grandson of the founder of the Bristol Aircraft Company, and son of its wartime Chairman), Air Chief Marshal Sir Wallace Kyle GCB KCVO DSO LLD KStJ (President of the RAF 2 Group Association, who had been Hughie Edwards's boss), Air Marshal Sir Ivor Broom KCB CBE DSO DFC** AFC (another distinguished former Blenheim pilot), and MRAF Sir Michael Beetham GCB CBE DFC AFC FRAeS (President of the Bomber Command Association), together with many other ex-Blenheim air- and ground-crews. They expressed sympathy, urged me not to waste all that we had learned in the course of our great achievement, and to try again if that was possible. The dice were being rattled in the cup – we were being directed inexorably towards square one.

I was being forced to decide straight away whether or not we should, or could, try again. This decision had been difficult enough the first time, but the dilemma had become far more daunting now, in that I was no longer able to call upon the resources of my garage company. I felt that it was my duty to try and organise a second restoration, and clearly many people wanted me to, and all the reasons behind the first one were still valid, apart from the fact that this time it would be entirely 'down to me'.

The historic importance of the Blenheim had been brought home to me during the first rebuild, I still wished to pay this special tribute to their courageous crews, and I had seen how the flying Blenheim had delighted Blenheim veterans. My aim to 'put the Blenheim back on the map' had become almost a personal crusade. I realised that, however sensible, easy and prudent it would be to simply turn my back and 'walk away', I would find that road too unsatisfying, too empty, too dull.

The wreckage was transported back to Duxford and laid out in the hangar, a process that we found very painful. It was distressing and disturbing to inspect at such close quarters the extent and severity of the damage. I spoke to the IWM to ascertain its attitude, then asked Richard Lucraft to call a Press Conference there for the following Monday, 29 June.

I had a long session with John Romain, his arm still in a sling, to seek his views on whether or not we should commit ourselves to another restoration, trying to keep my own attitude strictly neutral. Considering that he had just been subjected to such a traumatic ordeal, he was surprisingly positive. I should qualify that remark, for although I was pleasantly surprised at the time by his resilience in rising to this immense challenge, now that I know him better I realise that it demonstrated the great strength of his character. I saw the rest of the Team individually, over a drink or meal or at the airfield, to see if they too were willing to start all over again. It speaks volumes for their dedication that all bar Bill said, 'If you can provide the hardware we will rebuild it', or words to that effect. Bill was happy to work on our other aircraft but, quite understandably, could not bring himself to devote more of his time and effort to another Blenheim as he had seen his just completed pride and joy 'thrown away so soon, and so stupidly'. I respected his view, but we would miss his input as he had put so much first-class work into the Blenheim restoration.

But we, as a Team, had reached the decision to 'dust ourselves down, pick ourselves up, and start all over again'. So, the following Monday, having prepared a pile of press-packs headed 'A Blenheim Will Fly Again', I stood in front of the wreckage at the well-attended Press Conference and announced that we were going to restore another airworthy aircraft. I paid heartfelt public tributes to the Team, singling out John Romain especially as the person responsible for most of the restoration work and for resolving many of the major difficulties that had beset us. I restated my conviction that had he or John Larcombe been flying the Blenheim at Denham, the accident would not have happened. I said that we felt the Blenheim to be far too important to be allowed to fade away, that our team possessed the experience and the expertise to resurrect one, that the IWM would continue to make the facilities available, and that we had spoken to the Canadian Warplane Heritage about acquiring another derelict airframe. We had demonstrated that we could do it once and were determined to do it again – all that we needed was financial support.

I then launched The Blenheim Appeal, which would be needed to contribute towards the costs of this second restoration, for although the insurance money would enable us to get started and at least part-way along the road, I realised that I would not be able to fund it entirely from my own pocket. Due to the high premiums required we had been unable to insure the aircraft for its actual worth; indeed, with the premiums that we could afford in that first year it was insured for about half its probable open-market value. It is hard to establish the true worth of the only airworthy example of such an historic aircraft – to us it was priceless anyway! We intended to increase the agreed hull value the following season when we had a better guide to the annual level of income from air displays, for virtually all of this goes on insurance premiums! Rather rashly, I undertook to complete this second restoration in 5 years from starting again, rather than the 12 years the first had taken.

Exactly a week before, reports on the accident, mainly of the 'Blenheim Bunkered' variety, had appeared in all the national dailies, most with photographs, as well as featuring on the BBC and ITN news. The poor Blenheim had certainly 'hit the headlines', but not in the way we wished! So I was pleased to see that my briefing and 'The Blenheim Will Fly Again' press release received widespread coverage too. All of the aviation magazines – bar one – carried the Blenheim Appeal announcement, which explained exactly what we were trying to do, and it also appeared in the *Daily Mail*, *Evening Standard*, *Sunday Express*, and *Mail on Sunday*. A copy is included as Appendix 6. Responses and letters of support, many with small donations, started arriving by the hundred, and all had to be personally acknowledged. We were on our way, moving across the board and up the first ladder.

The Blenheim had been due to appear at the huge International Air Tattoo at Fairford that July, and the organisers asked us to take part of the wreckage down to exhibit as we couldn't take part in the air display. So we took down the broken rear fuselage with the tail assembly, which was put on show in the President's Enclosure and inspected by HM King Hussein, amongst other dignitaries. We sold photos and T-shirts and received donations in a small tent. I was interviewed by BBC TV alongside the wreck, emphasising the historic importance of the Blenheim and giving the Appeal a good mention.

I was anxious to keep our superb Team together, both before and after the accident, and thought I'd found the ideal project to follow up the Blenheim. Throughout that summer I had been negotiating to purchase a Bristol Beaufighter from Australia, in conjunction with my partner in the Lysander. This 'Beau' was complete and in good condition, so could have been put back into the air relatively easily to become the sole airworthy example. But it was owned by a small group that required unanimous consent to a disposal; to our great disappointment, this was not forthcoming.

We had commenced restoring the Lysander, which shared the Mercury engine and DH propeller with the Blenheim, to flying condition; the main fuselage frame was finished and we had started on an engine for it. But these plans had to be changed with the loss of the first Blenheim and the decision to start on the second. The Lysander was sold to the IWM with a long-term contract to rebuild it as a static exhibit – so the world was denied not only the airworthy Blenheim but also a flying Lysander. My half of the proceeds was put straight into the second Blenheim, as we had yet to receive settlement of our insurance claim.

We were running into serious difficulties and delays here. The insurance company – although they could find no fault in our operation of the aircraft – would not meet the claim until the Accident Investigation Board report was published. The draft report, as sent to interested parties, was severely critical of the pilot, so Roy entered into protracted correspondence with the Board and managed to get it toned down considerably. When it was finally published, the Senior AIB Inspector exonerated us completely and made it quite clear that the blame lay solely with the pilot, although you have to 'read between the lines' a little; the report is reproduced as Appendix 7. You will note that the last paragraph states, most unusually, that, 'The operating company had taken great pains to ensure that the aircraft was fully airworthy and that the pilot was capable of safely performing the display.'

The insurance underwriters were aware that the Civil Aviation Authority were also investigating the accident with a view to prosecuting the operators and/or the pilot, and were still unwilling to pay out despite the efforts of our broker. So when we as operators were also cleared completely by the CAA, I asked them to confirm this to our insurers. Our claim was finally settled some six months after the accident – six very harrowing months for me. We also negotiated the purchase of the salvage from the insurers, for we needed some vital engine components and various small airframe parts.

This too was very nerve-racking, as a company at North Weald were trying to buy it so that it could be burned while making a film! Despite appeals direct to the owner of this company, explaining our needs, it was motivated only by commercial considerations, so that we had twice to increase the price to be paid to better its offer.

Roy Pullan was charged with contravening Articles 47 and 48 of the Air Navigation Order: 'A person shall not recklessly or negligently cause an aircraft to endanger any person or property' or 'recklessly or negligently endanger an aircraft and the persons therein.' He was tried and, despite a bitter and lengthy defence by his QC, convicted of both of these criminal offences, fined heavily and ordered to pay the CAA's substantial prosecution costs. This was paradoxical, for we would sooner have seen those thousands of pounds benefiting the Blenheim Appeal, which we considered a far more deserving cause than the Treasury. There was a further irony in that his defence was, I understood, provided by BALPA, and their comment on the causes of the accident – causes totally denied by the defence – is given in the previous Chapter!

John, 'Smudge' and myself had to attend the trial as witnesses; we found it a wearying and draining experience that revived too many sad and painful memories. But that dreadful chapter had been closed at last; the nightmare of the loss of the first Blenheim could finally be put behind us, and we were free to concentrate entirely on the second one.

We drew up a list of all the known Bristol Type 149 Blenheim/Bolingbroke airframes worldwide, and considered their suitability and availability. Eventually we settled on the airframe of RCAF 10201, with the outer wings of 9703, at Strathallan. John Romain and I flew up there and carried out as detailed a survey as possible without

The airframe of RCAF 10201 standing out in Canada – it looks to be in better condition and more complete than it really was. The outer wings had been removed; the pair we acquired came from RCAF 9703.

further dismantling. It was generally in quite sound condition, had the advantage of being in the UK, thus saving transport time (the St Lawrence River was frozen over) and considerable cost, and of being stored under cover for the previous few years at least.

After protracted negotiations we managed to purchase it. John, with 'Smudge' and Colin, went to Scotland, split the fuselage from the centre-section and into its three main parts, then packed and loaded it all up for transport. The components arrived at Duxford in February 1988; now we could get weaving on the second Blenheim restoration. While waiting, over the preceding six or seven months, for this to appear, the team had kept themselves busy, as a kind of therapy, completely stripping and rebuilding our Auster AOP9 and DHC-1 Chipmunk.

At the Press Conference on 29 June I had also announced that we were forming a Blenheim Society, with a newsletter to keep supporters informed of progress on the second restoration. This was reported in several aviation magazines and resulted in many enquiries requesting particulars. All were answered, thanking them for their interest and saying that 'details of the Society would be sent in due course'. Among these was one to Hugh George, an ex-XV Squadron Battle and Blenheim pilot. He replied, mentioning that on a visit to France the previous year by some veterans of the RAF Blenheim, Battle and Hurricane Squadrons based there in 1940, they had talked about the desirability of 'setting up some sort of association', adding that 'we both have the same sort of thing in mind with your Society and our Association.' I was glad therefore to accept an invitation to a reunion dinner at Huntingdon on 4 September, arranged largely by Hugh's wife Betty, for some survivors of the Blenheim squadrons, so that I could look into this prospect. Although they had not taken any steps towards launching their Association, it seemed sensible to discuss forming one society, if the interests and aims were compatible, rather than two possible rivals.

Some of these ex-2 Group veterans had visited RAF Wyton the day before, 3 September. We had arranged to take our Blenheim to the former Blenheim base there

The airframe being loaded in Canada to start its journey to the Strathallan Museum; the centre-section is standing upright at the rear of the trailer unit.

at the request of the CO to mark the anniversary of the start of the Second World War, but could not as, of course, it had been reduced to a pile of wreckage.

The dinner was a great success. Those present had been appalled at the accident and were anxious to help put a Blenheim back in the air. An ad hoc steering committee was selected there and then, we retired to an anteroom, with Hugh in the chair and Betty as

The components arrive at Duxford in February 1988; now we could get weaving on the second Blenheim restoration.

secretary, and got down to forming the Blenheim Society straight away. We found that our aims and interests did coincide, and adopted three equal objectives:

1 To raise funds and offer expertise to assist in restoring the British Aerial Museum's Blenheim to flying condition.

2 To retrieve and record the true history of the Blenheim and its air and ground crews in RAF service.

3 To organise functions and events for the reunions of veterans of the Blenheim squadrons and others interested in the aircraft.

The Society had its first public meeting, which I arranged in the Officers' Mess at Duxford, one foggy day in November 1987. Some 350 people turned up, including many ex-Blenheim crews. I had contacted as many as I could of those Blenheim people who had written in or subscribed to the Blenheim Appeal and invited them. The day was a great success and got the Society off to a flying start. There are now some 850 members who receive a very good quarterly journal, which is an excellent way of keeping them up to date with the second restoration by means of regular progress reports.

The Blenheim Society also holds local reunion lunches up and down the country, and has a special enclosure and marquee – with refreshments both solid and liquid! – at various air displays at which the Blenheim performs. At the inaugural AGM, held at the RAF Museum, Hendon, in September 1988, the ad hoc committee were elected en bloc by the members, with Hugh George as Chairman and Betty as the 'Hon Sec', positions that they still hold. We were delighted when Air Marshal Sir Ivor Broom, a highly respected figure and distinguished former Blenheim and Mosquito pilot, agreed to be our President.

It has been my privilege to meet many ex-Blenheim crews over the years, not all of them members of the Society, and my admiration for them has grown as I have become closer to them and learned more of that extraordinary period in their lives. They have revealed, usually with commendable reticence and modesty, a wealth of fascinating and often incredible tales of their wartime Blenheim experiences. Most retain the traditional RAF reluctance to 'shoot a line', and play down their own part. Often remarkable stories had to be almost dragged from them. I found this a humbling experience and determined to see the full story of the considerable contribution to our war effort made by Blenheims and their brave crews published one day.

A couple of years into the second restoration, the Blenheim Team was shaken by the sad loss of our respected chief pilot, John Larcombe, as described in Chapter 5. His demise left a gap at the centre of our Team; a fine obituary notice by Stephen Grey, head of The Fighter Collection, is included as Appendix 9.

The need to organise some serious fund-raising was apparent as, after a few months, the initial wave of small donations sent with sympathy had virtually dried up, but the expenses of the restoration continued to mount inexorably month by month. We arranged a range of Blenheim 'merchandise' to sell at air displays and at Blenheim Society events. This was run on a voluntary basis by John Larcombe's wife Marrianne, helped by Andy Gilmour and various supporters. When it became too much for Marrianne, Andy and his family took it over. It is a hard slog setting out a sales stall at a dozen airshows, manning it in all weathers, and packing it up after each event. Andy's printing firm, New Granary Press at Linton, produced most of the sales items, the most popular of which was a T-shirt displaying a pair of Mercury engines on the chest and the slogan 'Happiness is Big Bristols'! This was, needless to say, another brilliant idea from the irrepressible 'Smudge'.

Andy, with some friends from Radwinter, staged a 'Blenheim Dance' in a suitably decorated hangar at Duxford in 1988 to the music of the Squadronaires; guests were encouraged to wear uniform or 1940s costume, food was served in individual 'ration boxes', and it was great evening that grew into a successful annual event. Apart from being a most enjoyable night out, these re-creations of wartime hangar dances to Glen

Only 3¹/2 years later, the largely completed fuselage and centre-section, with the rebuilt port power plant, was displayed at the launch of my first book, proceeds from which went to the Blenheim Appeal.

Miller music made useful contributions to the Blenheim Appeal. John Dibbs did a lovely cartoon of Father Christmas dropping coloured parcels from a Blenheim, which made a novel Christmas card.

Frank Wootton, the doyen of aviation artists, painted a superb portrait of 105 Squadron Blenheim Mk IVs flying low over the Dutch countryside – complete with a piece of broken branch caught in a wing-tip! Prints of this were marketed with great flair by Richard Lucraft as a limited edition, signed by Lord Rothermere and Blenheim veterans. Aided by an editorial feature and a double-page colour advertisement in *You*, the *Mail on Sunday* magazine, it soon sold out and made a substantial contribution to the Blenheim Appeal. Over the next five years Richard repeated the exercise with two superb paintings by Gerald Coulson: 'The First Blow', depicting Blenheims low over the sea on the first offensive sortie of the Second World War, published on the 50th Anniversary of that event; and 'Night Hunter', showing a night-intruder Blenheim over a moonlit coast – a print to which we will return later. Both of these limited editions, also generously supported by *You* magazine, also sold out, and made further worthwhile contributions to the Appeal. Purchasers of these prints, and the videos and books mentioned below, were invited to join the Blenheim Society.

At around the time of the completion of the first Blenheim we had made a dummy 250 lb bomb from fibreglass with metal fins, moulded on a real one borrowed from the IWM. We intended to fit four of these into the bomb bays so that we could perform a fly-past at air displays with the bomb doors open revealing the load. 'Smudge' had the bright idea of making a slot in the 'bomb' and mounting it on a stand next to the airframe, to form an unusual collection box for donations. Over the years several thousand pounds in coins have been dropped through that slot by generous visitors, again making a very helpful contribution to the Blenheim Appeal. Normally I write to thank people who make postal donations, but as I am unable to write to the many unknown donors who have put small change in the slot, I hope that they will accept this appreciation of their kind support. Thank you, folks!

We had put together, largely by 'Smudge', our own video on the restoration, called 'The Blenheim', which we sold on the stall, but I was anxious to promote a longer professional version. So, following an approach from a small independent production company, I arranged for the *Daily Mail* to finance a video on the Blenheim, royalties from the sales of which would benefit the Blenheim Appeal. I worked with the producer, Barry Heard, and arranged for him to film interviews with several ex-Blenheim crews; these were mixed with archive film and footage of our Blenheim, and the result was 'The Forgotten Bomber'. This was a good video that was bought and shown by Anglia TV, and then by most of the other ITV regions, so was seen by millions of viewers. It also sold several thousand copies, but alas the promised royalties did not appear.

To link the two together, the same title was also used for my first book *The Forgotten Bomber*, published by PSL in 1991. I am happy to say that it was very well received, and was reprinted, but is now out of print. This earlier book described the first restoration only, from the time of my own involvement up to the accident; many of you have probably read it, so I have tried to avoid repeating myself in the present one!

Mention is made of these behind-the-scenes but necessary activities to reveal that there is more to making, and keeping, a Blenheim airworthy than meets the eye.

Chapter Sixteen

Starting from scratch

While the various activities described above were going on in the background, the physical restoration work on the second Blenheim had started. As this work was essentially a re-run of the first restoration I will not bore you by repeating the details of the entire process all over again. But please bear in mind that the Team had no choice but to repeat the entire process all over again. No similar short-cuts were available to them! Moreover, we had made a rod for our own backs by setting ourselves the hard task of completing the second comprehensive restoration in only five years from starting again from scratch. Or rather, I made the rod by giving this undertaking so publicly!

The major difference between the two restoration programmes was that this time we rebuilt then fitted out each major section of the airframe in the workshops, rather than assembling the relatively bare airframe sections, then fitting them out in the hangar. During the first rebuild we were so anxious to see morale-raising RVP (Rapid Visual Progress!) that we tended, for example, to fit the major airframe components such as the three fuselage sections together and mount them on the centre-section, etc, first as trial runs in the workshops, then permanently in the hangar, there to complete them later by fitting the various systems and so on into them.

On the second rebuild we completed each major airframe component as far as possible in the workshops, including installing the systems. This made access much easier, especially in the nose section of the fuselage, which includes the cockpit with all its controls, instrument panels, and so forth. This was fully glazed, wired and plumbed, and most of the controls and instruments fitted, before it was moved to the hangar. So, to the public gaze, little progress was apparent for the first two or three years, but considerable progress was being made behind the scenes.

The aircraft was registered with the CAA as G-BPIV so that their surveyors could monitor the restoration. John Romain drew up the rebuild programme and work schedules, and as the CAA-licensed engineer responsible, supervised all of the actual work – apart from actually doing the lion's share of it with his own hands. He rose to this onerous challenge magnificently. We were aware that the CAA would keep a particularly beady eye on it, in view of the very public loss of the first restored Blenheim.

Once again the centre-section – the core of the whole aircraft – was the first major airframe component to be restored. This time we mounted it in a vertical jig, for we stripped it down further than the first one, and the rebuild was more comprehensive. The complete process of stripping, inspecting and repairing – or replacing with a fabricated new part using the removed one as a pattern – was carried through once more. This included re-capping the main spars with new formed and heat-treated sections of the special steel, which were riveted and bonded into place. A new alloy floor for the central well, which forms the roof of the bomb bay, was constructed, plus the wooden floor that covers it; new wooden supporting strips under the walkways were fitted, as were new 'fir-tree'-section alloy trailing-edges. Then we made a complete set of new skins, again a gauge thicker than the originals, using the time-consuming back-drilling method described earlier. They were fitted, etch-primed and painted internally, and the resulting structure has even greater structural integrity than the original. The bulk of this work was done by 'Smudge' Smith and Colin Swann, helped by Dave Swann, James Gilmour and Robert Sparkes.

The inner flaps – one rescued from the salvage of the first aircraft – with their operating system, hydraulic jack and piping, linking cables, etc, were refurbished, then fitted in the workshops, rather than in the hangar later. New tank bay panels and fuel-tank supports were fabricated and fitted, likewise the rebuilt and stove-enamelled undercarriage and engine mounting frames, then the entire reconditioned main undercarriage units themselves were assembled on to the centre-section, with all new nuts and bolts, in the workshops. Most of the control torque tubes were refitted, after reconditioning or replacement, on to the renewed 'D' brackets on the forward face of the front spar, and new leading-edge sections were made to cover them, together with new hydraulic pipes, fuel lines, wiring and plumbing. The wing attachment lugs at the ends of the spars were stripped, crack-tested and replaced with all new cross-bolts and nuts – the latter alone cost £2,000 per side. In November 1989 the entire centre-section, completed as far as possible, was moved to the corner of a hangar and covered over. There it sat and waited for a couple of years.

The main fuselage was then moved into the workshops to take the place of the centre-section. This in turn underwent the laborious and messy process of being paint-stripped inside and out. Every bare-metal former, stringer and skin panel was carefully

The partially stripped upper surface of the centre-section, showing corrosion on both the spars. The fuselage 'well' seen between the step-ladders fits just behind the cockpit.

The spars have been recapped, the ribs repaired or renewed, and the stringers are now being attended to from the trailing edge downwards.

inspected; fortunately relatively few repairs or replacements were needed, so it was all etch-primed. Work then commenced on replacing internal fittings such as the floors, renewing the control runs, hydraulic piping, wiring, and so on. This did not take nearly as long as the centre-section because the rear fuselage contains far fewer systems. Colin

Below left *The refurbished undercarriage frames are attached with all new bolts and nuts, and the main hydraulic ram is in place, as are the D-brackets on the front of the spar, with some trunking and pipework too; the pivoting arm in the centre is for the aileron controls.*

Below right *The centre-section completely re-skinned and painted internally. Note the cross-bolts for the lugs attaching the outer wings.*

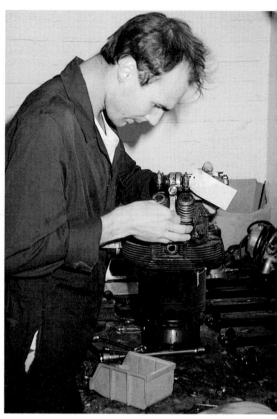

Above left *Once more we could see the Bristol Mercury engines being built up, and admire the machining on the crank and rods.*

Above right *Nev Gardner followed Chalky's example by working to the highest standards; here he is refitting the rocker assembly to a cylinder.*

Below *Over many months Nev, helped by his father Cliff, built up the engines in the workshops . . .*

. . . until they were completed, first the port unit shown here with the exhaust collector ring, then the starboard, the nine reclaimed cylinders for which are waiting on the floor, each tagged and carefully taped up to protect the bores.

The starboard engine is now mounted and Nev is connecting it up with advice from the chief plumber Colin and his mate Robert!

took the turret home to work on it in his garage. A few months later the virtually completed main fuselage was also moved into a hangar.

While this work on the centre-section and fuselage was being carried out, Nev Gardner, helped by his father Cliff, had stripped down, one after the other, both the engines torn from the crashed aircraft. They cleaned and inspected all the items that seemed undamaged and might possibly be made fit to use again. Most fortunately, after the most careful examination, measurement and crack testing, they were able to reclaim all of the cylinder barrels with their matching pistons. This saved many months, if not years, of painstaking work in preparing matching sets of these vital components, and completely justified our efforts in purchasing the salvage from the insurance company.

Over the next four years the two replacement engines were built up slowly but surely, first the port then the starboard, the rebuild of each taking about two years. As the crankshafts and the alloy crankcases had been severely shock-loaded in the accident, they were discarded and further examples were selected from the components available from the engines we had stripped down during the first restoration. After the most meticulous inspection, measurement and crack-testing process, these fresh crankshafts and crankcases, along with the sets of reclaimed cylinders, were used as the basis for rebuilding the second pair of engines.

Once more two superchargers, with their high-speed impellers, had to be meticulously assembled and balanced, and the supercharger cases fitted. Once more two pairs of the inlet and exhaust cam drums had the lift and dwell of each lobe measured and found to be perfect. They were installed together with their gear drives, and the roller cam followers and the push-rod assemblies, which incorporate the device that compensates for the differential expansion of the cylinders and push-rods to maintain tappet clearances exactly as set. Once more two sets of the epicyclic reduction gears, which bring down the speed of the crankshaft to the lower speed of the propeller shaft, had to be selected from those available. They too were stripped down, inspected, measured, re-assembled and checked for truth and correct meshing, then mounted on the front of the engines, together with their protective alloy domes. To my eye the pleasing symmetry of these domes is spoiled by an external oil-pipe that carries engine oil under pressure to the propeller pitch-change mechanism.

After a most thorough inspection, many of the ancillaries, such as the magnetos, oil scavenge and pressure pumps, starter motors, pneumatic, hydraulic, vacuum and fuel pumps, and the generator, were found to be serviceable; those that did not pass this critical examination were reconditioned. The valves and valve-gear were completely overhauled, as many of the rocker shafts and covers had been damaged; all 36 valves were lapped in carefully and their perfect sealing checked by the time-honoured method of leaving each cylinder inverted while containing petrol.

As Nev says, 'It's all right for the airframe guys – when they have finished one they are done; but when I have finished one, I have to start again on another one!'

'Smudge' was the exception to this, as he had the difficult task of fabricating two more new engine 'firewalls' in stainless-steel. These were fixed to the rebuilt engine mountings, so that when each basic engine was complete it could be located on to its mounting ring. Then the refurbished inlet and exhaust manifolds, the push-rods and their tubes, the new braided ignition harness, and all the ancillaries mentioned above, were refitted as the engines were built up into complete power plants. Another pair of oil-tanks, and another pair of oil-coolers, which had all been repaired and pressure tested, were installed, together with their ducting. The inner cowlings were repaired or replaced by 'Smudge'.

Among the last items to be fitted were the baffles between the cylinders and the exhaust collector rings that form the front of the cowlings. Moreover, this time we did far more work to build up complete power units in the engine shop in 'Blenheim Palace', where it was warm and dry, rather than on the aircraft in the hangar, where it was cold and damp.

While the engines were being built up steadily in our workshops, the de Havilland propellers for the second Blenheim had to be rebuilt on a commercial basis in Canada. We had sent the damaged props to British Aerospace at Lostock, who had rebuilt them for the first Blenheim, but – as expected – all the hubs and blades had been damaged beyond hope of repair. Then BAe closed its propeller shop, so we had to look elsewhere anyway! This was a pity, as it meant that we would have to bear the full cost of rebuilding and certifying the propellers on the second aircraft, which, with the shipping and insurance costs, and including a spare prop, was some £33,000.

In the meantime, the starboard outer wing of RCAF 9703 had been bolted into the jig in the workshops and stripped right down. Each one of the thousands of rivets was drilled out by hand, and all the skin panels were removed and numbered. The whole lengthy and painstaking rebuilding process from paint-stripping onwards was followed once more. Many damaged ribs and stringers were repaired or renewed, and new flap housings were made. Several sections of the booms and cornices of both spars were corroded, so new replacement sections were folded to one of the eight different profiles required, heat treated and spliced into place, using more of our dwindling stock of the special steel. These different profiles are needed to follow the curves of the upper and lower wing surfaces, as previously illustrated. Once more new spar-caps were folded to shape, heat treated and bonded and riveted into position. This highly skilled work was carried out over many months, virtually single-handed, by John Romain. Once more all the skins were renewed with panels in a heavier gauge – 'Smudge', Colin and Dave helped John considerably in making and fitting the new ones. A new wing-tip was fabricated, and everything was etch-primed and all internal surfaces painted. The aileron control system was overhauled and replaced, the outer flaps and their operating mechanism refurbished and installed, the wiring renewed. This process of rebuilding just one

The starboard outer wing, stripped and undergoing repair, mounted in the jig. The centre of the front spar is also supported on a carefully adjusted jack to keep it perfectly straight.

Now it is the turn of the port outer wing, which required the replacement of sections of the spar flanges, booms and cornices.

old, damaged, corroded, incomplete outer wing into a condition better (and stronger!) than new, takes but a few moments to describe but took two years to carry out!

The next major component to be tackled in the workshops was the fuselage stern section and tail unit. This was in generally poor condition, so had to be stripped right down. One source of concern proved unfounded as the central former, which carries the mountings for the tailplane and tailwheel oleo, is the only one in the aircraft manufactured of steel, and we feared might have suffered from corrosion, but it was found to be quite sound.

Again, the complete restoration process on the stern section was followed through once more. The one-piece tailplane was bolted in a jig, stripped, repaired as necessary and re-skinned; the fin and the fin post, which bolts to the rear of the stern section, followed suit. All were etch-primed inside and out, repainted internally, and reassembled. The fin was mounted on the stern section and the multi-curved fin/fuselage fairings reshaped by 'Smudge' – indeed, he did the bulk of the excellent work on the stern section and tail assembly.

At the same time that the rear end of the Blenheim was being worked on, the front end was receiving similar attention in the workshops. The fuselage nose and cockpit section, having been stripped and repaired, was being fitted out with its mass of piping, the many rods, levers and cables for the flying, engine and systems controls, and the instrument panel and all the instruments. However, each of the individual instruments had to be overhauled, re-calibrated and certified before fitting. Every component in the various systems had to be reconditioned, installed and connected up or plumbed in, then adjusted, inspected and checked before it could be signed off.

The pilot's seat chassis with the main flying controls, the rudder pedal assembly with

The interior of the rear fuselage being fitted out. The main electrical panel is to the right, the hatch opening above, with the turret mounting behind that. Two heat lamps help to control the humidity.

the brake balance valve, and all the ancillary controls were also refurbished, fitted, adjusted and checked. We 'pulled off' a complete set of perspex glazing panels from the moulds we had made for the first restoration, trimmed and fitted them, plus the flat glass windscreens and bomb-aiming panels in the nose. Now we had a virtually

A view of the Blenheim 'growing' in the hangar, showing the fin and tailplane in position; the wing-root fairing, rudder and elevators are yet to be attached.

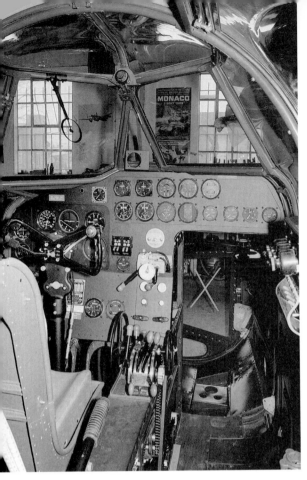

Left *The nose was glazed and the cockpit fitted out with the controls and instruments in the workshops before being joined to the airframe. Note the gun-sight, the engine and prop controls in the centre (above part of the chain-and-sprocket drive from the trim wheels), and the flare pistol mounting in the right-hand corner.*

Below *The nose and main fuselage sections are now mounted on the centre-section, and the port engine is on a stand in front of the starboard mounting as we had put up steps on the port side so that Blenheim Society members could see into the refitted cockpit.*

Below right *'Smudger' showing some ex-Blenheim crew members around the Blenheim, now on its wheels; this view shows clearly the height of the undercarriage and its mounting frame.*

complete nose and cockpit section. This was fascinating and satisfying to inspect, and demonstrated the most apparent and worthwhile progress.

Come July 1991 the centre-section was rescued from its corner, placed on trestles in the hangar and reunited with the main, nose and stern fuselage sections. Suddenly a

second recognisable Blenheim had appeared before the public once more. This was just in time for the launch of my first book, *The Forgotten Bomber* – we wheeled the almost completed port engine up on its mounting and stood it in front of the starboard side for photographs. The Blenheim Society had a marquee at the Classic Fighter Display that weekend, so members were given the first opportunity to see the substantial progress on the restoration. We put up a platform and steps on the port side of the nose so that they could look in and see that the cockpit was almost completely fitted out.

The keel-plate and side panels to the bomb bay were soon fitted, then 'Smudge' repaired the large but graceful wing-root fairings, and made them fit properly too. The completed fin and tailplane were added, then the wood tailplane tips and elevator gap shrouds, plus the overhauled tailwheel assembly. The repaired and pressure-tested main fuel-tanks were installed in their centre-section bays, using the new tank supports and fuel bay panels we had made earlier. There was a plethora of 'Rapid Visual Progress' to see at this stage.

Sunday 27 October 1991 was a good day, for the Blenheim was lowered from the trestles and moved on her own wheels for the first time. She was pushed out of the hangar, turned round and pushed in again, but with her nose pointing towards the airfield – as if she was impatient to become airborne again.

While all this activity was going on in the hangar, back in the workshops the port wing of 9703 had been bolted into the jig and stripped right down; this revealed some real horrors. Severe corrosion had completely perforated some sections of the front spar booms, and several sections of the cornices were in a bad way too. The entire spar had to be dismantled – the first time we had to do this – for the major repairs necessary. To prevent any movement of the wing structure, the rear spar had to be carefully supported on jacks while the front spar was removed. John found that we had only just enough of the special steel to fold into the various profiles and lengths required, and that was only achieved after a lot of juggling of the different lengths and sections needed. When formed, they were sent away as before for heat treatment to re-harden them. What a shock we had when they were returned – most had been distorted far too much during that process to be useable!

We could not obtain any more of the special steel, we did not know which mill had

made it, the Chairman of British Steel who had helped before was long since retired, and the whole of the steel industry had been privatised anyway. John beavered away to overcome this serious set-back and, with the aid of the Metallurgy Laboratory of a Cambridge University, a treatment was devised to re-harden the material – normally impossible – so as to retain all the characteristics of the original specification. The new sections were spliced into the front spar and it was reinstated; repairs to the rear spar were carried out in situ. Both spars were then capped, various ribs and stringers repaired or replaced, and all new skin panels were made for this wing, like the others. The comprehensive repairs to this wing took nearly three years, but satisfied the strict requirements of the CAA.

The airworthy Blenheim had been saved yet again. John deserves to be awarded a bar to his Distinguished Restoration Order!

On to John's shoulders, too, fell the demanding task of stripping and rebuilding two more of the delicate and complicated Claudel-Hobson constant-vacuum twin-choke carburettors with their automatic boost and mixture controls. The original pair, rebuilt for the first aircraft, had been torn from the engines in the accident and were now use-less. He and 'Chalky' had made a fuel flow rig to test and calibrate them to the figures in the manual, and he used this again to set the float levels, which are critical, and to measure the flow through each of the paired main, idling, intermediate and accelerator jets in both carburettors. The rebuild of each unit took John more than two months of meticulous work, calling for great concentration and application, but the final result was two spotless carbs that performed exactly as they were designed to – a tribute to his skill.

By this time we had decided that the aircraft would be painted in an all-black night-fighter scheme. This was partly to show the public that we had restored a different air-frame, and not just repaired the crashed aircraft, and partly as we wished to put into

One of the new 'beetle-back' rear nacelles is shown to the left of this shot of the rear fuselage, with its prominent RAF markings; the trailing edge of the wing-root fairing is as yet unpainted.

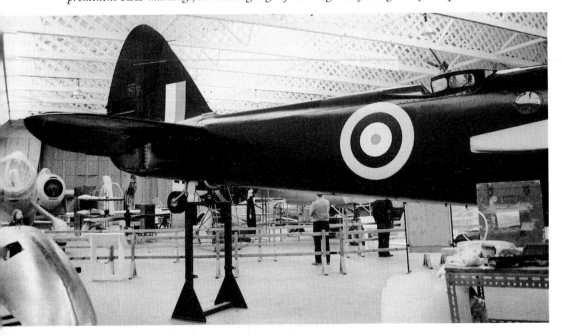

practice our previous intention of depicting in this way some of the many different operational roles undertaken by wartime Blenheims. We had not yet chosen the individual markings of a suitable Blenheim, but we could start to apply grey primer and black paint to the various airframe sections as we assembled them in the hangar.

The elevators and rudder had been rebuilt, recovered and fitted, including the trimming tabs, and the duplicated control runs to them installed, with new cables and bearings for the levers. All were tensioned, set and adjusted to give the correct range of movement. The completed starboard wing was then fitted so that 'Smudge' could start to fabricate the upper and lower engine nacelles that straddle the joint between centre-section and outer wing, where the dihedral angle commences. In the absence of a jig, these nacelles have to be made up on the airframe, and the pair on the port side could be made as mirror images ready for a final fitting, as we were still awaiting the port wing.

By mid-1992 the port power plant had been fitted and all the systems and engine controls were connected up or plumbed in. The hydraulic system was completed and tested from an external source of hydraulic power – the undercarriage and flaps went up and down as they should, and the rebuilt turret – which Colin had produced – turned from one side to the other and the guns and seat raised and lowered in unison. Most of the plywood skins of the eight bomb doors had been torn in the accident, but we were able to repair and re-use the wood frames, and made new skins in alloy. The fuel system was connected up and pressure tested, the oil-tanks and coolers likewise, and the electrical circuits were also completed and tested. The restoration was moving forward rapidly, but there was one pretty large fly in the ointment – the need for more funding.

Donations to the Blenheim Appeal had virtually dried up, and my own resources were fully committed. The only way to complete the restoration in anything like the five-year period we had set ourselves was to obtain a bank loan. So I arranged overdraft limits of up to £100,000, for then we would only need to pay interest on the amount of

Mike Terry rebuilding an aileron in the workshops.

the facility taken up, rather than on the complete sum; this overdraft was secured on my personal guarantee, which meant that at the end of the line my home was at risk. I was confident that we would be able to repay the loan from airshow income once the Blenheim was flying again, but at that time all it was doing was soaking up money month after month. This undertaking demonstrates the extent and depth of my personal commitment to the second Blenheim restoration.

Over the winter the starboard power plant was fitted to the airframe and everything connected to it. Finally the port wing, with the major repairs completed, was bolted into position. The upper and lower engine nacelles and the close-fitting cowlings had been completed and installed. The controllable cooling gills and their mounting rings, which contain the operating chains, had been rebuilt by Bob Sparkes and were now fitted. All the remaining panels and fairings, plus the control surfaces, had been painted black.

The ailerons had also been rebuilt; we had to make a new tubular spar for the port one as the spar on the aileron on the second airframe was corroded, and the one from the crashed aircraft was bent. After they were re-covered in Ceconite and painted, they became almost the last airframe components to be fitted. The control rods were connected up – these incorporate an off-centre pivot on one of the arms that gives the effective differential aileron action patented by Leslie Frise, the designer at Bristol.

The reconditioned propellers arrived from Canada and were fitted to the engines – they looked magnificent. Repairs completed and painted, the bomb doors – once more! – became the last components to be fitted. The completed aircraft was rigged, weighed and the full dimensional check carried out – once again the measurements were absolutely 'spot on'.

Nev started up both engines for the first time on a cold day in April 1993. They ran beautifully, and apart from a persistent leak from the hydraulic pump, were completely trouble free. John taxied the aircraft for the first time on 28 April, and the complete

The great day in April 1993 when the engines of the second Blenheim were started up for the first time. They ran perfectly apart from a leak from the hydraulic pump.

Above left *Nev working on this problem during the engine runs.*

Above right *The programme of engine tests was completed, including full-power checks with the aircraft tethered down.*

programme of engine runs and checks, right up to full power tests, took place over the next two weeks.

The second pile of paperwork, like the first, had grown in line with the aircraft. Everything was inspected, checked, re-checked, cleared and signed off. It was the spring of 1993, just five years after the small team had started the restoration work all over again. The second Blenheim had been completed to airworthy standards, and was ready to take to the skies once more. We had done it! Again!

Chapter Seventeen

Our finest hour

As the day of the first flight drew near, the excitement grew apace. So many people were telephoning to ask when it would take place that they were unwittingly disrupting the work, and we had to put in an information line, for which I recorded a series of messages – the line was so heavily used that the tape soon wore out and failed!

We did not in fact know when the actual first flight could take place, or when the CAA flight test schedule would be completed, mainly due to the vagaries of the British weather. But we did know that the Blenheim could not perform in public without holding a Permit to Fly. So we elected to hold an 'official first flight and naming ceremony', to which all our friends, Society members, and those who enquired, could be invited, late in May, by which time – hopefully – all the formalities would have been completed.

Selecting, several months ahead, the date for this event was not easy. Gerry Coulson had added the markings of our chosen Blenheim WM-Z to his superb 'Night Hunter' painting, and Richard Lucraft further complicated the choice of date by including an invitation to this event in his brochures and advertisements for the limited edition prints, as an added inducement to the 850 purchasers. Invitations needed to be printed and distributed, and I had to liaise on the date with Lord Rothermere's office as he had kindly agreed to name the aircraft 'Spirit of Britain First', as a tribute to the first Viscount Rothermere and to the original 'Britain First'. The Blenheim will continue to carry this name through the changes that we will make every couple of years or so to the individual serial numbers, squadron colours and markings, to illustrate some of the many operational roles undertaken by the RAF's hard-worked first multi-combat-role aircraft.

We had decided that the initial markings would be Z5722, coded WM-Z, the 'personal' Blenheim Mk IV-F of one of the RAF's most famous pilots, Wing Commander The Hon 'Max' Aitken DFC, the son of Lord Beaverbrook, the wartime Minister of Aircraft Production, when he was CO of 68 Squadron. I wrote to his widow, Lady Violet Aitken, to obtain her consent to this; she was delighted to give her blessing, and happy to endorse and sign the print too.

Maxwell had flown Blenheim Mk I fighters with 601 Squadron at the start of the war, leading a section on the attack on the German base at Borkum in November 1939. His Squadron was re-equipped with Hurricanes (paternal influence?) and played a leading role in the Battle of Britain. Max shot down eight enemy aircraft, including an He 111 at night. Tour completed, he was appointed to the Director of Operations at the Air Ministry and became increasingly involved in the problems of intercepting enemy aircraft at night, for the Luftwaffe had turned to the night 'blitz'. Aitken was given the

The aircraft was to carry the markings of Z5722 WM-Z, the personal Blenheim IVF of Wing Commander the Hon Max Aitken DSO DFC CzMC, when he was CO of 68 Squadron. His widow, Violet, Lady Aitken, gave her blessing to these markings.

command of 68 Squadron, a night fighter unit re-equipping with Beaufighters, but these experienced so many teething troubles that he preferred his trusty Blenheim for several months, although it was much slower and less heavily armed than the Beaus.

The original Z5722 had served with the Fighter Interception Unit at Ford and had one of the rare AI sets that actually worked. Max had the aircraft stripped down and repainted with a less matt black than standard, and removed as much equipment as possible to save weight. When the Beaus were 'sorted', the Blenheim remained on strength as the Squadron 'hack' until it was written off at Coltishall on 6 June 1942, by a pilot who forgot to close the cooling gills on take-off, striking a flagpole. Z5722 had survived exactly two years from being manufactured – an unusually long time for an operational Blenheim.

Wing Commander Aitken added five more German night bombers to his score, plus the DSO and Czech War Cross to his DFC; promoted to Group Captain, he commanded 219 Group in the Middle East. Although based at HQ he borrowed a Beau one day and shot down two Ju 52s, damaging two more! He then formed and commanded the famous anti-shipping Strike Wing of Beaufighters and Mosquitos at Banff. He flew an operation in a Mossie on the last day of the war, this ensuring his place in the history books as the only RAF pilot to fly an operational sortie on both the first and last days!

We therefore felt that Max Aitken deserved to join Hughie Edwards in having his own colours and markings carried by the only flying Blenheim in the world; we did this to salute their outstanding personal bravery, which exemplifies that of all the wartime Blenheim crews, and to bring this bravery to the attention of the present generation.

With all the correct markings of WM-Z applied, including the stencils, she looked very dramatic indeed, and refreshingly different; but being all black made her difficult to film or photograph against a light sky. Several airshow commentators christened her 'Black Beauty', but we discouraged this. I remember that Gerry Coulson balked at being asked to paint an all-black aircraft flying at night (!), but his great skill as an artist magnificently overcame this seemingly impossible task!

We had a running battle with the CAA about the pilot for the first flight; I felt that John Romain was by far the best and safest choice, and believed that he was well-qualified to fly this particular aircraft for the first time, for all of his 1,200 hours P1 had been flying piston-engined tailwheel aircraft, and no one knew or understood the Blenheim and the operation of its outdated systems better. However, the Chief Test Pilot (Light Aircraft) of the Flight Test Department, Safety Regulation Group, Design and Manufacturing Standards Division, Civil Aviation Authority, had informed John by telephone that he did not consider him to be suitable. This was before the CAA had been appraised of John's specialised experience, so naturally he was miffed. I wrote to express my concern at this high-handed attitude, and listed the reasons for our choice. They suggested two other pilots, but I felt them to be less suitable than John, and advised the Fight Test Department accordingly, as did the two pilots in question, but the Department 'closed ranks' and would not alter its position.

I arranged a meeting with the CAA Chief Test pilot at his Gatwick Office to 'seek clarification', advising that I would be accompanied by Sir Ivor Broom. The latter supported our view, and his opinion would carry considerable weight, for he was a former Commandant of the RAF Central Flying School, had been Controller of the National Air Traffic Services, and was Chairman of Gatwick Handling, as well as being President of the Blenheim Society. In an attempt at compromise we had proposed, at his suggestion, that the actual Flight Test Schedule should be flown by 'Hoof' Proudfoot, the Chief Pilot of The Fighter Collection, with John in the right-hand seat, after John had carried out the initial 'shake down' flights with 'Hoof' in the right-hand seat. But our entreaties were to no avail – the official mind was set. If we nominated 'Hoof' to do the test-flying he would be required to carry out the initial flights too. John accepted the position manfully, but I was very disappointed.

So it was 'Hoof', with John alongside him, who made the first flight on Tuesday 18 May 1993 – a great day indeed in the lives of all the Team who had worked so hard to achieve this success. It was a lovely sunny morning, in sharp contrast to the dull and drizzly day of the initial flight of the first aircraft in May 1987. But the memorable anti-climax of that earlier day was to be repeated – the second aircraft was at the runway threshold, just about to take off for the first time, having completed full power checks and all the cockpit drills, when the crew noticed a fluctuation on the fuel pressure gauge to the starboard engine. Although the engines were running beautifully, the take-off was abandoned and she taxied back to the stand. An urgent investigation showed that the gauge was incorrectly placarded: it showed the pressure in the cross-over fuel system, not the feed to the starboard engine. When it was sorted out the pressure reading was as normal as the actual pressure had been all the time! But far, far better safe than sorry.

The Wednesday was fine too, and 'Hoof' and John carried out the complete CAA special Flight Test Schedule, including single-engine climbs, establishing the minimum speed at which control could be maintained in the asymmetric configuration – known in my day as the 'safety speed' – exploring the handling characteristics at the stall, with undercarriage and flaps both retracted and extended, and measuring and recording the performance. They did a wonderful job – the aircraft was snag-free, and the full report was submitted to the CAA on Friday the 21st – the day that John was delighted to fly the Blenheim for the first time.

While all this was going on, I had been busy arranging the 'Official First Flight and Naming Ceremony' for our previously chosen date of Friday 28 May. It looked as if, barring serious snags, everything could just about be made ready in time. The invitations had been printed and some 1,500 sent out to those Blenheim Society

The wonderful day in May 1993 when the wheels left Mother Earth for the first time and once more the world could see the only airworthy Blenheim return to its true element – the sky.

members, and other ex-Blenheim crews, plus the print purchasers, and friends and supporters of ours, who were able to attend. Press and television were invited too. Michael Turner had painted the Blenheim taking off on her first flight, and we hoped to have limited edition prints available at the event, but were too late. Without the backing of the *Mail on Sunday* (*You* had become a women's magazine in the meantime) it was far more difficult to sell.

For the event on 28 May we had arranged to prepare the Blenheim for flight in a closed hangar, tow her out and park in front of our special marquee and enclosure alongside the Control Tower, where Lord Rothermere and Lady Aitken would be introduced to the Team and carry out the naming ceremony. Jerry Mead's commentary kept our guests in the enclosure amused and informed; they could meet old friends, eat and drink; and the sun appeared for the first time in a very dull day just as the Blenheim was towed into view! Champagne was laid on for the christening, plus some steps to a platform so that the name, signwritten in a 'Gothic Gilt Script' just below the pilot's window, could be unveiled by pulling the tasselled cord attached to a taped-on black cloth.

John Romain with Nev Gardner would then start up the newly christened 'Spirit of Britain First', taxi out and take off. John would then carry out a fly-past closely escorted by a Spitfire and Hurricane, who would break away and perform solo slots, then the Blenheim would return and John would commence his full display routine. After landing, he would park back by the enclosure, and we would escort small groups of guests out to the 'live side' for a close inspection. That was the theory, anyway!

I had invited a few special guests to luncheon in the Officers' Mess; these invitations had to be strictly limited and I was sorry not to be able to include more – especially from the Team – but it was not possible. Lord Rothermere, Vyvyan Harmsworth and Dee Nolan represented Associated Newspapers; Max's widow Violet, Lady Aitken, and his son Maxwell, the present Lord Beaverbrook, with Lady Beaverbrook, represented the Aitken family; Sir Ivor and Lady Broom the Blenheim Society; John and Amanda Romain the Blenheim Team; Ted Inman the Imperial War Museum; Gerry Coulson the artists; Lord Harmsworth, the publishers; and myself and my wife Shirley, the British Aerial Museum. Amanda joined us but, most unfortunately, John Romain could not as he was still battling in the office with the CAA surveyors and the paperwork – he finally prised the Permit to Fly out of them, and it arrived by fax less than an hour before take-off time! Very nerve-racking for both he and myself.

When I led the convoy of special guests over from the Mess at the appointed time, we found the enclosure completely swamped, and hordes of press, photographers and TV cameramen swarming round the aircraft. In all 1,538 numbered tickets, each for two persons, had been given out, so we expected about 3,000 people at the most – but some 5,000 turned up! The section of the enclosure reserved for the disabled, and the front row of seats for the special guests, were both fully occupied. The Spitfire had gone unserviceable, so a P51 Mustang was substituted, and the Air Traffic people in the Control Tower were 'going spare' at the number of people on the live side. The little table with the champagne and glasses set neatly on a white cloth had disappeared. The lead to the microphone would not reach the aircraft, so Lord Rothermere – after being introduced to the Team in front of the Blenheim – had to go back into the throng to say a few well-chosen words in memory of his grandfather, adding praise for the skill and determination of the Team, and naming the aircraft. He then went back to it and climbed the steps with Lady Aitken, pulled the cord, and named it again; I had found

Left *Lord Rothermere named the Blenheim and with Lady Aitken poured a libation of champagne over the nose.*

Below *More toasts were drunk and everyone was delighted – 28 May 1993 was indeed a memorable day.*

The Team in front of their pride and joy, with Nev using his height to peep over the shoulders of Lord Rothermere and Lady Aitken. John Romain, looking remarkably cheerful considering the pressure he was under, went on to give a beautiful display.

and opened the champers and a libation was poured over the nose. So the Blenheim was well and truly named!

While we moved people back behind the barrier, I am sure that John and Nev were glad to get away from the crowd and into the cockpit to carry out their sortie. John flew a spirited but smooth and sensitive display, which was greatly appreciated by the 500-odd ex-Blenheim crew members there – their largest gathering since the war. I had arranged for several of these veterans to be interviewed on film in the Mess, and also for the events on the airfield to be filmed, for another video that we hoped to make. Later we cancelled a planned photo-sortie, and towed the Blenheim back to the public side of the barrier, as the crush to get out to the live side for a close look became intense – once out there people were reluctant to return to the enclosure! I had to apologise to guests about the overcrowding in the marquee and enclosure, and to those who were unable to get out to inspect the aircraft or meet members of the Team. We had become the victims of our own success! But, all in all, it had been a wonderful day and I received dozens of letters of thanks and congratulations.

Twenty fateful years had passed since those derelict old hulks were first rescued from their Canadian resting place to start the long and eventful journey that took them back to the skies.

That weekend the Blenheim went straight to the big Air Fete at Mildenhall. The organisers were pleased as she had appeared on television on the Friday evening, mentioning that the first public display would be at Mildenhall. The next event was a repeat of the 1987 events at RAF Cosford and the Biggin Hill Air Fair; when she appeared at

Biggin from Cosford there was spontaneous applause from the crowd – something that Raymond Baxter, the highly experienced commentator, had not heard before. She starred at the 'Classic Fighter Display' at Duxford, appeared at the huge International Air Tattoo at Fairford – where pieces of wreckage from the two Migs that collided in mid-air fell within a few yards just as John was about to start up – and at Sunderland, Leicester, Alconbury, 'Great Warbirds' at Wroughton, Zoersel in Belgium, RAF Finningley, and the main 1993 event at Duxford. All the programme compilers and commentators had been sent fact-sheets and information about Blenheims in general and WM-Z in particular. Over two million spectators saw the Blenheim perform at these air displays, plus several millions more on television – no longer was she the forgotten bomber!

The Blenheim also had a couple of somewhat sad goodwill appearances to make that year: the closure ceremony at RAF Wattisham, and an event to mark the closing of Ipswich Airport, from both of which airfields wartime Blenheims had operated. Blenheims of 107 and 110 Squadrons were the first RAF aircraft to be based at Wattisham in 1939, and later 236, 18 and 13 Squadrons were located there, and over 300 Blenheim crews lost their lives on operations from that one base. So it was fitting that a Blenheim should be the first and the last aircraft in the Wattisham skies. We feel that it is our duty to attend such events free of charge where possible, but alas such noble sentiments do not pay our heavy operating costs, of which the insurance premiums are by far the largest, although we do pick up some fuel from time to time.

Another nostalgic event in 1993 would have been the opening by HM The Queen Mother of the Battle of Britain Memorial at Capel-le-Ferne on the cliffs of Dover, for we had arranged with the organiser, Wing Commander Geoffrey Page DSO DFC*, for the Blenheim to fly over in close formation with a Hurricane and an early Spitfire – the two principal day fighters and the principal night fighter – forming a true Battle of Britain Memorial Flight at last! I had notified the national press and television of this, but alas

The Blenheim coming 'over the hedge' with wheels down and full flap, showing how the scalloped nose allows the pilot a view of the runway on the approach. The gun-pack was not fitted at this stage, but the light bomb carriers were.

We later fitted the correct Mk IVF four-Browning gun-pack, as well as the light bomb carriers used on intruder missions.

some really filthy weather prevented any aircraft from appearing. Our President attended the ceremony and confirmed the atrocious weather; he was relieved that we were not tempted to risk the Blenheim in such conditions. However, the weather gods have made amends by providing fine days in the following years, and we are proud that the Blenheim has formed a central part of the ceremonies held annually at this fine memorial.

The 1993 display season had kept the Team pretty busy, but constant inspection and maintenance ensured that the Blenheim remained trouble-free throughout. We checked out John Webb as a back-up pilot – he had flown our Beech 18 for several seasons – and he handles both aircraft safely and sympathetically, and gets along very well with the Team. Being a little on the portly side, he was given the nickname 'Mr Blobby' by Bill; when at the Red Lion, long after a display, John said that if he didn't get home soon he would have to spend another night in the garden shed, we sent his mail with the address commencing 'Captain Blobby, The Garden Shed'!

The fees received from our appearances enabled us to start repaying the bank loan that we had taken out to complete the aircraft in the five-year period we had set ourselves. Unfortunately the 1994 display season was not nearly as good; airshows were affected by the recession and organisers were reluctant to pay the fees we needed to operate the aircraft, and several did not wish to book it two years running. Indeed, none of the major displays mentioned above took the Blenheim for 1994. Apart from non-paying events at Duxford, the Blenheim appeared in the UK only at the 'Fighter Meet' at North Weald – where John Romain won the Trophy for the best individual display, which was very commendable as several Air Forces were vying for it – and the SBAC show at Farnborough.

Fortunately the picture was brighter on the continent, and the Blenheim appeared at Le Bourget, Falaise, La Ferte Alais, and Lyons in France, Tirstrup in Denmark, and Eindhoven in Holland. But overall the fees paid barely covered our operating costs, and the loan was not being reduced as rapidly as we had intended, so was still incurring interest charges.

The popular annual Blenheim Dances had grown so much that Andy and his family found it too much to handle alone, so the ubiquitous John Romain took care of much of the organisation. The proceeds from the 1994 event enabled us to purchase a GPS satellite-controlled navigation system, which certainly made for safer operation and eased the strain of flying in bad weather. The 1995 Dance paid for half of the insurance premium, and a couple of thousand people thoroughly enjoyed their evenings of nostalgia-tinged fun.

The Blenheim also made several interesting goodwill trips in 1994. She did a fly-past over the RAF Museum in Hendon to mark the opening of a Coastal Command exhibition there, and flew over the Royal Yacht, packed with visiting Heads of State, for the D-Day Anniversary celebrations. She returned to her birthplace at Filton, escorted by two Luftwaffe Tornados – how times have changed! – and was parked with a Concorde outside a Gala Dinner held by the Bristol Aero Collection. She visited British Aerospace at Lostock for their open day, and did fly-pasts at the Battle of Britain Memorial on the Dover cliffs mentioned above, and at the opening of a memorial at the site of RAF Castle Camps, but was prevented by bad weather from appearing at a similar event at Steeple Morden.

However, the saddest event was her appearance at the closing ceremonies at RAF West Raynham, another famous wartime base used by Blenheims of 139, 114, 614 and 18 Squadrons – one of the latter's pilots was Wing Commander Hugh Malcolm, who won his VC when the entire force of Blenheim Mk Vs he was leading was shot down in North Africa. Appropriately, our Blenheim – flown by 'Hoof' Proudfoot on this occasion – opened the air display, as Blenheims of 101 Squadron were the first RAF aircraft to be based at the station when it opened in 1939. She was followed by examples of most of the other RAF aircraft that had been based there over the years, and the display

Our Bristol Blenheim posing for a brochure at Duxford with its namesake, hand-built at Filton by Bristol Cars . . .

. . . and at Filton with the car and Concorde by invitation of the Bristol Aero Collection and British Aerospace.

was concluded by the Red Arrows. Many ex-Blenheim crews were among the guests, and after various march-pasts, with the salute taken by the AOC 11 Group, AVM John Allison, he went into the cockpit of the Blenheim and she took off – the last aircraft to do so from West Raynham. After the Sunset Ceremony, the 'Last Post' was sounded and, just as the RAF ensign was being lowered for the last time, the Blenheim passed low right over the dais in a fine final salute on a most moving occasion. Many were the handkerchiefs dabbed at moist and misty eyes, especially those of the Blenheim survivors. To me, this was an unforgettable moment that made all of our efforts to put a Blenheim back in the skies seem worthwhile.

We were lucky to meet Stephen Connor, a laid-back young man who puts together excellent video programmes. He wrote and directed the one with the same title as this book, which I recommend strongly! It is narrated by Raymond Baxter, who gives a beautiful reading of the poem by Richard Passmore (Roger Peacock) set to suitable images. The video contains some lovely air-to-air and in-the-cockpit sequences, as does his later title, 'Flight of the Blenheim', which is almost as good as actually going for a flight in it!

Arrangements for the 1995 season were changed. Up to then I had sent out all the letters and photographs to organisers, made innumerable telephone calls, negotiated the fees, and booked and invoiced all the air shows from my office at home, as well as sending information sheets for commentators and programmes. But John Romain felt that it would be better to centralise this and run the operation of the Blenheim from his Duxford office, with the help of his assistant Anna McDowell, who was good at 'chatting up' airshow organisers on the telephone and had some good contacts on the continent. They felt confident of improving on the 1994 bookings, so I was happy to agree with these changes, although I missed the day-to-day involvement.

In 1995 the Blenheim performed in the VE Day celebrations at Duxford, Southend and Chatham, and in the televised fly-past over Buckingham Palace – I was in the bomb-aimer's position in the nose and saw quite clearly HM the Queen, the Queen Mother and the Princess Royal on the balcony.

Displays were also carried out at the North Weald 'Fighter Meet', the Air Fete at Mildenhall, RAF Cosford and RAF Halton, the IAT at Fairford, 'Flying Legends' and the main IWM display at Duxford, Elvington in Yorkshire, Shoreham and Shepway on the South Coast, Newtownards in Northern Ireland, the Battle of Britain event at

Biggin Hill, and at Eindhoven in Holland. Goodwill visits included the Capel-le-Ferne memorial, and two to Filton. One of these, sadly, was for the funeral of Sir Archibald Russell, the famous designer who had worked at Bristol's drawing office from 1925 until retiring as Managing Director in 1969. He related to me much of the information in the chapters on the pre-war days at Filton, and the genesis of the Blenheim, when I conversed with him at length at a lunch Lord Rothermere kindly hosted, and at Filton the previous year.

Once more the Blenheim undertook the doleful duty of performing an important role in the closing ceremonies of another famous RAF station, for in September 1995 Swanton Morley followed Wattisham and West Raynham in the previous years. The Blenheims of 105 Squadron had been the first to arrive when the station opened exactly 55 years earlier in September 1940. Hughie Edwards led his Blenheims from here on the Bremen raid that resulted in his award of the VC – if only we could have brought our first restored Blenheim carrying his markings as GB-D back to Swanton Morley! Most appropriately, the salute was taken by AVM Richard Kyle, the son of ACM Sir Wallace Kyle, who as Group Captain 'Digger' Kyle had promoted Hughie Edwards to command 105 and sent them on the Bremen raid. Once more the Blenheim opened the air display, and once more it was the last aircraft to take off, returning after the Sunset Ceremony, to dip over the flag-pole in a perfectly timed and positioned final salute as the RAF ensign was being lowered, and the 'Last Post' sounded.

In the past $2^1/2$ years the Blenheim has been admired at air shows by over four million spectators, and seen on video and television by many millions more. Most people seem to be aware now that there is a flying Blenheim; we seem to have succeeded in our aim of 'putting the Blenheim back on the map'.

The Autumn Air Show at Duxford, held in the 'Indian summer' of mid-October 1995, was a most satisfying day. The crowd was large, the flying magnificent, the weather glorious. The Blenheim Society had an enclosure and marquee alongside the Control Tower, and on show there was the new painting, 'Blenheim Boys', a striking portrayal by Trevor Lay of a section of Coastal Command Blenheims returning from a wartime sortie. This was most appropriate, for this event saw the last appearance by our Blenheim in the all-black scheme of WM-Z, for it was put into Coastal Command camouflage and markings over the winter – the first of many fresh identities that we intend to adopt.

This time the Blenheim was painted in the 1941 grey, green and sky scheme of Coastal Command – which drastically alters the appearance – with the markings of *L8841* QY-C of 254 Squadron. For what is in effect our third Blenheim, we chose 254 – based mainly in the Scottish Islands – to represent the many little-known but hard-working Coastal Command Squadrons, with their anonymous crews, as opposed to the famous and high-profile pilots such as Hughie Edwards and Max Aitken of our first two Blenheims.

As a prelude to performing a stirring solo display in John Romain's capable hands, the Blenheim, flanked closely by a Hurricane and an early Spitfire, led a formation fly-past as a true memorial flight to the Battle of Britain. The trio flew in from the west, low and tight, with a backdrop of a cloud-flecked blue sky, the unchanging vista of the Duxford countryside unfolding behind them, sun glinting on perspex, the singing of the two Merlins and two Mercurys underscoring the incomparable scene. This splendid spectacle brought to vibrant life the history of our nation's 'finest hour' in 1940; all present shared a moving and memorable experience.

The commentator said, 'These three aircraft form the perfect flying tribute to all of the RAF pilots and aircrews who served during the war.'

I can live with that.

Obituary of Ormond Haydon-Baillie

Ormond was an extraordinary man. His death in Germany early in July came as a very great shock to us all. His enthusiasm for collecting and flying rare and interesting aircraft and keeping them in excellent condition set a high example in historic aviation. He knew what he wanted and his single-minded energy in trying to achieve his ideals left us standing. He loved Duxford and his part in it and wanted to see it succeed as an exciting, lively, flying aircraft museum. He tried very hard and waged many battles. He was debonair, knowledgeable, difficult, charming, enthusiastic, and very hard working – in any capacity required from grease-monkey to negotiator and, above all, a leader of his team and his many followers. He was always helpful and encouraging to those of like mind, contemptuous of petty officialdom, and anathema to bureaucrats. We all miss his bubbling enthusiasm for flying and Duxford, and have lost a great ally in helping Duxford come alive.

This obituary first appeared in Duxford Aviation Society News

Bristol Aeroplane Company Type Numbers

*Multi-engined aircraft with specification numbers – those produced are in **bold** type.*

130	Bombay type to C26/31	2 x Pegasus
130A	**Bombay Mk I**	2 x Pegasus
131	Bomber to B9/32	2 x Pegasus
135	Commercial Monoplane	2 x Aquila
137	130-based Commercial Monoplane	2 x Pegasus (137A 14-str, 137B Freight)
141	3-str Fighter to F22/33	2 x Aquila
142	**'Britain First'**	2 x Mercury
142M	**Blenheim I** to 28/35 & 33/36	2 x Mercury
143	**10-str Commercial Monoplane**	2 x Aquila (135 revised to 142)
143F	Military version for Finland	2 x Mercury (proposed)
144	Night Bomber to B3/34	2 x Perseus (version of 130)
145	Long-Range Bomber	2 x Phoenix (145A and 145B)
148	Army Co-Op 2-str	2 x Perseus (146-based to A39/34)
149	**Blenheim IV** to 34/36 & 10/37	2 x Mercury (and Bolingbroke I)
150	Torpedo Bomber M15/35	2 x Perseus
152	**Beaufort** Bomber G24/35 & 10/36	2 x Taurus
153	Day/Night Fighter to F37/35	1 x Hercules (proposed)
153A	Day/Night Fighter to F37/35	2 x Aquila (proposed)
155	Composite Bomber B18/38	2 x Taurus (Albemarle spec)
156	**Beaufighter** to F17/39	2 x Hercules
157	Beau Bomber	2 x Hercules
158	Slim fuselage Beau	2 x Hercules or Griffon
159	Four-engined Bomber B1/39	4 x Hercules
160	**Blenheim V** to B6/40	2 x Mercury (and Bisley I)
161	Beaumont to B7/40	2 x Hercules
162	(both Beau-based)	2 x Merlin
163	**Buckingham** to B2/41	2 x Centaurus
164	**Brigand** Mk I to H7/42	2 x Centaurus
165	Brigand Mk II	2 x Centaurus
166	**Buckmaster** to 13/43	2 x Centaurus
167	**Brabazon** 1 to 2/44	8 x Centaurus
	Brabazon 2 to 2/46	4 x Double Proteus
169	Buckingham to PR.8/44	2 x Centaurus
170	**Wayfarer/Freighter**	2 x Hercules
175	**Britannia** to 2/47	4 x Proteus
223	Supersonic Transport	4 x Olympus (Concorde prototype)

Some Blenheim 'firsts'

FIRST flight of Bristol Type 142 'Britain First'   12.04.1935
FIRST all-metal monoplane of stressed-skin construction ordered for the RAF   24.10.1935
FIRST flight of Bristol Type 142M 'Blenheim I' K7033   25.06.1936
FIRST delivery of 'Blenheim I' K7036 114 Squadron, Wyton   17.03.1937
FIRST flight of Bristol Type 149 'Blenheim IV' K7072   24.09.1937
FIRST aircraft in the world equipped with air-to-air radar; 25 Squadron
   had 15 Blenheim Mk IFs with AI Mk 1   30.08.1939
FIRST aircraft to reach 1,000 deliveries under pre-war RAF expansion Scheme
   – 1,089 (more than any other type) were on charge   01.09.1939
FIRST Second World War sortie against Germany, Mk IV N6215 of
   139 Squadron, 1202 hours   03.09.1939
FIRST bombing raid of the war, against German fleet off
   Wilhelmshaven – five Mk IVs from each of 107, 110 and 139 Squadrons   04.09.1939
FIRST decorations of the war – DFCs to Blenheim pilots F/Lt Doran,
   110 Squadron, and F/O McPhearson, 139 Squadron   10.10.1939
FIRST Fighter Command attack on a German base, Borkum
   – six Mk IFs from each of 25 and 601 Squadrons   28.11.1939
FIRST Finnish Air Force attacks on invading Russian forces   01.12.1939
FIRST Night Intruder sorties against enemy airfields
   – Mk IFs of 23 Squadron   21.12.1939
FIRST ever radar-controlled interception (by CH Station at Bawdsey Manor),
   He 111 destroyed 45 miles off Suffolk coast by Blenheim IV P4834 from
   Martlesham Heath   05.02.1940
FIRST RAF aircraft to sink a German submarine (*U31*)
   – Blenheim IV P4852 of 82 Squadron   11.03.1940
FIRST RAF sortie against Italy, attack on El Adam airfield
   – 26 Blenheim Is and IVs from 45, 55 and 113 Squadrons   11.05.1940
FIRST ever successful interception using air-to-air radar
   – Mk IF Blenheim from Fighter Interception Unit, Ford   22.07.1940
FIRST flight of Bristol Type 160 'Blenheim V' AD657   24.02.1941
FIRST deep-penetration unescorted low-level daylight raid, Cologne/
   Knapsack Power Stations – 54 Blenheim IVs   12.08.1941
FIRST RAF sorties against Japanese forces – 62 Squadron Malaya   08.12.1941
FIRST 'Combined Operation' with Army and Navy, South Vaagso, Norway   28.12.1941
FIRST RAF aircraft to sink a Japanese submarine – Mk IV of 84 Squadron   23.02.1942
FIRST RCAF aircraft to sink a Japanese submarine – Mk IV of 155 Squadron   07.07.1942
FIRST and ONLY RAF aircraft to serve in every wartime RAF Command
   (Fighter, Bomber, Coastal, Army Co-operation and Training Commands)
AND in every Theatre of War

Principal Bristol piston aircraft engines

Giving details of cubic capacity, development of power output by year, and examples of aircraft to which the engine was fitted.

Poppet-valve radial air-cooled engines

Jupiter
9 cylinders, bore 5.75 in x stroke 7.5 in (146 x 190 mm) giving 195 cu in (3,189 cc) per cylinder, and a capacity of 1,753 cu in (28.7 litres)
From 360 bhp (unsupercharged) in 1923 to 580 bhp (supercharged) in 1932
Bulldog, Flycatcher, Bloodhound, Sidestrand, Wapiti, Hinaidi, Virginia, Gamecock, HP Heracles and Hannibal

Mercury
9 cylinders, bore 5.75 in x stroke 6.5 in (146 x 165 mm) giving 169 cu in (2,765 cc) per cylinder, and a capacity of 1,520 cu in (24.983 litres)
From 420 bhp in 1928 to 1,050 bhp in 1941 (all supercharged)
'Britain First', Blenheim, Lysander, Gladiator, Gauntlet, Skua, Master, Martinet, Hamilcar X, Sea Otter, Fokker G1, PZL P11

Pegasus
9 cylinders, bore 5.75 in x stroke 7.5 in (146 x 190.5 mm) giving 194.7 cu in (3,191 cc) per cylinder, and a capacity of 1,753 cu in (28.723 litres)
From 590 bhp in 1932 to 1,010 bhp in 1937 (all supercharged)
Hampden, Harrow, Bombay, Swordfish, Wellington, Wellesley, Walrus, Vildebeest, Sidestrand, Overstrand, Sunderland

Sleeve-valve radial air-cooled engines

Aquila
9 cylinders, bore 5 in x stroke 5.375 in (127 x 136.5 mm) giving 105.56 cu in (1,734 cc) per cylinder, and a capacity of 950 cu in (15.6 litres)
500 bhp in 1934, not developed further
Bristol Type 143, Vickers Venom

Perseus
9 cylinders, bore 5.75 in x stroke 6.5 in (146 x 165 mm) giving 169 cu in (2,765 cc)
   per cylinder, and a capacity of 1,520 cu in (24.983 litres)
From 515 bhp in 1932 to 960 bhp in 1939
Lysander, Flamingo, Botha, Skua, Roc, Short Empire Class,

Taurus
14 cylinders, bore 5.0 in x stroke 5.625 in (127 x 143 mm) giving 110.7 cu in
   (1,814 cc) per cylinder, and a capacity of 1,550 cu in (25.4 litres)
From 935 bhp in 1938 to 1,060 bhp in 1941
Beaufort, Albacore

Hercules
14 cylinders, bore 5.75 in x stroke 6.5 in (146 x 165 mm) giving 168.6 cu in
   (2,764 cc) per cylinder, and a capacity of 2,360 cu in (38.7 litres)
From 1,325 bhp in 1936 to 2,080 bhp in 1948
Halifax III, Stirling, Lancaster II, Beaufighter, Hastings, Viking, Varsity, Albemarle,
   Freighter, Lerwick, Wellington III and V, Solent, Hermes, Nord Noratlas

Centaurus
18 cylinders, bore 5.75 in x stroke 7.0 in (146 x 178 mm) giving 181.65 cu in
   (2,978 cc) per cylinder, and a capacity of 3,270 cu in (53.6 litres)
From 2,000 in 1938 to 2,980 bhp in 1950
Tempest II, Fury and Sea Fury, Brigand, Beverley, Warwick, Ambassador, Firebrand,
   Buckingham, Shetland, Brabazon I

Please note that the Jupiter, Mercury and Pegasus poppet-valve engines shared the same 5.75 in bore as the Perseus, Hercules and Centaurus sleeve-valve engines, while the Mercury, Perseus and Hercules also shared the same 6.5 in stroke, as did the Neptune (a 7-cylinder version) and the Titan (a 5-cylinder version).

This common bore of 5.75 in was also shared by the Jupiter and Pegasus with their 1-inch longer stroke.

This combination of bore and stroke of 5.75 in by 7.5 in (146 x 190 mm) was used on the original Jupiter in 1917, and with the shorter 6.5 in (165 mm) stroke in 1927. The same bore from 1917 continued in the Centaurus, which was still in use well over 40 years later!

The Jupiter, Mercury, Pegasus, Aquila and Perseus are single-row 9-cylinder radial engines; the Taurus, Hercules and Centaurus are double-row radials, the first two with 14 cylinders, the third with 18. All these engines are air-cooled.

Citations for Victoria Crosses

HUGHIE IDWAL EDWARDS
No 105 Squadron
Extract from 'The London Gazette' of 22nd July, 1941
'Acting Wing Commander Hughie Idwal Edwards, DFC, No 105 Squadron.
Wing Commander Edwards, although handicapped by physical disability resulting from a flying accident, has repeatedly displayed gallantry of the highest order in pressing home bombing attacks from very low heights against strongly-defended objectives.

On 4th July, 1941, he led an important attack on the Port of Bremen, one of the most heavily defended in Germany. This attack had to be made in daylight and there were no clouds to afford concealment. During the approach to the German coast several enemy ships were sighted, and Wing Commander Edwards knew that his aircraft would be reported and that the defences would be in a state of readiness.

Undaunted by this misfortune he brought his formation 50 miles overland to the target, flying at a height of a little more than 50 feet, passing through a formidable balloon barrage.

On reaching Bremen he was met with a hail of fire, all his aircraft being hit and four of them being destroyed. Nevertheless he made a most successful attack, and then with the greatest skill and coolness withdrew the surviving aircraft without further loss.

Throughout the execution of this operation, which he had planned personally with full knowledge of the risks entailed, Wing Commander Edwards displayed the highest possible standard of gallantry and determination.'

HUGH GORDON MALCOLM
No 18 Squadron
Extract from 'The London Gazette' of 27th April, 1943
'*Acting Wing Commander Hugh Gordon Malcolm (Deceased), No 18 Squadron.* This officer commanded a squadron of light bombers in North Africa. Throughout his service in that theatre his leadership, skill and daring were of the highest order.

On 17th November, 1942, he was detailed to carry out a low-level formation attack on Bizerta airfield, taking advantage of cloud cover. Twenty miles from the target the sky became clear, but Wing Commander Malcolm carried on, knowing the danger of proceeding without a fighter escort. Despite fierce opposition, all bombs were dropped within the airfield perimeter. A Junkers 52 and a Messerschmitt 109 were shot down; many dispersed enemy aircraft were raked by machine-gun fire. Weather conditions became extremely unfavourable and as a result, two of his aircraft were lost by collision; another was forced down by enemy fighters. It is due to this officer's skilful and resolute leadership that the remaining aircraft returned safely to base.

On 28th November, 1942, he again led his squadron against Bizerta airfield which was bombed from a low altitude. The airfield on this occasion was heavily defended and intense and accurate anti-aircraft fire was met. Nevertheless, after his squadron had released their bombs, Wing Commander Malcolm led them back again and again to attack the airfield with machine-gun fire.

These were typical of every sortie undertaken by this gallant officer; each attack was pressed to an effective conclusion however difficult the task and however formidable the opposition.

Finally, on 4th December, 1942, Wing Commander Malcolm, having been detailed to give close support to the First Army, received an urgent request to attack an enemy fighter airfield near Chouigui. Wing Commander Malcolm knew that to attack such an objective without a fighter escort – which could not be arranged in the time available – would be to court almost certain disaster; but believing the attack to be necessary for the success of the Army's operations, his duty was clear. He decided to attack. He took off with his squadron and reached the target unmolested, but when he had successfully attacked it, his squadron was intercepted by an overwhelming force of enemy fighters. Wing Commander Malcolm fought back, controlling his hard-pressed squadron and attempting to maintain formation. One by one his aircraft were shot down until only his own aircraft remained. In the end he, too, was shot down in flames.

Wing Commander Malcolm's last exploit was the finest example of the valour and unswerving devotion to duty which he constantly displayed.'

ARTHUR STEWART KING SCARF
No 62 Squadron
Extract from 'The London Gazette' of 21st June, 1946

'Squadron Leader Arthur Stewart King Scarf (37693) (Deceased), Royal Air Force, No 62 Squadron.

On 9th December, 1941, all available aircraft from the Royal Air Force station, Butterworth, Malaya, were ordered to make a daylight attack on the advanced operational base of the Japanese Air Force at Singora, Thailand. From this base, the enemy fighter squadrons were supporting the landing operations.

The aircraft detailed for the sortie were on the point of taking off when the enemy made a combined dive-bombing and low level machine-gun attack on the airfield. All our aircraft were destroyed or damaged with the exception of the Blenheim piloted by Squadron Leader Scarf. This aircraft had become airborne a few seconds before the attack started.

Squadron Leader Scarf circled the airfield and witnessed the disaster. It would have been reasonable had he abandoned the projected operation which was intended to be a formation sortie. He decided however, to press on to Singora in his single aircraft. Although he knew that this individual action could not inflict much material damage on the enemy he, nevertheless, appreciated the moral effect which it would have on the remainder of the squadron, who were helplessly watching their aircraft burning on the ground.

Squadron Leader Scarf completed his attack successfully. The opposition over the target was severe and included attacks by a considerable number of enemy fighters. In the course of these encounters, Squadron Leader Scarf was mortally wounded.

The enemy continued to engage him in a running fight, which lasted until he had regained the Malayan border. Squadron Leader Scarf fought a brilliant evasive action in a valiant attempt to return to his base. Although he displayed the utmost gallantry and determination, he was, owing to his wounds, unable to accomplish this. He made a successful forced-landing at Alor Star without causing any injury to his crew. He was received into hospital as soon as possible but died shortly after admission.

Squadron Leader Scarf displayed supreme heroism in the face of tremendous odds and his splendid example of self-sacrifice will long be remembered.'

The Blenheim Appeal announcement

A Blenheim Will Fly Again

Canada 1974

Duxford 1985

Duxford May 1987

Denham June 1987

On 22nd May 1987, a Bristol Blenheim took to the skies for the first time in over forty years to become the sole airworthy example. This first flight followed a meticulous restoration which took twelve years, a small fortune, and some 40,000 man-hours to complete. On 21st June 1987 it was virtually destroyed in an accident at Denham, not due to any mechanical fault, and mercifully with no loss of life.

Despite this devastating blow the British Aerial Museum Team, in response to overwhelming public demand, are ready, willing and able to put a Blenheim back into the air.

They have the experience and expertise, access to the necessary airframe components, the facilities (thanks to the Imperial War Museum at Duxford) *and* the determination and dedication. The Team have demonstrated that they can do it by the superb job they did (virtually unaided) on the first Blenheim rebuild, greatly admired by all who saw it fly during that brief, glorious month. **But they need your help and support to do it again.**

We are honoured that The Master of the Guild of Air Pilots and Air Navigators has kindly agreed to administer the Blenheim Appeal Fund and all donations, large and small, will go directly towards the rebuild. We also need help in kind and can offer commercial sponsorship schemes that will enable you to benefit from the enormous public interest.

The Blenheim was a mainstay of the RAF in the first two desperate years of World War II and the bravery of its crews was unmatched as they fought against heavy odds, often in operations made far more dangerous by the unsuitable tasks they had to perform. No less than 94 Squadrons of the RAF operated Blenheims and they were the only aircraft to serve in every RAF Command and in every Theatre of War.

The British Aerial Museum wish to restore not just the airframe but the proper historic importance of the Blenheim by displaying it at Air Shows in the same way that the RAF Battle of Britain Flight perpetuate the fame of the Spitfire, Hurricane and Lancaster. The Blenheim too, and the extreme courage of its crews, deserves to be commemorated and must not be allowed to fade from the public memory.

Please help us put a Blenheim back in the air once more – the greater your response the sooner the job will be done.

Graham Warner
Founder, British Aerial Museum

The Blenheim Appeal

Building 66, Duxford Airfield, Cambs CB2 4QR.

Please make cheques payable to 'The Blenheim Appeal' – Thank you

Accident Investigation Board Report No 11/87

Accident Investigation Board Report

No: 11/87   Ref: 1a

Aircraft type and registration:	Bristol 149 Blenheim Mk IV G-MKIV
No & Type of engines:	2 Bristol Mercury XX piston engines
Year of Manufacture:	1942
Date and time (UTC):	21 June 1987 at 1345 hrs
Location:	Denham airfield, Buckinghamshire
Type of flight:	Air display
Persons on board:	Crew – 3 Passengers – None
Injuries:	Crew – 3 (minor) Passengers – N/A
Nature of damage:	Aircraft damaged beyond repair
Commander's Licence:	Airline Transport Pilot's Licence
Commander's Age:	60 years
Commander's Total Flying Experience:	15,639 hours (of which $4^{1}/_{2}$ were on type)
Information Source:	Aircraft Accident Report Form submitted by the pilot, report by engineer and video film.

The aircraft was making an appearance at an air display. On board were the pilot and 2 engineers who were part of the team that had rebuilt the aircraft. One of the engineers, who knew the aircraft well and held a Private Pilot's Licence Group B, occupied the right-hand cockpit seat for take-off and landing. The other engineer sat in the turret. The runway in use was 25 with a usable length of 667 metres; the wind was from the north-west at 3 to 5 knots and there was no significant weather.

When the display was planned the pilot had declined to land at Denham because of the relative shortness of the runway, **and it had been agreed that no landing would be**

attempted. Nevertheless, on the day, after demonstrating the aircraft at both high and low speeds the pilot decided to carry out a touch-and-go landing. He later stated that he had been asked to do this by the display organisers but no evidence was found that any such request was made to him at the time of the display. The touch-and-go landing was thus not part of the planned display and had not been rehearsed.

A setting of 15° flap was used for the approach, which was shallower and slightly faster than it would have been if landing flap (60°) had been used. The aircraft touched down some way beyond the landing threshold and bounced slightly. The pilot controlled the bounce and applied power to take-off again. The sound of misfiring was heard from at least one engine and black smoke was seen behind the aircraft. The aircraft veered to the left and ran on to the grass. The pilot stated that after touch-down he steadily opened the throttles to +2 psi boost pressure then, sensing that the aircraft was not accelerating normally, he opened the throttle further. Acceleration was still below normal so he opened the throttles fully and then held the aircraft on the ground to achieve flying speed. He had no recollection of the engines misfiring or of the aircraft swinging to the left. The engineer in the right-hand seat said that, after controlling the bounce, the pilot rapidly opened the throttles and both engines suffered rich mixture cuts. He said that he advised the pilot to close the throttles and open them up again more slowly but the pilot did not respond; some seconds later the right engine picked up to full power and the aircraft left the runway. The engineer in the turret confirmed that he heard on his headset the advice given by the other engineer to the pilot.

A video film of the landing showed the aircraft rolling along the runway with the tail-wheel off the ground for about 12 seconds, for the last 8 of which the sound of an engine or engines misfiring could be heard on the film. The right wing then began to rise and the aircraft ran off the runway with the right wing still rising, at a speed said by the pilot to have been about 80 mph but thought by the engineer to have been about 70 mph. It became airborne, banked some 15° to the left, and climbed to between 50 and 100 feet with the left bank increasing and the airspeed reducing. A few seconds later the left wing hit trees and the aircraft cartwheeled along the ground. Both engines were torn from their mountings, both wings were severely damaged and the fuselage was broken in half. The occupants suffered only minor injuries; the two engineers were able to evacuate the aircaft unaided and the pilot was released from the wreckage by the airport fire and rescue services, who arrived at the scene very quickly and covered leaking fuel with foam.

The operating company had taken great pains to ensure that the aircraft was airworthy and that the pilot was capable of safely performing the display. Prior to flying the Blenheim the pilot had been given experience on a Beechcraft 18, an aircraft with similar handling characteristics. He had flown 4^1/$_2$ hours on the Blenheim but had not practiced a touch and go landing on the aircraft. The Pilot's Notes stated that on take-off the throttles should be fully opened in a time of only 2 to 3 seconds and it had been found that any attempt to open the throttles in less than that time caused rich mixture cutting. The pilot was aware of the need to avoid rapid throttle movements.

Flight Test
Notes G-BPIV

Mr. R. Cole
Flight Department
Civil Aviation Authority
Aviation House
Gatwick Airport South
West Sussex
RH6 OYR

British Aerial Museum
Imperial War Museum
Duxford Airfield
Cambridge
CB2 4QR

REF:
1. TEST SCHEDULE NO 233
2. FLIGHT TEST SCHEDULE NO 3 ISSUE 3
3. LETTER MR R. COLE/PROUDFOOT DATED 9 MAY 1993
4. AIRTEST LETTER G-MKIV - FIRST AIRCRAFT FROM MR. J. LARCOMBE 24.5.87

Dear Bob

BLENHEIM : G-BPIV - AIR TESTS

1. The Blenheim G-BPIV has been airtested in accordance with the criteria laid down in References 1, 2 and 3. The completed documents are contained as annexes to this letter. All references to the first aircraft are to the BAM G-MKIV aircraft previously tested.

2. SPECIFIC TEST RESULTS

   a) LOADING.   Ref 1, 3.1. Ref 2 Para 3.

   The aircraft has been weighed and it will be noticed that the C of G position differs from that of the first aircraft. The reason for this is because the C of G datum for G-BPIV has been taken from the datum plate position, whereas on the first aircraft it was taken from the spar centre line. If the datum plate had been used on the first aircraft this C of G position would be 42.9" aft, i.e. within 1.76". Both are obviously within the allowable range of 28.5" to 45.87" aft of datum.

   b) TAKE OFF.   Ref 1 para 5. Ref 2 para 7

   The take off was normal in all respects with an estimated ground roll (still air) of 450m.

   c) CLIMB PERFORMANCE.   Ref 1 para 6. Ref 2 para 8.

   The two pitch propellers fitted are not usual on modern twin engined aircraft as full feathering is not possible in an engine shut down situation. The propellers can be placed in the coarse pitch position to reduce drag but will continue to 'windmill' the engine. Therefore, for test purposes, the simulated dead engine was not shut down using mixture cut off as the fuel lubricated engine driven fuel pump would run dry as the engine windmilled, and the subsequent risk of failure would be high. Engine shut down was therefore simulated using idle power and course pitch.

This procedure was also used for the VMCa and VMCl tests later. It will be seen that the Single Engine Climb performance of G-BPIV more superior to that of the first Blenheim. I can not explain this as a repeated test on the opposite engine still gave almost identically better results.

d) STICK FORCES PER 'g'. Ref 1 para 7. Ref 3 para 4

These were linear, qualitatively assessed, and agree with the first Blenheim test results, para 8 of Ref no 4.

e) STALLS. Ref 1 para 8. Ref 2 para 9.

All straight forward and also agree within 3 mph of the first aircraft. The aircraft did not display the 'violent' characteristics described in Pilots Notes - on the contrary, it was very docile.

f) RATES OF ROLL. Ref 1 para 9. Ref 3 para 7.

These were carried out and results are similar to the first aircraft.

9.1.   Gear, flap, approach speed, M.C.P. 30^0 to 30^0 - 3.5 secs.

9.2.   Clean at safety speed (recommended at 85 mph) 30^0 to 30^0 - 4.5 secs.

9.3.   175 mph clean 30^0 to 30^0 - 2.5 secs.

Note: Opposite roll direction produced the same results.

g) ASYMMETRIC HANDLING. Ref 1 para 10. Ref 3 para 8.

The results match those of the first aircraft using the simulated engine shut down already described. Neither engine was critical. Using plus 4 1/4 lb boost (max t/o) control could be retained down to 82 mph with relative high rudder loads (estimated at 130 to 140 lbs ft). Recommend VMCa to be 85 mph. Using the BCAR 23 guide for an approach on one engine it was demonstrated that the required criteria could be met at 84 mph. Recommend VMCl to be 85 mph.

h) CHANGES OF STICKS FORCE WITH POWER AND FLAP. Ref 1 para 12 & 13. Ref 3 para 5. Ref 4 para 12 & 13

All carried and the results are in agreement with the first aircraft. The VDF of 260 mph was achieved with no problems - trim and control forces being normal. I note that the VNE speed of 245 mph recommended by the CAA Flight Test Report (first aircraft) dated 28 May 1987 is 245 mph. Should this be 234 mph (i.e. .9 of VDF?) We would prefer a VNE of 245 mph in the future and will go to VDF of 272 mph with your approval to achieve this.

i) LATERAL AND DIRECTIONAL STABILITY. Ref 1 para 15. Ref 3 para 6. Ref 4, para 15

Carried out to the criteria in Ref 3. In both the idle power and powered approach configuration (approx - 2 lb boost) the aircraft has positive lateral and directional stability. Normal characteristics were demonstrated.

j) MINIMUM TRIM SPEEDS. Ref 1 para 18.

The aircraft can be trimmed load free in all cases from minimum to maximum speed and in all configurations.

3.   OBSERVATIONS

        a) TEST CRITERIA

        All previous air test material and original Pilots Notes (as amended for this aircraft) plus
        past operating procedures used on the British Aerial Museum's first aircraft were studied by
        the pilot and observer. Apart from amendments and additions, as recommended by Mr. Cole of the
        Authority, airtesting followed the same format of the previous aircraft.

        b) ENGINE HANDLING

        The rebuilt Bristol Mercury XX engines were limited to short periods of full boost (plus 4 1/4
        lbs). Both engines handled very well at all power settings and are extremely well matched.
        RPMs, oil temperatures and pressures and CHTs being almost identical under the same operating
        conditions. It should be remembered that the mixture controls are not conventional (forward -
        weak, rear - normal) and carburettor 'Warm Air' should be used more than on modern aircraft.
        CHT's should also be monitored carefully to be maintained at 'about 160°C'. All this is well
        documented in the Pilots Notes.

        c) PROPELLERS

        The propellers are two speed only and cannot be feathered.

        d) AIRCRAFT HANDLING

        The aircraft handles well and displays docile characteristics. Elevator forces become fairly
        heavy in steep turns but overall the aircraft is nicely harmonised. No unusual or potentially
        hazardous characteristics were encountered within the normal flight testing envelope.

4.   SUMMARY

        The Blenheim MKIV, G-BPIV, is extremely well constructed, was very carefully and methodically
        prepared for testing and delightful to fly. A great credit to all involved in this aircraft.

Yours sincerely,

M. B. PROUDFOOT
TEST PILOT

Enclosures:

1.   Airtest Schedule No 233, completed

2.   Twin Piston Engine Test Schedule. No 3 Issue 2 May '86, completed

3.   Pilots Notes (Blenheim IV) AP1530B as amended.

Obituary of John Larcombe

John Larcombe's passion for flying extended far beyond his professional work as a Boeing 747 Training Captain for British Airways.

From the sober uniform of that commercial airline would often emerge the youthful-figured silver-grey crewcut and steely eyes of the eternal fighter pilot. Whilst always beaming, or at least carrying a quizzical smile, it was around vintage aircraft that Larcombe became most radiant.

He lived close to the Imperial War Museum at Duxford Airfield and spent so much of his leisure-time there, helping restore and fly vintage aircraft, that his wife Marianne was obliged to join him. This extraordinary couple ran their home as an officer's mess for groundcrew, pilots, friends and wives. Larcombe was always able to win at whatever the mess game, be it spoons or darts.

'Larks' was a gifted pilot who first flew with the Manchester University Air Squadron on Chipmunks in 1955. He recently returned to his first love and acquired a part-share in a Duxford-based Chipmunk.

He joined the RAF in 1958 and flew for the major part of his RAF career as an instructor on fighter types. He was awarded the Air Force Cross for exceptional flying just days before leaving the RAF in 1970. Thereafter, at BOAC and BA, he flew the big aircraft: 707, DC10 and then 747. Duxford, however, was the outlet for his wider aviation interests. Whether Tiger Moth, Blenheim or Mitchell Bomber, Messerschmitt 109, Spitfire or training types, he always displayed the same sympathetic, cautious and enquiring approach to flight.

He was generous with his experience, knowledge and skill, always prepared to advise, teach or train others, particularly in safety and emergency procedures. Shortly to retire from flying the Jumbos, he had planned to start a specialist, military-style training school where one could learn the now exotic art of flying high-performance tailwheel aircraft.

Away from flying, Larcombe was a proud family man, a keen golfer and a fine shot. The gentle side of his character had started to prevail and he could no longer bring himself to shoot game-birds in an age of plenty. His sense of fun and fair play passed not just to those people around him but genetically to his son and two daughters. He was about to become a grandfather and it is ironic that his own father had died prior to his birth.

Wonderful images of him stand out: the wall-to-wall grin on his face when he first flew a Spitfire; the sheepish look, as he had lent his uniform to a British Airways hostess who had always wanted to dress up as a Captain – and in the spirit of the event he appeared in hers. John Larcombe was a person who died doing what he loved.

This obituary by Stephen Grey, proprietor of The Fighter Collection,
first appeared in The Guardian

Letter from AOC 11 Group, Royal Air Force

From: Air Vice-Marshal J S Allison CBE RAF

Headquarters No 11 Group
Royal Air Force
Bentley Priory
Stanmore
Middlesex
HA7 3HH

081-950 4000 Ext 7400

Air Officer
Commanding
11G/1/AOC

Mr G Warner
British Aerial Museum
Duxford Airfield
Cambridgeshire
CB2 4QR   2 June 1994

Dear Graham,

    I write to thank you for so generously allowing the Blenheim to take part in the flying display to mark the closure of Royal Air Force West Raynham.

    It was a sad but significant day for the Royal Air Force because, as you know, West Raynham has been part of our history for 55 years and it was important to mark its closure with due ceremony in a way which properly honoured its past, and in particular recognised the courage and sacrifice of those who served there in the Second World War.

    The return of the Blenheim to West Raynham was not only historically significant, but powerfully symbolic of the war years, given the type's long and honourable operational record from West Raynham, and it is indeed a blessing that, through the dedication of your team at the British Aerial Museum /Aircraft Restoration Company and the support of the Blenheim Society, the Blenheim was put back into the air so that it could play a part in such events.

    I thought it particularly appropriate that, having opened the batting at West Raynham in 1939, the Blenheim should be the aircraft to make the final flypast in conjunction with the Sunset Ceremony. This was perfectly positioned and timed by Hoof Proudfoot and was of course in addition to his earlier excellent display. I also very much appreciated your inviting me, as the reviewing officer for the day, to be on board the aircraft as it made that last salute. It all added to the symbolism of the occasion.

    Thankyou for allowing the Blenheim to play a pivotal role in the closure of Royal Air Force West Raynham.

Yours sincerely,

John Allison

'Blenheim': a poem by Richard Passmore, 1987

So once again, after these many years,
And in the evening of my days,
(As in their early dawn),
I stand and marvel at the grace,
The unimpassioned beauty,
Of this machine.

Again, as in times past –
Too long past –
I climb down through the once familiar hatch,
Bend my now clumsy shape
Under, over, up until
Again I sit where in that magic time I used to sit,
A boy, ecstatic, thrilled,
Waiting.

The engines start,
Spit and bang and roar,
And as the metal shakes
So too does my incorporated flesh.
Beyond the tail
The near horizon sways
This way and that, until
At last we stop and wait.

And now the engines gather up their strength and roar.
The earth flows past and falls
Away. Again at so long last I am indeed
A god.

Below the downthrust wing
The fields revolve even as once they did;
Again I know myself
Filled with that other power, moved
Across the endless undulations
Of the invisible air.

Why did I not, then, anticipate
This quite impossible Me
Who in after years
Would return?

Truly it has been said
We walk into the future looking backwards,
Our eyes forever fixed
Upon the irrevocable past. That boy
Could surely not foresee
This grosser flesh, this tired mind,
World-weariness, all joys
Abandoned and passed by.

And yet now, suddenly
I am once more
Indeed the boy that once I was – and now
Too near to tears
At this undreamed-of gift
Of youth renewed.

'The many men, the beautiful
And they all dead did lie' –
So now I must return
To everyday.

Valhalla must indeed be full;
And I, who die in age
And not as they, at dawn,
May never join them there.
Domine, non sum dignus;
Lord, I am not worthy
Indeed.

Acknowledgements

I would like to thank all the ex-Blenheim crews and ground-staff who have written or talked to me about their Blenheim days, and those of them who kindly supplied some of the photographs used.

Most of the excellent photographs of the first Blenheim, both under restoration and in the air, were taken by John Smith – 'Smudge' – of the Team. The front cover photograph and many of the other beautiful air-to-air shots of the second Blenheim were taken by John Dibbs, now a leading aviation photographer, who we were happy to encourage in his earlier days.

It is impossible to attribute all of the illustrations, as many are now 50 or 60 years old, but they include photographs made available by: Wes Agnew, Ian Blair, The Bristol Aeroplane Company (now part of British Aerospace), Chris Burkett, Bill Burberry, Ken Collins, Colin Craxton, John Dibbs, Ian Frimston, Wensley Haydon-Baillie, Sqn.Ldr. F. Hoblyn RAF (Ret), The Imperial War Museum, Steve Jefferson, James Kightly, Cliff Knox, Stan Lee, Richard Lucraft, Sqn.Ldr. R. Muspratt DFC RAF (Ret), Clive Norman, the *Daily Mail*, Group Captain W. Maydwell DSO DFC RAF (Ret), Richard Paver, Roger Peacock, John Rigby, John Romain, Maurice Rowe, Robert Rudhall, Stuart Scott, John Smith, Robert Sparkes, Reg Stride, Colin Swann, David Swann, and the late Ken Whittle.

The evocative drawings 'Pre-Flight' and 'Last Briefing' used on the endpapers are by Gerald Coulson, doyen of aviation artists.

My thanks are due to John Romain and the Blenheim Team for answering my many technical questions about the restoration process, so that I could describe it in layman's language.

Especially, I would like to thank all who have made donations, large or small, to The Blenheim Appeal, for without their unstinted support there would not be a Blenheim in the sky today.

Above all, my deep appreciation and heartfelt thanks is given to the individual members of the Team – for it was their sterling efforts and unremitting hard work throughout so many years that twice turned a derelict hulk back into a beautiful flying machine. My sincere tribute to each one of them is the central theme of the 20-year saga that I have related here.

Graham Warner,
Saffron Walden, 1996

Last briefing. (From a drawing by Gerald Coulson)